The Owner-Builder Book

*How You Can Save More Than $100,000 in the
Construction of Your Custom Home*

Third Edition

Mark A. Smith
with
Elaine M. Smith

The
Consensus
Group

The Owner-Builder Book:
How You Can Save More Than $100,000 in the Construction of Your Custom Home.

Third Edition
Copyright © 2003 The Consensus Group, Inc.

This book is distrubuted to the book trade through Ingram, Baker & Taylor, and Partners Publishers Group.

ISBN: 0-9661428-8-8
Library of Congress Card Number: 2002094408

Designer: Jon-Cameron Gull
Cover: Jon-Cameron Gull

Third Edition 10 9 8 7 6 5 4 3 2 1

The Consensus Group, Inc.

Toll Free: 1-888-333-2845
www.OwnerBuilderBook.com

Reader Comments

"I took your book out of the library because my friend said it was a good one. Before I finished reading it, I had found the confidence to go out and build. We read the Special Reports to each other on the way back from Montana. We read all the ones that go to the budget and we broke it down to our parts where each of us get bids."
Melanie & Jeremy T.   Riverton, UT

"I read it, my husband is in the process, and we are sold on the idea. My husband was up til 3:30 this morning reading this, it was so enthralling to him. He says it is very helpful and he is looking forward to using the software templates. I enjoyed the website, especially the moms that are on there."
Lyn & Phil S.   Kansas City, MO

"I was in the library yesterday and found your book. What a Godsend!! I have been reading it and decided to check out the website. We have already been doing a lot of what is recommended by the book; getting estimates on jobs, pricing materials, calling banks, etc. I have found two banks willing to loan us the money with us being our own g.c. I know I am rambling on, which is out of character for me! I guess my reasons for writing are to ask if there is any advice you can give to me and to just thank you for the book. It has encouraged me that Jim and I CAN do this ourselves and have a nice home without an enormous debt."
Jodenia & Jim M.   Blacksburg, SC

"I liked it. I like the fact that it's very easy to read. I like the way it's laid out."
Mike W.   Molalla, OR

"It makes sense that you make your money in planning."
Kevin T.   Lawton, OK

"You've got some good stuff in here. The savings emphasis and the encouragement helped me. It agrees with the things my buddies in contracting tell me. It breaks it all down so you can understand it."
Eric R.   DeSoto, TX

"I'm so glad to find your book. I feel like we can get started now. I felt so alone, but now all of a sudden after reading your book, I see that it's not just me."
Judy & Chris P.   Bothell, WA

"I enjoyed reading the book. We gathered about thirty different books, and yours had things like Realtor input that no one else had. Many lists of things that we liked."
Tom W.   Logan, UT

"I've been enjoying your book. I've done some projects as a project manager. That's my forte, so house building seemed like a natural. I had a contractor last time, and that convinced me never to do that again. Everything you say in your book is true."
Suanne D.   Rio Rancho, NM

"I bought your book, "The Owner-Builder Book" and found your personal signature in it, we think it is cool. I am now halfway thru book and really like how you organize the contents. I was going to plan to

owner-build my house in only one month but after reading your book, I extended it to one year. So I am going to continue renting the house we live in now and plan aheaaaaad."
Eric Emmons (via e-mail)

"It's a good book. I'm in construction, and I've been reading books on this for 20 years and I really enjoyed it. It was more practical, and the numbers seemed more real than other books I've read over the years. I see 50% and 60% off all the time, not just 10%. Subs will charge what they can get away with. The best part was how you talked about the planning. For me, planning is about 90% of it. It all should be done in your mind first."
Jim & Mary F.   Northboro, MA

"I thought it was very great. We are doing a major remodeling, start to finish, and it's very helpful, very good info and things you learn. The numbers that hit you when you get your plans are so high, you know you have to be able to do it cheaper than that. You need to hear it over and over. Very, very good book. I was shopping around. This is very easy to follow. Easy to read and highlight. It had everything in it. Like a one stop shopping. Eye-opening, but very good. We've been doing a lot of shopping around."
Bonny P.   Andover, NJ

"We've owner-built once before 24 years ago without any kind of help like this. We didn't do any of the trades. We just cleaned up and bought everything. This time we'll downsize. We have wonderful plans, and wonderful people because we've been here in this small town for a lot of years. I wish I'd had some literature like this the first time I did it. I just knew that I could shop better than a contractor could. We saved a lot of money the first time, and we'll do a lot better this time."
Gene P.   High Springs, FL

"I read your book in two days! I really appreciated it. I'm looking forward to the CD-ROM."
Gina L.   Fountain Inn, SC

"I was very inspired by your book. We're getting ready to build a house. It's going to be fun."
John O.   San Rafael, CA

"I build apartments by trade, I've built about 10,000 units. I stumbled onto your book a couple of weeks ago, and I think it's the finest publication I've ever read on the subject."
Chris V.   Federal Way, WA

"My husband and I are getting ready to build a home in town and we are so much more excited about what we can accomplish because of what we have read in your book. Thanks so much for the information and tips and encouragement. We are picking up our final design plans tomorrow to submit to the city and then the real fun begins."
Shawn & Amy H.   Provo, UT

"Don't change a thing. It's easy reading. That's a big plus. I've used this as a Bible, throughout the whole project. It's hard to put down."
John J.   Higganum, CT

"It was very refreshing to see the comments you make about referrals and subcontractor certification and the other games that go on in our industry."
Mike M.   Bonham, TX

"It's a good book. I write in it and fold the pages. I like the letter to the reader that says you can do it. I've got my wife thinking we can do this. My friend is having a contractor build his house, and he says 'I think I can do it. All you have to worry about is having the subs show up.' And you cover that in chapter 13."
Greg T.   Harrison, OH

"I started by reading *The Complete Guide to Contracting Your Home* which was full of valuable information. Then I got your book and liked it even better. Your book covers a different side of owner-building. What a perfect complement the two books are!"
John & Pat W.   Crystal Lake, IL

"I just finished building my wife and I a house. Where I ran into problems was in the planning stage. When you say go, you are running down a hill that's too steep, and you keep up or fall. I was thinking of going to a psychiatrist because this first project caused such emotional stress, but bought your book instead and now I know that I have control of those factors, not the construction workers."
Tom M.   New York, NY

"Very interesting. It's a good read that at the very least will prevent you getting ripped off. One of the most fascinating books I've ever read."
Ivey S.   New Strawn, KS

"I love your book. It's great. We were trying to decide whether to act as general contractor. After reading the book we got so excited about it we are doing it now."
Becky & Steve G.   Waterloo, IA

"Been in the Corps of Engineers, and have extensive homebuilding experience. I've looked at a lot of books, and yours was by far the most comprehensive, especially in getting your construction loan. There's a lot of owner-building here. If you want a decent house, you have to do it."
Clinton B.   Anchorage, AK

"The book is simply great. My wife and I are in the planning stages of building our own straw bale house in Tucson. I especially liked the concept in your book that a dollar saved is equivalent to 10 dollars in wages that does not need to be earned (or at the very least not spent needlessly). This is why I'm interested in the budget templates. Your ideas are very similar to the thinking in the book *Your Money or Your Life*. Following the basic principles in that book have culminated in being able to do what's in yours."
Robert G.   Tucson, AZ

"I was telling a friend of mine, my lender, that this book was probably the best investment I've made in the last twelve months. You emphasized many things the average person doesn't think about. I can save a lot of money with this book, there is no doubt in my mind."
Julio L.   Austin, TX

"I'm a management consultant, have done a 6,000 square foot house, a 5,000 s.f. house, and now a 4,000 s.f. and concur with all that you said in the book. Obviously you had to be a good management consultant to create the level of detail that's in the book. I owned the book for six months, and finally took it on vacation where I read it. I want to commend you. It's written very well, and very very practical."
Jim V.   Reno, NV

"I do property management, and I know that preparation is everything."
Rob B.   Mesquite, TX

The Owner-Builder Book

"We really enjoyed your book. We noticed that it was the only one in the group that acknowledged and referenced the other books on the subject. It's nice to know that when you wrote the book you had already assimilated everyone else's philosophies. And you're the only one with internet support where you can share ideas with others."
Steve & Kathryn H.   Spanish Fork, UT

"It's a great book. I finished it in three days, I was so engrossed. It was extremely good."
Emmanuel G.   Oak Brook, IL

"Your book was the most interesting in the bookstore. There was nothing in any other book that was so practical."
Chris F.   Plainfield, VT

"My friend had your book checked out of the library so much that the librarian bought him his own copy."
Dale B.   Tucson, AZ

"I enjoyed your first edition very much. I was very glad to find this second edition at the bookstore. Because I remodel houses, I watch for all the books on this subject. I've probably read them all. There are so few books out there that you can use. The majority of the construction books are just written to sell. Yours is written to inform. Some of the books I just get maybe a paragraph out of that's new. Yours I can use."
Cliff S.   York, SC

"We are working on a huge apartment project, and this is coming in really handy. The book gave us the inspiration to get started in the first place."
Edmund & Emily M.   Coppers Cove, TX

"This book fell into my hands last year. It was like an answer to prayer. I just devoured the book immediately. I have 20-30 sticky tabs sticking out of it all over."
Dorethy H.   Topeka, KS

"Excellent book. A lot of useful information a lot of people don't have. Very informative. As a contractor, I sat down with the book. At first I was wanting to toss it out the window. Either this guy is clueless, or he's been there before. I finally realized that the realities of running your own project are right on target. You can run your own project and become your own construction manager. Often the client doesn't have a clue and they are running fifteen subs and don't want to cut loose control and it turns into a nightmare. They are never there, but they hold the power of the purse. When the subs know that you're not cutting the check, they don't paying attention to you.

It was very informative and very on target. And this is the wave of where construction will go. A great book to pass on to clients. I've got a client now where they can't get a hold of a contractor. They've done a lot of footwork, but don't have enough information to take the reins and do it. It's very hard to get contractors right now and this is a great resource for people who could do this on their own. This will give them enough to know what they are getting into at the very least. It gets crazy with people who don't know what they are doing.

A contractor's perspective. We hear how to sell. And we find contractors that just slam-dunk people, and we are trying to build a reputation for doing what's fair. I've laid my books open to people. Everyone talks about leveling the playing field, but that's difficult when there's no one to reinforce the certification of contractors. We find scabs out here who undercut the price but don't carry the insurance, the Workmen's Comp., and they're not above board. We often have to go out and clean up a bad mess. If people really want to level the playing field they have to reinforce the certification of contractors.

Instead, let's give everyone the information to be a true owner-builder. We're trying to run a square game. We try to make enough profits to stay in business for another day. We get slammed with high liability insurance, workers comp., and all the overhead. I'm all for people being fully informed. If someone had this information and had their project as well-planned as it should be, it would be a joy to work for them. There would be very few problems. That does everybody a service."
Larry T.   Santa Rosa, CA

"I love your book. You talk about a software project in the beginning of the book. I've used that as an illustration for the need for planning at my own work."
Scott A.   Walnut Creek, CA

"It was very well written. I liked the summary level detail."
Gerry R.   Austin, TX

"It's inspiring. The testimonials in there are amazing. It's very tempting to do this."
Kathy N.   Truckee, CA

"This is one the best books I've found on this subject."
Terry H.   Santa Fe, NM

"I appreciate your book. I thought it was a very good source. I also appreciate the postings on the web site."
Dave M.   Sunnyvale, CA

"This book is done very practically. I like the way it's put together. It's not theoretical, it's my type of book. Thank you for doing this. You did a great job putting this together."
Anthony L.   San Jose, CA

"The book reinforced our thinking that this is all do-able.
Ken & Linda L.   Silver City, NM

"This is the best thing I have gotten my hands on. I checked it out at the library and decided I needed my own copy to make notes in."
Mark F.   Lynnwood, WA

"I found the book very useful. I found the information you gave on making a contract very helpful."
Richard R.   Huntingtown, MD

"This book has been just tremendous. I read it once and marked it, and now I'm going through again. It's been so helpful, I would highly recommend it. I'm thrilled with it."
Bill H.   Sacramento, CA

"It's very helpful, especially for someone new to this sort of thing."
Jason A.   Lake Station, IN

More than 50 pages of user comments are viewable on our web site.

Letter to the Reader

I had no idea I could build a house.

I didn't know the first thing about carpentry, or cement work, or any of the trades; I had no tools; and I certainly didn't have enough money to build the kind of place I knew I wanted.

Yet here I sit in the nicest office I've ever had in the nicest home we've ever owned enjoying every comfort and a breathtaking view of the mighty Wasatch Mountains.

Elaine and I built this place. We truly love it. It's a gorgeous house that has everything we want in it and works very well. It's a great comfort because we can manage the mortgage payment and because we go to sleep knowing that we have more equity in it than we owe.

I never thought we could do this because people assume you can't. And the thought that you could do it far less expensively than a general contractor really causes resistance. People told us "no" all the time.

We decided to write a book that would tell you "yes".

Enjoy this book. It's loaded with every tool, technique, and tip that we used, most of which we couldn't find in any other book.

One more thing. We sometimes felt very alone building our house. Because we don't want that to happen to you, we have provided a web site where you can interact with other owner-builders. Elaine and I are accessible via toll-free number and e-mail as well.

Don't let anybody tell you you can't do this.

Table of Contents

Chapter 1: You Can Save $100,000 1

Amazing Cost Savings 1
Best Tax-free Way to Make Money 2
"Cold Sweat" Equity 3
Lowering the Threshold 4
Other Benefits 4
Myths and Propaganda 5
Owner-Builder Misconceptions 9
Qualifications of an Owner-Builder 11

Chapter 2: Learn The Wealth-Building Secret 13

People in Construction Know the Secret 13
Free and Clear Step-up Strategy 14
Owner-Builder Exclusive 16
Retirement Plan 17
"Open Up Your Veins" 18
D.S.D.E. 18
Rock Star Wages 19
Guerilla Economics 20

Chapter 3: General Contractors Aren't What You Think They Are 21

Contractor Games 21
You'll Shop Better 24
You'll Be More Organized 25
You'll Give It More Attention 26
You'll Keep Your Savings 26
How Much Can You Save? 27
When is 10% Not 10%? 28
Contractors Mark Up Their Costs to You 29
Get Bids from Three Generals 29

Chapter 4: You Can Manage Better Than a Contractor 31

Management Concept One: "People Often Ingest M&M's" 31
Management Concept Two: "Plan Hard, Work Easy" 32
Why Plan 33
I Want a Thousand Hours! 34

Act Like You're a Business 36
Planning Steps 38

* Key PP 36-48

* *Key chapter*

Chapter 5: You Will Profit By Building a True Custom Home 51

Starter, Step Up, Custom, Dream House 51
Four Ways to Make Money 52
Your Dream Home Notebook 53
You or the Market? 54
Real Estate Survey 58
Sub and Supplier Input 59
Features of a Custom Home 60
A House that Works 62
Quality Considerations 63
Comfort and Convenience Considerations 65
Energy Saving Features 66
Forum Thread from Our Web Site 68

*

Chapter 6: Conquer Details Room By Room and Save 20% 69

Change Orders Are Costly 69
How Specs Save You Money and Get You a Better House 71
How to Develop Room by Room Specifications 72
Architect vs. Designer 77
You Are Ready to See Your Designer 79
Good Design Saves Money in Four Ways 80

Chapter 7: How to Get the Subs on Your Side 85

How to Find Good Subs 85
How to Interview Subs 87
Detailed, Accurate Bidding 88
Get Three Bids from Subs on Each Item 91
How to Get Bids 92
Follow Up Your Bids 93

Chapter 8: How to Build a Budget That Is a Powerful Miracle Tool 95

Start with Your Bids from General Contractors 95
Spreadsheet Budgeting 96

Riverbottoms House Budget 99
Budget Worksheet 105
"Shop" Your Budget for a While 106
Sample Links from Our Web Site 118

Chapter 9: Commando Shopping Techniques 119

The Price of Marshmallows 119
Bargains..121
Identify Your Suppliers...123
When You Pay for Materials Separately You Save 125
How to Use a Computer to Save 126
100 Construction Bargain Strategies..128

Chapter 10: How to Schedule the Work
at a Savings 159

Another Miracle Tool 159
Picking the Right People is Half the Battle 160
Computer Scheduling..161
Live in Your Schedule for a While 162
Sample Construction Work Schedule 164
Schedule Worksheet..166
Back-up Plans to Keep the Work Going..170
Schedule Reinforcement Program 171

Chapter 11: How to Make Your Lender Swoon 173

Your Next Thousand Hour Payoff...173
What the Lenders Want...174
Your Loan Proposal Book 175
Lenders Want to Put a Copy of the License in the File 177
Don't Budget Self-Work 178
Your Loan Presentation...179
Shop for the Right Terms 180

Chapter 12: Paperwork Before You Begin....................................... 183

Anatomy of a Lawsuit...183
Get Good Protection 185
Lien Waiver 186
Write Good Contracts 188
City Permits 189
Contracting Agreement..190

Chapter 13: Six Months to Victory 191

"Integrate" 191
Step One 192
How to Get Subs to Show Up 192
Rules of Work 193
Running the Job 194
Cost Accounting 195
Daily Record 196
Your Video Camera and Other Unlikely Tools 196
Emotional Roller Coaster 197

Chapter 14: Smooth Execution Saves Money and Improves Quality 199

Other Daily Duties 199
Why You Need to Be On-Site 202
Consensus Breeds Creativity 204
Clean Job Saves Five Percent 205
The Inspector Is Your Friend 206
You Can Get Independent Inspections 207
Inspections Checklist 208
Staying on Schedule 210
If You Do Self-Work — Control It 210
Rules of Self-Work 213
Sub Recognition 215
Owner-Builder Connections from Our Web Site 216

Chapter 15: Mistakes You Can Avoid And Successes You Can Achieve 217

Mistakes 217
Disasters 218
Successes 219
How to Score Yourself 220
If You are Married 222
The Ten Commandments of Owner-Building 223

Chapter 16: If You Decide to Use a Contractor 225

There are a Lot of Reasons to Use a General 225
How to Hire a General 226
Who's Got the Risk? 227
You Know What You are Getting Into 229

Afterword: Once You're In... 231

Minimize Punch List.........................231
Punch List 232
Lower Your Property Taxes..................236
Better than Wall Street......................236
Help Someone Else 237
Web Messages 238

Appendix: Free Special Report 239

✱ page 240 KCr

Index 245

Resource Guide.........251

Special Reports 252
Books 257
DVD's 264
Free CD-ROM 270
Free E-mail Newsletter.....................271
www.OwnerBuilderBook.com..............272
Paperless Coupons...........................274

Chapter 1: You Can Save $100,000

Amazing Cost Savings

You are driving down a beautiful street and you see houses that you would like to own. These are spacious custom homes with many upgrades and custom features. They cost around $350,000. You want to build a house like that, but not at that price. You sigh and drive on. But wait a minute. What if you could save 35% on construction and build that $350,000 house for $254,000?

Adjusting for land value, the average owner-builder ("O-B") I studied saved that much on the same type of property. How does $226,000 strike you? That's what it would cost if my own owner-builder savings were applied to that $350,000 house. How about $207,000? One of the O-B's I studied saved that much building a similar house.

In these examples, I have assumed that the $350,000 house was built on land with a value of $75,000 and construction costs were $275,000. And I have applied savings of 35%, 44%, and 52% — actual achievements of people like you.

Savings Comparison					
Price of House	Cost of Land	Construction Cost	O-B Savings	O-B Cost of Construction	Total Cost with Land
$ 350,000	$ 75,000	$ 275,000	35%	$ 178,750	$ 253,750
$ 350,000	$ 75,000	$ 275,000	45%	$ 151,250	$ 226,250
$ 350,000	$ 75,000	$ 275,000	52%	$ 132,000	$ 207,000

Sources Say

"Most people think that to build a home you have to know a lot about architecture, bricklaying, carpentry, electricity, and plumbing. Not so. Most professional builders are essentially managers. They leave the actual hammering, nailing, and wiring to specialists."

From *Everything You Need To Know About Building the Custom Home*
(See page 259)

The 35% savings example comes from my interviews with owner-builders from around the country. Their average savings on construction costs were 35%. These savings are calculated either against actual builder estimates of construction cost, or against appraised values after completion.

The 44% savings example is our own. Elaine and I built our home in 1996 for $50 per finished square foot after it was estimated by a general contractor at $90 per foot, exactly as specified, with the addition of many upgrades. We saved about $140,000, or 44% of the estimated cost.

The 52% savings example is that of Vince Miner, a college tennis coach I interviewed. He saved 52% on the cost of his custom home by owner-building.

Best Tax-free Way to Make Money

"You can make more tax-free money building houses for yourself than any other way."

Rod Allred, general contractor.

Owner-building is the best kept wealth secret around. I first understood this when we struggled our way into our first house in Denver, 25 years ago. We tried painstakingly for a year to save up the $3,000 down payment from my IBM paycheck, and wound up putting part of it on a credit card. I just barely squeaked in before the house got over my borrowing limit. The house cost $55,000.

Sources Say

"As the developer and general contractor of your own house, you perform the most important (and best paid) roles in home building."

From *Build Your Dream Home for Less*
(See page 259)

A year and a half later, when we moved out of town, I sold the house for $84,000, paid commissions of $4,000 and had $18,000 left over. Since I purchased another home right away, I owed no taxes. The $18,000 was mine! I put $10,000 down on the new house and had $8,000 in cash. With the cash, I paid off two automobiles. I didn't even have $500 in savings from the years at IBM. But I had $18,000 in cash from my house. And I found out an amazing thing about that house profit. It spends just like any other money!

Living expenses and taxes had eaten up my generous IBM salary, but the money we made from our house was intact. We made that money from appreciation, one of the ways that home ownership pays off. Colorado was in the midst of a real estate boom, and we made a phenomenal 15% gain per year on our home. I was ecstatic. It wasn't until years later that I discovered an even better way to make money on a home.

Building booms come and go, and house appreciation fluctuates. It is rarely more than ten percent per year, and it can be flat, or worse. In the 1990's, homes in some parts of California actually lost value. A surer, faster way to make money is through owner-building your home, because you can accomplish your gain in a very short time, usually less than six months. We saved 44% on our home in the first year by owner-building, and we continue to add five percent or so to its value each year through appreciation. The appreciation amounts to more than $1,000 a month, but during the time we built our home we made about $20,000 a month through construction savings.

This sizeable income is protected from taxes in two ways. First, money saved building your house is not taxed at all when you save it. You don't pay federal, state, social security, sales tax or property taxes on what you save. It goes direct and untouched into your home equity and your net worth. Second, when you sell it, the 1997 Taxpayer Relief Act allows you to keep your profit tax-free.

If you are married and file a joint return, you can keep up to $500,000 in house profits without paying a dime in taxes. You must live in the house for two years to enjoy this tax-free bonanza. But you can do it again and again, as long as Congress maintains the current law. You no longer even need to build or buy a new home with the proceeds.

Some people think that winning the lottery is the best way to make money, but it's hardly tax-free. You can "make" a million dollars on the lottery, yet with the $50,000 checks you would get once a year (they usually pay the million over a 20 year period), the various taxes you'd pay (more than 50%), and the things you'd spend it on, very little if any would go to your net worth. In fact, I added more to my wealth each month I was building my house than a million dollar lottery winner does in a whole year. All the savings in building a house for yourself go to net worth. It's pure wealth!

"Cold Sweat" Equity

To achieve this wealth, you don't need to swing a hammer or do much self-work on your home. On the contrary, I advocate limiting self-work and emphasizing your role as manager of construction.

The big savings in home costs that build value are often called "sweat equity" — you provide labor to reduce costs on a new home or to improve an existing one. The value of the property and your equity in it rise. This book will teach you "cold sweat" equity — the savings and value you get through your worry, planning and management. Most of the savings described in the chapters that follow are in planning, organizing, and controlling construction costs.

> **Readers Say**
>
> "I have a friend who built a house with four kids under 7 and a husband going to graduate school and she did it for a pretty good price. If she can do it I know we can."
>
> John & Jessica N.
> Lehi, UT

> **Readers Say**
>
> "Did $8,000 in sweat equity, all in the last 6 weeks of the house. Very productive, but very stressful."
>
> Gary & Linda Z.
> Stansbury Park, UT

Sources Say

"Here are the major ways to save money: Real estate commission, 7%; Builder mark-up, 20%; Savings on material purchases, 4%; Cost-saving construction, 2%; Doing work yourself, 9%; Total: up to 42%."

From *The Complete Guide to Contracting Your Home*
(See page 260)

Lowering The Threshold

For many, home ownership is an unattainable dream, beyond the financial reach of the average person. The owner-builder process can change that.

If the median new home cost is $200,000 and the mortgage payments are $1,750 per month, only people with household incomes of $5,250 per month, or $63,000 per year can qualify (rule of thumb: income should exceed three times payment). This amount of monthly income ranks at about the 60th percentile of U.S. households. At a savings of 25% of construction cost, that same average home could be erected for $160,000, requiring a monthly payment of $1,400 and a household income of $4,200 or $50,400 a year, hitting the 50th percentile of incomes in the U.S.

For those who are just trying to enter the market in the smallest possible way, you may be looking at a project in the $100,000 range. Kyle and Rachel Echols purchased a starter home for $120,000 and in two years were thrilled to know its value had climbed to $140,000. Look at those numbers. The $120,000 mortgage requires a monthly payment of $1,050 for a household income of $3,150 a month or $37,800 a year. This comes in at the 40th percentile in the U.S. Saving 25% on the construction portion would put that project at about $96,000 for a monthly payment of $850. The qualifying household income would be $2,520 a month or $30,250 a year, about the 30th percentile of U.S. households.

Saving 25% or more on construction costs can make home ownership available to an additional ten percent of U.S. households or about ten million more families. Ownership of nicer homes is also available to a wider group. I live in an exclusive neighborhood that includes the ranch of former football star Steve Young, and the home of TV personality Donny Osmond. This is a neighborhood far above our means. Typically the mortgage on a home like we live in would require a monthly income of $9,000. Because we saved $140,000 on the home we were able to save $1,200 on the monthly mortgage. Multiplying times three, we were able to get into the house at an income of about $3,500 a month less than otherwise indicated.

Other Benefits

We saved 44% building our home, but the benefits didn't stop there. Our satisfaction has been enormous — real daily pleasure in our new home and a sense of pride that we accomplished what we set out to do.

In doing this, we didn't cut any corners. In fact, we always chose the "upgrade" while trying for the best deals we could get on the improved version. We upgraded the carpet, cabinets and appliances from the original specifications. We bulked up the framing, the insulation, the wiring and the concrete work. We upgraded the fixtures and added flexibility for future upgrades to the house as each opportunity presented itself. In many cases we found an upgrade available at the same or lower cost than the going price for standard levels of finish. For instance, we actually saved money shifting from Corian™ to solid granite countertops when a bargain arose.

Readers Say

"We were with a package plan at first. This is where they provide you all the materials at a discount and you get to hire your own subs. I decided by the time I went and got labor-only bids, I might as well get my own materials, too. I saved a lot of money."

Dan M.
Green River, WY

As your own contractor you get to buy cafeteria-style. You may have things you want to do which vary from the norm, and which save labor dollars. You don't have to argue the merits with a contractor, like using pre-built roof trusses instead of "stick-built" roofs. Or using insulated panel sheathing instead of conventional stick built exterior walls. You can realize increased savings on labor because you negotiate with each trade directly.

You get the extras you want without the surcharges occasioned by fixed-price bidding. One of the pleasures of our new home is ceiling fans. They can move the heat out of a bedroom quickly on a summer evening and provide a very pleasant breeze through a summer night. Builders will add ceiling fans as upgrades to custom homes at upwards of $300 apiece. We put in each high-end fan ourselves for about $75 and each economy fan in children's rooms for about $35. At that price we installed as many as we wanted, and controlled the quality closely.

We saw just the right vinyl siding at a home & garden show, and met an award-winning craftsman to install it. We removed the original siding subcontractor from our plans and engaged the new craftsman without a hitch. We found a solid vinyl deck material we wanted to use. We negotiated for a contractor price and got it installed at far below market value. In the course of construction, other ideas and improvements occurred to us. We implemented them without having to negotiate with a contractor. We found many bargains, and exploited them on the spot.

There are unexpected benefits when you build your own house. You have control over quality and features. You get inexpensive extras. You ensure low maintenance and ease of repair. You control energy-efficiency and comfort. You derive a continuing sense of accomplishment, make new friends, experience family and personal growth and gain prestige.

In the course of interviewing architects for *The Owner-Builder Book*, I talked with an architect from Louisiana who was curious about our owner-built home. I described the specifications and asked him what a house like ours is worth. He said that in his market, our home would appraise for "at least $150 per square foot". After being told so often that one cannot achieve a success like ours, this brought me a deep sense of satisfaction.

Myths and Propaganda

One of the biggest satisfactions in owner-building our home has been that we "beat the system". The system tends to be a closed one, reserving the privilege of owner-building to construction industry "insiders". Many myths about owner-building have been spread about as propaganda by general contractors. Even some construction lenders have voiced the stereotypes you see here.

Since contractors have their own industry groups and associations with their own publicity machines, they can perpetuate attitudes about something like owner-building that they consider to be a threat. Very little exists to counteract the flow of misinformation. Owner-builders have no organized voice, no association, no official magazines, no propagandist. As a result, many of the following attitudes have come to be accepted as fact.

"You Can't Save Any Money"

This is a widely circulated idea that has no basis in fact. Every owner-builder that I surveyed saved something over the cost of a general contractor-built house. I know of several instances of "civilian" O-B's (non-construction people) completing their new homes with 50% equity or more. Among construction tradesmen who owner-build, instances exist of savings of 60% and more in terms of cash expended. (Part of their savings is due to trading labor with other tradesmen.)

This is not to say that O-B's don't exceed their construction budgets. Budget overruns are common in all branches of construction. Mistakes, surprises, and upgrades caused my own budget to go over by $20,000. But I still saved 44% against contractor estimate.

"The Professional Builder Passes Inspections With Flying Colors"

Building inspectors tell me they catch instances of contractors cheating frequently, although less so on custom homes. A veteran general contractor whom we hired to do air conditioning and furnace work caused me one of my few failed inspections. He had framed up the furnace closet three inches too shallow to pass code. He had been general contracting and doing furnace work for 40 years. He had to re-frame the closet, and since I was dumb enough to pay him by the hour, I got to pay for his indiscretion.

Owner-builders on the other hand are regarded as a good bet by inspectors. They are building for themselves, not to protect a contractor's bottom line. As a result, they are seen as interested in quality, durability, and safety.

"Contractors Get Better Prices Than the Public"

I had trouble getting a good price on the lumber for my house. My initial quote came in at $21,000. A general contractor I used as an advisor sent me to his lumberyard to get his prices. He had built many homes with his lumber dealer over the years. The dealer priced the package at $19,000. I was pleased but decided to give it another try. Then a prestige builder friend of mine who buys $250,000 a year in lumber had his lumberyard estimate it. This time the price came in at $16,000. The materials were identical, and I was able to beat the price of my construction advisor by $3,000, and the initial quote by $5,000. The advisor was amazed. He had never questioned his prices at the lumberyard.

A retired cement contractor told me that he had a deal with the cement plant to buy concrete at $10 a cubic yard, many years ago. At the time, contractor prices for concrete were $16 a yard. He kept his prices a secret by signing a non-disclosure agreement with the plant. His conclusion: "There are contractor prices, and then there are contractor prices." This contractor got wealthy by sourcing the material at secret prices, and passing it on to his customers at street prices. Note well that any contractor who gets a special price may have no motivation for sharing his savings with you.

There is always a better price to be had, usually through research and effort. Chapter 9 provides you a guide to construction buying at a savings.

"Contractors Take the Risk and Relieve the Owner of That Burden"

Author Ronald Horne says that increasingly, contractors work without risk: "There is no risk for the builder any more." This is particularly true if a home is built on a fixed-bid contract, as 90% are. If a contractor agrees to a fixed price with you, he knows that he can meet it because he has control over materials and workmanship, and can cut corners to protect his profit. For the owner, the risk is the viability of the single greatest investment he will ever make. For a review of relative risks, see Chapter 16.

"Contractors Can Get Better Quality Materials Than You Can"

One contractor told me that owners were liable to get "crooked lumber" because they don't know any better. That wasn't a problem for us. Before we signed our lumberyard credit agreement, our framer advised us to cross out the paragraph that said we had to pay a restocking charge for any returns. He then inspected all the stock that was delivered, and refused to accept anything that was hard to work with. I hired the framer; the framer checked the lumber.

"The Contractor is There to Protect Your Interests"

The interests of a contractor and his customer are frequently at odds. The customer wants every upgrade and attention to detail possible. The contractor wants every bit of his planned profit, and that means economizing on costs. Most of these trade-offs are decided by the contractor during the course of construction. Who do you think he decides for?

"Owner-Builders Build Shoddy, Cheap Houses"

This makes no sense. The owner wants the best for his comfort and his investment. Unless he is doing the work himself (not recommended) he is contracting for the best quality he can get. In reality, owner-builders are known for upgrades and extras, not for shortcuts and cheating.

"Owner-Building Isn't Legal"

Unless you buy land in a developer-restricted subdivision, there is no law against owner-building in the United States. You must own the land, obtain necessary permits, and make timely requests for municipal inspections. You may be required to carry certain forms of insurance.

"You Have to Have a License"

Not to build your own house. In a few areas there are restrictions against doing some of the mechanical trades yourself, (electrical, plumbing, heating and air conditioning). But even those restrictions are rare.

"Banks Won't Lend to You Unless You Have a Contractor"

In nationwide telephone interviews of bankers, I found that 15% of banks refused to make construction loans to owner-builders. 40% made the loans with some restrictions. 45% made the loans with no special restrictions.

"You Can't Possibly Get It Done in Six Months"

The National Association of Home Builders says that the average owner-built residence took 9.5 months to complete last year in the U.S. Contractor-built residences took six months on average.

My survey of owner-builders indicates that the average planned schedule of completion was five months. Average actual time was seven months. Most O-B's could use some help in this area. About half of my respondents finished in under six months. Vince Miner, owner-builder extraordinaire, finished his 4,000 square foot house in four months.

"You Will Save Enough In Interest Alone To Pay a Contractor"

My carrying charges on a seven month $150,000 construction loan were an average of $625 a month. The National Association of Home Builders says average completion time on contractor-built houses is six months. As it took me seven months to build, completing the house in six months would have saved me $625 in interest.

But many contractor customers complain about how slow contractors are to finish a job. Particularly on custom homes, the contractor time to complete can be much longer. My neighbor built a 9,000 square foot dream home with a contractor. The original schedule was 14 months, and they got the job done in a mere 30 months.

"You Can Make More at Your Job Than What a Contractor Costs"

The average American saves less than ten percent of his salary. However, all of the savings you realize building your home go directly to your net worth. If you build a $350,000 house for $250,000 you enrich yourself by $100,000 in equity. If you make $100,000 at work, you enrich yourself by less than $10,000 on average, a savings rate of less than $1,000 a month. The average owner-builder I studied completed their house in seven months. Which is better, $100,000 saved or $7,000?

Few people have to quit their jobs to act as their own general contractor. However, you will have to make some choices during the construction period.

"The Subs Won't Show Up for You"

A good portion of this book is devoted to the problem of managing subs effectively, starting from subcontractor interviews and references, to the bidding process, to on-site management. Some of the O-B's I interviewed had no problem with subs showing up. Much more to come on this subject.

"You Can't Do It Because You Lack Know-How"

You may indeed lack construction skill. However, contracting a home is not a construction skill; it is a management skill.

One contractor told me that no one should expect to come in and do what a contractor does any more than expect to do what a doctor does. He said, "What if my wife needed surgery — do you think I could cut her open with a knife and start messing with her organs?"

I have to laugh at the gruesome illustration. I can just see a couple hearing this harangue and the wife squirming at the vivid analogy. And then placing themselves wisely in the hands of this surgeon of brick and mortar.

But the analogy is a scare tactic and hardly apt. This builder went on to say that he had seen windows framed into owner-builder walls without headers, and later on, the walls would sag, he said. Well, O-B's rarely do their own framing. This is the province of the framer. It is inspected by the inspector. You choose the framer you trust.

A better analogy is that of a homemaker. A builder is more like a homemaker than a surgeon. He shops or should shop for good values; he coordinates the efforts of different members of the group, and manages a budget. The task is a management task, not a medical one.

Owner-Builder Misconceptions

For their part, prospective owner-builders labor under some misconceptions, too. Lenders tell me that O-B applicants for construction loans are almost never prepared. They tend to underestimate the size of the task, or their own ability to contribute. Many don't understand the risks involved and how to manage them.

"I Could Do This With My Free Evenings and Weekends"

The general contracting task will actually take owner-builders about one man-year of effort, though you could spread the planning part over several years of time. Most of that can be done on evenings and weekends. The construction phase

Sources Say

"We (contractors) aren't tradespeople or very handy do it-yourselfers. We are professional managers of people, time and money. Those are the required skills for managing your own renovation project."

From *Be Your Own Home Renovation Contractor*
(See page 258)

requires about four hours per working day of the O-B's time. At least half of that during working hours.

"Once I Get the Ball Rolling, the Project Will Manage Itself"

This could be true for someone who has done dozens of houses and had systems and routines in place to manage the process. The construction phase of building a house has been called "Mr. Toad's Wild Ride" for good reason. Many things will go wrong if not managed, and many opportunities for improvement of house comfort, longevity and value will be missed.

"Subs Will Show Up as Promised and Do What They Promised"

Almost never.

"There Is Only One Way To Do It"

Some O-B's will not take counsel from the subs they hire for possible improvements in design or approach.

"My Construction Drawings Provide an Infallible Guide for the Subs"

One key to saving time and money is to be decisive. Many questions as to the owner's desires and intent arise every day on a custom home project, in spite of detailed drawings.

"The Subs Know What They Are Doing and Take Care of Everything"

One O-B went on vacation and returned to find that the roof had been placed on his house, but that the second story had been omitted.

"The Subs Will Do Everything They Can To Save Me Money"

Most savings come through persistence and planning. Help from any quarter is welcome, but it rarely comes spontaneously.

Qualifications of an Owner-Builder

1. You come to the job each day prepared to fire people if needed.

This consists of being clear about what you expect and holding subs accountable for it. You are writing the check, you are in power. You stage your payments so that you can pay for performance to date and release the sub if necessary. You can put your foot down if needed.

2. You are somewhat familiar with construction.

You have interest in the subject of building and some aptitude, and are willing to learn. You talk the talk of the business. This can be learned from building shows on television, from builder magazines to which you can subscribe, from interviewing subs, and from observing building projects, among other places. Even though you may not perform a given trade, you can talk about it knowledgeably.

However, overemphasis on building knowledge can interfere with the exercise of good planning and management, your principal tools.

3. You communicate well.

You make clear your expectations, and make certain they are understood. You can talk to all kinds of people. You can win loyalty and build relationships with the team. You are capable of making endless phone calls to check on things.

4. You pay patient attention to detail.

Winston Churchill, who liked to lay brick on his English country estate and was a competent oil painter, said, "Genius is the capacity for taking infinite pains." The tiny details done right add up to a distinctly superior house. The O-B must be prepared to take the time to see that things are done right.

5. You have job flexibility.

Either you or your spouse need to spend four hours a day or so on-site during construction. Many construction lenders interview their applicants about the circumstances of their employment to ensure this flexibility.

6. You have determination and problem solving ability.

You don't lie down at the appearance of the first knotty problem. There are several every week during construction. You will stick with them until they are solved.

7. You are financially motivated.

Parkinson's Law is that work expands to fill the time allotted to it. A corollary is that a construction budget expands to the borrowing limit of the owner. If your limit is low, you will be more ingenious in finding ways to meet it.

8. You are organized.

If not in general, at least for this project, you are organized to a fault. You will tend to the agreements, paperwork, schedule and budget tirelessly.

9. You are a good shopper.

You can tell differences in quality, can find bargains, and won't overspend on anything.

10. You are a good student.

You watch well and learn quickly. You can get answers to your questions.

I possessed, or Elaine did, nine out of ten of these qualifications, though we had to work at number two. It cost us dearly that I was utterly incapable of number one. If you lack one or more of these, perhaps you can hire someone to compensate. In my case, an independent inspector would have been a great help. *See Chapter 14.*

Chapter 2: Learn The Wealth-Building Secret

People in Construction Know the Secret

Readers Say

"I was a plumber for 21 years. I'm going to build a house for $250,000 and the one I saw built to the same plans on a lake sold for $1.2 million."

David D.
Lilburn, GA

We've all heard of "inside information" and "insider trading". In building homes, industry people have the "inside track" on a wealth-building secret, the building of houses for themselves. Probably half of all owner-builders are construction people. For them, owner-building is something of a side benefit to their profession. But you shouldn't be excluded from the privilege if you aren't a construction person.

The average American's net worth is equal to about four times their annual compensation. Thus, if you make $50,000 a year, you would hope to have a net worth of $200,000. And many people toil their entire lifetimes to develop it. But people in construction often have homes that contribute that much to their net worth.

One of the general contractors I interviewed was an executive in a large construction company. He owner-built his $650,000 house with help from company tradesmen for $450,000. It was finished in four months. He added $200,000 to his wealth practically overnight. This approximates the net worth that many of us work for over our entire lifetimes. For him it was an employment perk.

Sources Say

The Well-Built House has a good section on choosing a lot.

(See page 260)

Sources Say

Your New House lists 20 questions to ask before buying a piece of land such as, 'Are there any impact fees?'

(See page 260)

Sources Say

Build It Right! has a good chapter on lots.

(See page 258)

Sources Say

Independent Builder has a chapter on choosing a house site.

(See page 259)

One of the subs on my house built his own 4,500 square foot house for $88,000 plus land, making a total cost of about $120,000. It took less than six months. Yet that house has a valuation over $250,000. In six months, he added more than $130,000 to his net worth!

Free and Clear Step-Up Strategy

As an owner-builder, you may not feel very rich when you take on the increased mortgage payment that comes with your larger home. In fact, you may not see the financial effects until you step up to a house with a reduced mortgage payment or no payment at all, what I call the Free and Clear Step-up Strategy.

Custom Home Step-Up Strategy: Shrinking Payment

House	Land and Prev. Home Equity	Projected Builder's Estimate	Actual Monthly Payment	Net Cost to Build	Monthly Payment	Two-Year Sale Price	Current Value of 1st House
First	$100,000	$337,000	$2,370	$152,750	$1,528	$350,480	$350,480
Second	$197,730	$385,528	$1,878	$91,416	$914	$400,949	$364,499
Third	$309,533	$441,044	$1,315	$21,250	$212	$458,686	$379,079
Fourth	$437,436	$504,554	$671	$0	$0	$524,737	$394,242

• Improvement in Scale over original house: 1.3
• Assumptions: 2% appreciation, 9% mortgage rates, 25% construction savings, 10% Increase in house scale, self-sold.
• First house example is a 3,000 square foot home at $90 per foot.

I have heard it said that you can own your home free and clear if you build seven of them, over 14 years. South Carolina owner-builder Alex Acree says that you can do it in three builds. My calculations say that the average owner-builder can do it in four builds over eight years under certain somewhat conservative assumptions. Those are: two percent inflation in home prices, nine percent mortgage rates, 25% construction savings, 10% successive increases in house scale, and self-sold. The analysis above assumes that the owner-builder starts with the land paid for and modest proceeds from a previous home — $100,000 in initial equity. It assumes that the initial owner-built home is a 3,000 square foot custom home with a market value of $90 per square foot. In this example, the O-B takes advantage of increasing equity by making a smaller monthly payment on each successive house.

The owner-builder in the next scenario could own a home free and clear after three builds in six years through the simple expedient of keeping the monthly mortgage payment level. This means that even though the required mortgage payment shrinks on succeeding houses, the owner-builder intentionally makes the same monthly payment on each house. The non-required portion of the level payment goes to reduce loan principle each month. This builds equity faster, and in the example below, the third home is owned free and clear after paying off the nominal residual balance of $6,530:

Custom Home Step-Up Strategy: Level Payment

House	Equity	Builder's Estimate	Projected Monthly Payment	Net Cost to Build	Actual Monthly Payment	Two-Year Sale Price	Current Value of 1st House
First	$100,000	$337,000	$2,370	$152,750	$1,528	$350,480	$350,480
Second	$197,730	$385,528	$1,878	$91,416	$1,528	$400,949	$364,499
Third	$324,253	$441,044	$1,168	$6,530	$65	$458,686	$379,079

- Improvement in Scale over original house: 1.2
- Assumptions: 2% appreciation, 9% mortgage rates, 25% construction savings, 10% Increase in house scale, self-sold.
- First house example is a 3,000 square foot home at $90 per foot.

This example can be improved upon even further. Here's where the 1997 Tax Law gives you a dramatic benefit. In the past, homeowners had to spend more money on each successive home they owned to escape capital gains taxes on the sale of their previous home. Thus, if you sold a home for $250,000 you would need to buy or build another home at a cost of $251,000 or more. The Taxpayer Relief Act of 1997 changed this. Now you can replace your home with a less costly one without penalty. For those who want to own a home free and clear as rapidly as possible, the tax law opens up a third scenario. This example illustrates a way to own your own home free and clear after only two builds in four years. The strategy is to downscale the second house by 20% in order to own it free and clear after only a small cash payment:

Custom Home Step-Down Strategy

House	Equity	Builder's Estimate	Projected Monthly Payment	Net Cost to Build	Actual Monthly Payment	Two-Year Sale Price	Current Value of 1st House
First	$100,000	$337,000	$2,370	$152,750	$1,528	$350,480	$350,480
Second	$197,730	$280,384	$827	$12,558	$126	$297,599	$364,499

- Improvement in Scale over original house: 0.8
- Assumptions: 2% appreciation, 9% mortgage rates, 25% construction savings, no increase in house scale, self-sold.
- First house example is a 3,000 square foot home at $90 per foot.

In my case, I will achieve a free and clear home in two builds because house and land prices went up dramatically fast at the right time for me, because I had a low mortgage rate, and because I saved 44% on construction of the first house.

Author Marian Robinson says: "Owning your own home free and clear — that's the key to all the rest. Once you have your snug harbor, your safe base, all else comes easy. You can tell the rest of the world to go to hell if you want, once you own the roof over your head."

A third of the owner-builders I studied have built or plan to build more than once. As one wit put it, some believe that "You have to build two houses to get one right." Some O-B's are motivated by the "hands on" pleasure of trying new trades or by the pleasure of negotiating better deals. I found many ideas building my first one that I am anxious to include in our next house. My net worth rose dramatically during this project, and that becomes a major motivation to repeat.

One owner-builder who is a commercial freight pilot contributed this case study example of the financial effects of stepping up:

Case History

Two pilots, one with a commercial airline, one with freight. "A" makes $160,000 a year. "B" makes $80,000. Four years ago both bought houses. Both paid $150,000. "A" started paying his mortgage down, owes $120,000 and his house is worth $160,000. His equity is $40,000. "B" sold the $150,000 house for $240,000 in a stronger market. He then built a $240,000 house for a mortgage of $165,000. That house is now worth $300,000. His equity is $135,000 — more than three times what "A" has. He lives in a nicer neighborhood now with half the salary that "A" earns. And he has something for retirement.

Owning your home free and clear knocks out more than a third of your family budget, while potentially improving your level of home comfort and utility. The free and clear strategy reduces your need for salary. For instance, if you have a gross salary of $75,000, your discretionary income is $45,000:

		Percent of Income
Gross Salary:	$75,000	100%
Net Income:	$45,000	60%
Housing Costs:	$25,000	33%
Other Costs:	$20,000	27%

If you eliminated housing costs from your expenses, you would save $25,000 per year (property taxes and insurance excluded). Your need for salary would decrease by much more than that, due to typical income taxes and payroll deductions:

		Percent of Income
Housing Costs:	$0	0%
Other Costs:	$20,000	27%
Needed Income:	$20,000	60%
Needed Salary:	$33,333	100%

This means that if you eliminated $25,000 in annual housing costs, you could eliminate $42,000 in needed salary.

Owner-Builder Exclusive

Due to the Taxpayer Relief Act of 1997, U.S. owner-builders are in a unique position to profit from their homes. The law now allows you to sell a home every two years with no tax consequences (unless your profits exceed $500,000). In actual practice, only owner-builders can sell a home profitably every two years. An ordinary homeowner who buys a custom home usually does not get enough appreciation in two years to profit from selling the house. Now that taxpayers need not step up to more costly houses to avoid taxes, upward pressure on house prices will diminish and house appreciation will slow down. The "in and out costs" of Realtor commissions, mortgage origination fees and closing costs consume the profit of two years of house appreciation for typical homeowners.

This leaves the owner-builder in a unique position to profit from the provisions of the 1997 Tax Law. Because O-B equity stems from building at a reduced cost, owner-builders have a handsome profit to reap, tax-free, as often as every two years. If you build a $350,000 house at a savings of $100,000 every two years, you can enjoy a tax-free bonanza of $50,000 each year until the law changes.

Retirement Plan

This tax benefit builds your net worth along the way at a dramatic pace. In an economy where less than a quarter of retirees are financially independent, you have three very pleasant options during retirement.

Option One:

According to the banking industry, Social Security and your company pension will typically provide less than two thirds of the income you'll need for retirement. Since people spend about a third of their income on housing, if you have your home paid off via your step-up plan, you only need two thirds as much for living expenses. You can retire without worries on Social Security and your pension. You stay in the dream home you built for yourself.

Option Two:

After you own a home free and clear, you can continue to build and sell residences as often as every two years and bank the tax-free profits. After about five builds over the course of a lifetime, with the value of the home you live in, and with normal inflation, you will have amassed a net worth over one million dollars from the process. You are free to move into smaller retirement quarters or into a facility providing convalescent care and live off your wealth.

Option Three:

Through a financial vehicle known as a "reverse mortgage" you could stay in the house you own free and clear and tap the value of your dream home to lavishly finance your twilight years. You draw payments monthly against the equity in your home until it's gone or you are.

"Open Up Your Veins"

Money saved on the construction of your house is different and financially more powerful than money you save buying groceries or insurance, or even paying taxes. Your house is an appreciating asset, much like a savings account, but even better. A bank won't credit you with $350 if you only deposit $250 into your account. But you can build a $350,000 house for $250,000 and have the market count it as $350,000. You can sell it for that much and keep the difference.

Money you save on building your house goes directly to your net worth. It reminds me of the buffet at a recent Chamber of Commerce reception I attended. I chided the caterer on the high cholesterol in the hors d'oeuvres including bacon-wrapped chicken livers skewered with toothpicks. She answered, "Yup, you might as well open up your veins and mainline the stuff." In a different way you get to mainline money right to your net worth when you build a house. Everything you save goes direct to net worth. No processing, no withholding, no deductions.

If the accepted market value for a custom home at your level of finish is $100 per square foot, and you build it for $70 a foot or for $60 a foot, you get to keep the difference. Every bargain you find, every price concession, every savings adds directly to your wealth.

D.S.D.E.

Benjamin Franklin made famous the expression, "A penny saved is a penny earned." He said this about 150 years before we had income taxes in our country. I say now that "a dime saved is a dollar earned". That is, you typically have to earn a dollar to set aside ten cents. The savings rate in our country is well below ten percent, thus when an American earns a dollar, he will save a dime, or less, of it. The rest goes to payroll deductions, taxes, and consumption.

When I built my house, I discovered that my humble efforts at contracting were far more valuable than my professional salary as a planning consultant. If I earned $100,000 in salary, $10,000 or less, maybe much less, would make its way into savings. But when I saved $140,000 on my house, it all went into savings, into my net worth.

To have saved that much otherwise, I would have had to earn ten times that amount, or $1,400,000 in salary, which would have taken many years. I call this principle "D.S.D.E." or "a Dime Saved is a Dollar Earned". Every dime I save building my house would be the savings equivalent of ten times that much in salary.

Suppose you are making a mortgage payment of $1,000. How much goes to equity? On the mortgage that I hold, our monthly payment for principal and interest is $1,200, and only $65 goes to equity, about five percent. But the dollars you save building your house go straight to equity — 100%. Say you are building a $200,000 house, and the lumber is $30,000. If you find a way to get it for $25,000, your savings of $5,000 goes straight to equity. It "should" cost $30,000; but it costs $25,000. The savings reduce your cost but don't change the value of your house.

This book will present this special style of economic thinking and how it creates a new view of money for you. DSDE thinking (pronounced "dazdee") changes the way you see both construction savings and costs on your home. If you can save the $5,000 on lumber, you value that savings as much as you value $50,000 of salary. If you made $100,000 a year it would take you six months of work to save or set aside $5,000. If you can save $5,000 on lumber through a few hours of research and effort, you have perhaps saved the equivalent of six months of striving on a good salary.

When you are into DSDE thinking, you multiply any savings times ten to see the equivalent in units of salaried work. If you save $50 on a ceiling fan, was it worth the hassle? If you consider it to be the equivalent of $500 in salary — ten times the 50 dollars — and it only took you an hour or two to find the savings, it was well worth it. It may take you two days or a week to earn $500 at your employment.

When you are into DSDE thinking, you multiply any cost times ten when you consider it. What if trash hauling service adds $500 to my construction cost? That would reduce the equity on my house by $500. It would take ten times the $500 or the equivalent of $5,000 of salaried employment to set aside that amount. $5,000 in salary could be weeks or months of work. And I can haul away the trash in a day or two. It would be well worth it to save that expense.

At 44% of the contractor-estimated cost of my house, general contracting would have cost me $140,000 (contractor profit and overhead). The $140,000 cost would have done nothing to change the value of my house. The house is worth $350,000 in our market without a contractor, and it would have been worth $350,000 with a contractor. The $140,000 I saved on contractor costs went straight to equity. I realized that I would have had to earn the DSDE equivalent of $1,400,000 to replace that equity otherwise. That made me think twice about using a contractor. Especially when in less than a year's time I eliminated that cost. And you can, too.

Turn the DSDE principle around for a moment. Suppose you pay $100,000 for contractor costs on your house. Say it increases the cost of your house from $300,000 to $400,000. You've used up your cash for the down payment, so naturally, you mortgage the amount to cover it. Your mortgage payments on the additional amount add $1,000 to your monthly payment on the house. Since bankers multiply monthly payments by three to determine qualifying salary, you have to make an extra $3,000 a month to qualify - an extra $36,000 per year. Over a 30 year mortgage you must make an extra $1,000,000 to cover an extra $100,000 borrowed.

Rock Star Wages

It is worth being conscientious in the management of your construction. You are being paid handsomely to do it — DSDE thinking means that savings of $100,000 equate to earnings of a million dollars — rock star wages.

For the time I was building my house, I made rock star wages. Over a ten month period, Elaine and I put in 3,000 hours of effort. A year and a half's work for one person. We saved nearly $150,000 or about $50 for every hour we spent, whether planning, shopping, or sweeping the concrete. The DSDE equivalent is $500 per hour in salary. In a normal work year, someone making $500 an hour will gross $1,000,000 — about what Donny Osmond's salary was in his pop music days. Ironically, Donny and another musical performing star (less famous) live in the neighborhood we now enjoy.

Why can I afford a house like these megastars? For a brief shining moment, I made the equivalent of rock star wages, in savings on my own house. And you can too.

Guerilla Economics

Take a moment to consider the widely disseminated myths and propaganda about owner-building described in Chapter 1. This is what you are up against. No one will simply provide you with savings, although many will deprive you of savings on your project in the blink of an eye. The constant struggle over those savings is something like a war. And as in war, the first casualty is the truth.

Your truth is that you can save an amazing amount of money on the construction of your custom home and that those savings go straight to your net worth. You must hold on to this knowledge in the face of many naysayers and much resistance. If you do you will prevail.

Your attitude may seem like a guerilla or rebel insurgent one to the opposition. Because it is. You need to stretch a dollar to accomplish your goal, and you can. You may also need to temporarily forego some income, and it's worth it.

A lot of people are what independent inspector Joe Stark calls "checkbook rich, and savings account poor". They can't owner-build because they don't have the patience and discipline to come up with the land cost. But your reward for your guerilla savings efforts and attitude are a superior home and a galloping net worth.

Chapter 3: General Contractors Aren't What You Think They Are

Contractor Games

Perpetuating Myths

You call a general contractor for a bid on your project and he shows up in a nice pickup truck wearing jeans and a work shirt and work boots. Perhaps he's carrying a clipboard. The impression is that of a tradesman, and of technical expertise. The contractor will reinforce some or all of the Myths described in Chapter 1. Most non-construction people would hesitate to question the word of this "expert".

The big myth is that you can't do without this "technical expertise". It's a specialized field, and you need an experienced specialist. But the work of a contractor is to "contract", that is to hire and manage independent craftsmen, known as subcontractors. His work is management work, much like the work of any of us who have ever run a household with its myriad expenditures and activities.

Almost any independent construction inspector, (usually a retired contractor) has equivalent knowledge of the process and the details as does the contractor before you. They are paid as consultants, and can advise in detail on custom home construction for fees of less than $1,000.

Scare Tactics

Relying on the impression of exclusive expertise, a general contractor may play on the fears of prospective homeowners. An illustration comes from the recent text for general contractors, *Building Contractor* by R. Woodson Dodge:

"The Fear Factor Can Sell Jobs"

If you prepare yourself with stories to tell, you can increase your in-home sales. People are often nervous about the dependability, ability, and performance of contractors. This nervousness stems from fear created by the media. When people read a news story about how a homeowner was cheated out of money by an unscrupulous contractor, they become concerned. This type of news can hurt business for contractors, but it can also be your ace in the hole.

Once you have developed a portfolio of contracting-related horror stories, you can use the fear factor to sell more jobs. People generally assume you wouldn't be educating them in the risks that are present with contractors if you were one of the bad guys. Automatically, when you begin warning the consumer, you are building the image of one of the good guys.

After telling your stories, tell the customer how you operate to put their mind at ease. By showing the consumer what could happen, and why it won't if they work with you, you're on your way to signing a new deal.

What does that tell you?

Pursuing Self-Interest

The danger is that you believe that the contractor is there to protect your interests. In reality, the contractor is set up to make sure that his own interests are met over the course of your project.

In the same book, *Building Contractor*, out of 20 chapters, only one deals with schedule and budget. In fact, almost nothing in the book deals with your concerns. If you count the Customer Relations chapter, only two of the chapters, or ten percent of the book pertain to you. Lots of them deal with taxes, insurance and retirement plans, image, sales, marketing, and pricing. There's lots to learn about handling money, employees, vehicles, and your office location, but you don't care about that. You care about subs, schedule, and budget.

Offering Self-Serving Agreements

The typical bid-price construction contract is an example of the orientation general contractors have to their self-interests. The contract sets a price for your construction. You agree to pay so much for the house no matter what. It gives total control to the contractor. He can procure materials and labor at a savings, and keep the savings. He can substitute cheaper materials or cut corners on craftsmanship and is paid to do so by keeping the difference. If you want something better, you generally have to pay extra.

Most residential construction contracts are fixed-bid agreements. The general contractors I interviewed used them 90% of the time in preference to the little used "Cost-plus" agreements, which are less profitable to them. But cost-plus agreements are self-serving too. These are agreements that require you to pay the "cost" of construction and give the general a fee or commission of, say, ten percent on the whole amount. It's self-serving, because the contractor controls what the costs are, and the higher they are, the more fee you pay.

With cost-plus, it is hard to pin down cost. In many cases where the contractor uses an outside source for material or labor, he receives the invoice, tacks something on for his overhead and sends you a separate billing. When the contractor's own forces do work, he always adds in for overhead before sending you the invoice. It is common, for instance, to multiply wages paid to workers by 2.75 before listing "labor costs" on your invoice. At the end, the contractor is allowed to apply his profit to the whole amount, including the extra overhead added to each item. You are not permitted to scrutinize the detailed charges, nor can you control what he calls overhead.

Enforcing Package Buying

As an owner-builder, you get to buy cafeteria-style, selecting your materials and labor from the best source in each case. Contractors deprive you of this privilege. For instance, they will use their own cement crew or framing crew. You have no idea if the prices charged are competitive. Nor is there an assurance of quality. You take the service because it is part of the package. You have some comparison in the beginning by getting bids from multiple general contractors. But once the deal is signed, you are captive, and any extras are at the price the contractor quotes.

Lowball and Change Order

Some contractors take advantage of this situation by quoting a low price initially and claiming later that certain things were not included. For example, you may think you've paid for oak trim, and you visit the site to discover that the carpenters are putting up paint-grade economy trim. You object and a price is quoted to you for the "upgrade". Time is short, the carpenters are waiting, and you agree without any chance to check out price and availability. Such contractors are free to follow the old rule of crooked auto mechanics: "Double the usual price, and if the customer doesn't flinch, go with it."

Readers Say

"I got one house package estimate, (lumber, doors, windows, and trim) and was going to go with it, then went to Menands, and had them price the same take-off for a savings of $30,000. The original contractor and lumberyard were surly about it."

Yvonne B.
Caroline, WI

Readers Say

"We built a home for $110,000 four years ago, recently appraised for $210,000."

Joe & Connie W.
Olathe, KS

Exploit Your Ignorance

At an early point in my construction project, I got cold feet because I couldn't answer some of the questions posed by the subs. I began belatedly to look for some on-site supervision. My designer told me that the going rate in our market was $2,500 – $3,000 for assistance from a general contractor, including use of the general's license and some of his subs, answering questions, and providing some on-site supervision. I put the word out for help, and a wily general contractor called me and offered the assistance for nearly $1,000 a week. That would have been $25,000 for a six month project, 15% of my budget. I felt desperate, but I wasn't ignorant. I found the needed answers elsewhere for no charge.

Cuts Corners

Inspectors have told me many stories about corners that contractors have cut to improve their profit. Some examples: plumbing running uphill, roofs without base felts, gutters without flashing, reduced beam sizes, bowed walls, foundation walls two inches thick in spots, or poured five inches thick throughout instead of six, short roof shingles extended to provide minimal coverage, inadequate roof bracing, collar ties missing on every other rafter or omitted completely.

Are these shortcuts the fault of the general or the sub? Some work is done by the general's own forces, and he controls it directly. Other work is done by subs, but the general dictates what he will pay them, and he is responsible for their supervision.

You'll Shop Better

Contractors are poor shoppers. Witness my construction advisor, a general contractor who has built hundreds of homes. He offered me the lumber price mentioned in Chapter 1. With a little checking, I was able to beat his price by $3,000 in a week's time. He couldn't believe that his prices at the lumberyard were high. He had built over 200 homes with that lumberyard, and had never "shopped" their prices against other lumberyards.

The contractors I interviewed had few or no ideas on saving money, other than to speed up the project, which they all mentioned. That doesn't save you much money — some on interest. It makes them money because they earn their fee over a shorter time, and can go earn another fee from the next customer sooner.

The contractor looks at his fee based on time to complete:

Example: Overall Fee of $50,000

Months to Complete:	Twelve	Nine	Six	Five	Four
Fee Earned Per Month:	$4,166	$5,555	$8,333	$10,000	$12,500

You will shop better because you are not in a hurry. You will shop better because you will start long before you break ground. You will shop better because it's your money.

You'll Be Better Organized

A survey by Custom Builder Magazine a few years ago revealed that only 33% of custom builders use a computer for estimating project costs. This is an indication of how disorganized, how "seat of the pants" general contractors are. Spreadsheet budgeting is a very valuable technique that we will teach you in Chapter 8. It is easy and fun to do. We estimate that it will save you five percent on your overall project, when used as a tracking device.

If you have kept your own ideas about your custom home in your head, or in a dream home notebook, you are prepared to track details you expect. Since many bills will be paid out of your own checking account, you already have in place a very personal and controlled system for financial management.

If you can keep a file of bids for your job, along with product literature, you are already far ahead of what a general contractor will do. The list below contains some suggestions from other owner-builders to get organized. We will explore most of these ideas in more detail in later chapters:

Owner-Builder Ideas to "Get Organized"

○ develop written "flow chart" schedule of construction

○ maintain loose-leaf binders for bids from subs

○ fill a box with hanging files for product literature

○ keep a binder for insurance work

○ use a box for samples of wall and floor coverings, swatches and finishes

○ use a spreadsheet budget, make sure is complete

○ get all prices before starting

○ keep a business card reference file of subs and contacts

○ keep a binder of subs you hear about, both good and bad

○ know your running tally of expenses at all times

○ know what week of your schedule you are on

○ interview contractors and take notes

○ keep a phone list of contacts

○ file all invoices and attach copy of check and lien waiver

○ list all items you must purchase, record price comparisons

Readers Say

"As a contractor, I can cut the price $20,000 on a three bedroom, two bath house, and still make $30,000. I can build a $90,000 home for $40,000 and sell it for $70,000.

T.L.W.
Elizabeth City, NC

Readers Say

"I have 42 binders of ideas and specifications for my project. I have been planning actively for eight years."

Rich H.
Sandy, UT

Readers Say

"I'm building 4,700 sq. feet on a golf course, and I have a full-time secretary who helps me to do the bidding and sourcing."

Jim K.
Elk Grove Village, IL

You'll Give it More Attention

Building inspector Jim Wright told me "Contractors usually call subs, and get started, and then are somewhere else right away. In my opinion they probably spend one to two hours a week on-site."

I asked generals how much time they spend on each job and found they were a little evasive about this. Most tell you about how they are on-site "all the time". One general contractor building custom homes admitted that his superintendents handle a dozen jobs each at a time. In a 40-hour week, this means they could be at any given job no more than four hours a week. Allowing for travel time, office meetings, and paperwork, I would guess the actual on-site time is two hours a week per project.

Even at that low level, inspector Joe Stark complained to me that the superintendents in the industry today tend to be "kids". "They may know how to order, or schedule, but they don't know quality." This is not comforting when it's your house.

It is indisputable that you will spend more time on your job than a contractor would. But the less costly the house the more true it is. You might get a general who builds three a year to be on-site an hour a day, or about 100 hours overall. But the builder who handles 50 a year will probably be there an hour or two a week, maybe 35 hours altogether. As an owner-builder, I was at my job site nearly 2,000 hours, and Elaine was there about 500. This is about 25 times as much attention as a general can give.

The time they are there doing their own trade work doesn't count. How can they supervise themselves? If providing more care would cost them money, they have a conflict of interest deciding whether to provide that additional care. Something about being watched all day long makes people provide more care. You do the watching and get a better house.

You will also give more attention to quality. The builders I interviewed had a difficult time describing quality. Mostly they said it was finishing quickly. Good and quickly seldom meet, and quickly usually helps their bottom line, not your quality.

You'll Keep Your Savings

The contractor isn't motivated to save your money, only to complete the job faster. He will let you pay for any overhead expense he thinks is justified. In my initial budget to build the house, I allocated $500 for cellular phone service. When my budget began to get tight I decided to sacrifice the service to save money. I carried a roll of quarters in my car for use at the pay phone at the nearest gas station. I spent less than $20 for phone calls over the remainder of the project. Would a builder deny himself the use of his mobile phone to save you money? Most likely not, and every general charges this luxury and many others to his customers in the form of overhead.

The contractor isn't paid to bargain-hunt, find less expensive but equal quality components, or find superior products at special prices for you. The contractor is more loyal to himself and his subs than to the owner. He actually has a conflict of interest in trying to save you money.

Contractors routinely get promotional rewards or "Spiffs" from lumberyards and other suppliers for spending their customers money there. These are prizes or incentives which may include clothing, tools, cash, or trips to Hawaii. Have you ever heard of a contractor passing on the benefit to his customers — even though the customers paid for it?

How Much Can You Save?

One way to look at potential savings when you eliminate the general contractor is to look at how much contractors make.

I got a simplified look into contractor economics from a decking subcontractor who ran a crew but didn't do any of the work himself. He estimated my deck at $1,935 for labor only, as I was purchasing the materials separately. I called him back and asked him to break down his bid.

Reluctantly, he told me that it was $900 for labor, $800 for overhead, and $235 for profit. The labor was 60 work hours at $15. He paid them $8 an hour and charged them out at $15 per hour to cover payroll costs. What was the overhead? "We'll be on your job for parts of two weeks, and we only have two other jobs going on. My expenses and salary are $1,200 a week, so divided by three jobs, that's $400 a week. Somebody has to pay that. The profit we earn for managing your job."

This deck subcontractor resembled a general contractor in that he contracted with others to do the work and he handled multiple jobs. On the face of it, it appears that his margin (overhead plus profit) was $1,035 or 53%. But it might be even more than that.

I hired two carpenters at $15 per hour to build the deck and I provided unskilled help. They finished the project in 20 work hours at a cost of $300. It is hard for me to imagine that an experienced crew that builds decks for a living would be slower than two general purpose carpenters. True work hours would be 20 or less, not 60. If you take my actual costs of $300 and compare them to the estimated costs of $1,935 the margin for the contractor in this instance would be $1,635 or 84%!

In my survey of owner-builders, total savings added up to an average of 35% on the overall cost of construction. On a custom home in today's market, this would amount to a savings of from $100,000 to perhaps half a million dollars.

When is Ten Percent Not Ten Percent?

Usually general contractors claim to make "only ten percent profit" on custom home construction. Yet, owner-builders report a 35% savings. So what gives? The builder makes something on everything else. He makes it on overhead on all labor, he makes it on material mark-ups, trade mark-ups, overcharging for work not bid out, and on general overhead.

One contractor I interviewed told me he added overhead to materials and labor and then imposed profit on the entire amount. For example, on one job, lumber was $20,000 but they billed it at $30,000. Framing labor was $15,000, but they billed it at $25,000 for a total for framing of $55,000. Then they tacked on a ten percent profit of $5,500. However, direct costs were only $35,000. The contractor charged $60,500, which is a difference of $25,500 or a 42% margin. But technically, his profit was only ten percent.

A contractor from Indiana told me he makes 60% margin on a custom home. Like other contractors, he probably shows no more than ten percent profit each year so he doesn't have to pay excess taxes. He may make profits of 30% on a given job, but with the slow seasons of the year he only shows overall company profits of ten percent or less for the year.

The great variable is overhead. This is what a contractor *spends*.

If you make a healthy margin and want to pay less in tax, you spend more money on your company. You may put in place a retirement plan for your full-time employees, life insurance for your key people, medical coverage, higher salaries for the partners, and any manner of personnel expense. But it doesn't stop there. You may buy the biggest and best earth moving equipment, new expensive vehicles, build a bigger, better building, buy office computers, furnishings; almost anything under the sun could count as overhead.

I had one general contractor executive tell me insistently that his company only made ten percent on their work. Then I asked him if the company had built a home for him. He admitted they had, at a cost of $95 a foot. "And what would your company have charged for that?" His answer, "$135 a foot." Even though the company claimed to make only ten percent profit, they managed to save 30% on the executive's house.

The average for all the general contractors I surveyed was an overhead of 29% on residential projects and profit of 14%. They may only admit publicly to profits of ten percent, but that's the tip of the iceberg. The overhead is something every customer must also pay, and that is more than two times greater than profit, on average.

Contractors Mark Up Their Costs to You

Part of the contractor's standard formula is to add something to every cost in a job. Hourly employee wages, for example, are marked up considerably to pay for various indirect personnel costs. A common formula is to multiply hourly wages by 2.75. Thus an $11 an hour worker could be billed out at $30 per hour.

The book *Building Contractor* teaches budding general contractors how to price their services. The first key point is a hidden freebie: mark-ups on materials. The author confines his discussion to a range of from 10% to 35%. How would you like to pay a mark-up of ten percent on a $30,000 lumber package? The lumber supplier delivers and offers credit. What does the contractor need to do to procure that lumber that you couldn't handle yourself for a savings of $3,000?

In the 1980's, I consulted for several contracting firms in Ohio, and spent two years as a vice president for one of them, responsible for marketing and sales. I never "swung a hammer", so to speak, but I reviewed many construction budgets. In one instance the principals of the firm had bought farm land for $3,000 per acre and after building infrastructure, bundled some of the land for around $200,000 per acre into an office building project. Allowing $20,000 per acre for infrastructure, that land was marked up about 900% to the customer.

In my survey of general contractors I found that they marked up materials by an average of 24%. But the number could be even higher. An architect in Nevada told me that he set up a purchasing company to help his clients save money on materials. He said his firm openly marked up the materials by 35%. Yet, they almost always beat the material prices offered to clients by contractors.

One possible explanation is that some contractors may start with a list price, far above actual cost, and mark that up. Or they may be practicing the double whammy of marking up an item, and then adding a standard profit to the marked up number. Or they may not buy scientifically and simply pay too much for material. Either way, these contractor mark-ups increase your cost and decrease your equity.

Get Bids from Three Generals

While a contractor can hurt you, they can also help you. Even if you don't intend to use a general contractor you need to take advantage of a free service they offer and get three general contractor's bids on your plans and specs once they are detailed. If you provide all three general contractors the same detailed specifications (Chapter 6 will show you how) you will get an apples to apples comparison. This sets the bar height for what you can save.

One expert tells me that bids may vary 15% on the same house at different times based on market conditions. You may get a real bargain and decide to skip the effort of owner-building. More likely, you will get an education in specifics that will help you save far more money. Insist on line item estimates on each thing with an indication whether it is to be done by "own forces" or who will likely do it. And have them prepare a written schedule showing sequence and indicating how they will finish in six months, the "deadline you must meet".

Readers Say

"We looked at the contractor bids, and said - 'hey, we can save a lot of money doing this.'"

Eric & Ember M.
St. George, UT

"We are currrently remodeling a 25 year old house. It's been a fairly good process. We put our possessions in storage, and have lived in the midst of it for 3 1/2 months. We think we want to do it again. We hired a general for the addition we did, but after that we managed our own subs. Flat roofed block framed house. $70,000 expense. We've learned a lot. Next time we will sub everything. We learned a lot about selecting the proper people. You have to take your time more, and get more bids. We took out all the old insulation, and blew in cellulose, and it makes a big difference. We cut in the ceilings foot-wide openings in each room. Next year we are thinking about putting in an evaporative cooler, and A/C, and heat pump. They are about $4,000, though we know we can beat that. Swamp coolers save a lot of money here. Every month you save $200 at least. Now I am three minutes from work. We have an acre of land now. We will put in shade trees later. You do recirculating air under the ground, and use evaporative cooling if you want to build without A/C. It can be done, even here."

Jody & Andrew P.
Scottsdale, AZ

"We hired a general for our home back east. We worked our fannies off on that one and thought maybe we'll go it alone next time. We've done our own purchasing, and I have been the negotiator. We spent more than we anticipated, but still okay. $67 a foot vs. more than $100 for a contractor. That includes everything."

Kathi D.
Tucson, AZ

Sources Say

"A general contractor usually takes the cost of labor and materials and adds a 50% mark-up."

From *Be Your Own Home Renovation Contractor*
(See page 258)

The *Complete Guide to Contracting Your Home*
Recommends spending 6 months planning and 6 months building.

(See page 260)

"Incredibly, in some areas of the country, there is no systematic check to determine whether contractors are licensed or not. Therefore, unlicensed contractors can 'pull a permit' to build a house and dupe consumers into thinking they're legitimate."

From *Your New House*
(See page 260)

"Even more amazing, loopholes in laws also let contractors build houses *without permits*. A few states allow unlicensed contractors to build houses without a permit if the house is for their personal use. Some builders use this loophole to claim they're building a house for themselves, only to quickly turn around and sell it."

From ***Your New House***
(See page 260)

"As a manager, the builder should know good and not-so-good materials and workmanship. Scheduling and coordinating material deliveries and subcontractor work are critical, and oversight during construction is crucial. Inept and don't-care builders turn things over to the subcontractors and accept whatever happens while good builders stay right on top of the work, with frequent visits to the site to insure coordination and to get boo-boos fixed before they get locked into the fabric of the house."

From ***Build It Right!***
(See page 258)

Chapter 4: You Can Manage Better Than a Contractor

Time line: One year before groundbreaking

Management Concept One: "People Often Ingest M&M's"

Even though I have been a management consultant for more than 15 years, I am going to restrain myself and only include two management concepts in this book. However, these concepts will really help you to get a handle on your project and save money.

The first is the duties of a manager. They apply to any general manager. These are the tasks that a contractor should perform when building a house, and they describe your duties in doing the same:

✓ Plan   ✓ Organize   ✓ Integrate

✓ Measure   ✓ Motivate

These five words form the acronym "POIMM". The device I use to remember them is the phrase, "People Often Ingest M&M's".

✓ Plan

Later in this chapter we will suggest high value planning items that will change the outcome of your project. Planning will be about half your work in building a home.

✓ Organize

Organizing (making an organization) is bringing together your team. "Contracting" means organizing because it describes making arrangements for various specialists to work with you.

✓ Integrate

"Integrate" is a good management word. In my seminars, I have found people who thought the "I" in POIMM was "implement". But a general manager doesn't actually implement. He or she "integrates" or coordinates the functions of the team so they complement one another.

✓ Measure

"Measure" refers to management control, as in the job of a corporate controller. To measure is to see that all the measures of the project are met. In particular this means budget and schedule.

✓ Motivate

Motivating your team includes clear communication, payment for services and special recognition.

That's it. These five functions are the work of a general manager. They are the work of a contractor. My experience is that contractors usually neglect more than one of these functions, and sometimes every one of them. As an owner-builder, you will be trying to perform for the first time the functions that a general contractor has performed many times. If you think of them as POIMM you may find you do some or all of them better than the best contractors.

Management Concept Two: "Plan Hard, Work Easy"

Your first task is Planning. Years ago I discovered an amazing thing about planning. It saves time and money. This idea was made clear by Crawford Greenewalt, president of DuPont in the 1940's. DuPont had done manufacturing studies to see if planning was worthwhile. I call the conclusion the Greenewalt Principle:

"Top-notch workers first plan and then follow a relaxed rather than a frantic pace. Planning their time makes this ease possible, for every moment spent planning saves three or four in execution."

DuPont discovered that a twelve month project could be shortened to nine months by first spending one month in planning. Then, an average of eight months more was required to complete the project.

One of my associates tested this on programmers in a computer testing division of a major software company. Two programmers of the same average productivity were given the same program to write. Much like general contractors, both programmers indicated they would like to jump right in and begin work. One was permitted to start programming without any preliminaries. The other was instructed to plan and diagram the work in detail before programming.

The first programmer jumped right into the task, and with changes and rework, he had the finished program ready in eight and a half months. The second programmer merely planned. He planned for a month, then two months, and finally was ready to program after two and a half months. He was finished three weeks later. Both programs were considered equal in quality.

Why Plan?

We all know the old tailor's maxim, "Measure twice, cut once." It only takes a few seconds to make a cut with a power saw. Measuring takes just as much time. But construction tradesmen know it saves effort, time and money. I have heard carpenters exclaim with mock irritation, "I keep cutting this piece, and it's still not long enough!"

My then college-age son, Ben, supervised a crew of American high school students a few years ago in the construction of a low-income house in an impoverished area of Mexico. He instructed the sophomore girls on the first day to cut the lumber lengths for the frame of the small structure. In the space of a half hour they cut all the lumber to the wrong length. There was no more lumber available, and the crew had to work around the problem for the rest of the project.

When you plan a construction project, you are "measuring twice". It costs nothing to plan. It causes no one a delay. You are off the interest clock that starts when you break ground. Later, when you follow a good plan, you can work at a relaxed pace and get done much sooner. You naturally save money on interest but also on all your other expenditures. Planning time uncovers bargains, opportunities, and superior options that you don't turn up in haste.

General contractors and some owner-builders seem in a rush to break ground. I felt the impatience to do so. Even though I did much with planning, I glossed over the planning for the unfamiliar task of doing the electric wiring for the house. Confucius said, "Nothing done in haste is thorough." This proved painfully true for me.

"The more you sweat in training, the less you bleed in battle." Navy SEAL Slogan

Readers Say

"We do a better job than experts because we care. They tend to just get through it and they slop around."

Wilma B. Tampa, FL

Readers Say

"Banks think that owners are total dummies. They are used to working with developers who have a nice little pat package. When you walk in with something to present, they don't know how to deal with you."

Jean & Bill H. Lansdale, PA

Readers Say

"We were way over budget and it took a lot longer than we thought. You almost get into a panic state. We had to do a lot of building during the winter, couldn't find a roofer, went into a panic and grabbed whoever... If we had gotten the city to move a little faster on our permits, that would have helped."

Jim and Carol T. American Fork, UT

I spent an hour or two planning the electric work, thinking that my construction advisor would show me what to do. He never showed up to help me, and it took Elaine and me 800 hours and lots of anxiety to do the job. We saved money, about $5,000, but the task was excruciating. Real electricians can finish a house like ours in about 80 work hours. It's amazing but true that we beginners took ten times as long as the pros do.

Having been through it, I now estimate that if we'd spent a month, or 160 legitimate hours planning the task in detail, we could have saved three times that much in implementation, (480 hours), as the Greenewalt principle indicates. That means we would complete the electric work in 320 hours total, about four times what an experienced team would take.

Electric work is interesting, as are the other trades in a house, but only a small portion of our savings came from doing self-work. We saved about $20,000 on the four trades we did ourselves: electric, ceramic tile, painting, and landscaping. The big swinger is the management of the job at a savings. The rest of this chapter gives you a look into the possibilities that planning affords.

I Want a Thousand Hours!

You remember the wartime expression "Uncle Sam Wants You!". My version is "I want a thousand hours!". I want you to spend 1,000 hours planning the construction of your house. There are 2,000 hours in a work year (40 hours times 50 weeks). I want about a half year of planning, even though you and your spouse may share the duties and possibly spread them over several years of time.

Once our job started I found that I was too short on time to do a number of crucial things properly. Inevitably, the things you rush cost you more money than they should. As owner-builder Debbie Crosby told me, "You find you are under the gun to figure out windows, for example, in two days." I regretted that I had not done more planning. The most common regret of O-B's I interviewed was the same.

The average owner-builder I interviewed, after doing some mental arithmetic, reported 238 hours of planning. Elaine and I spent about 700, and it was relatively easy to do. Some of the tasks, like shopping for fixtures and attending the "Parade of Homes", are actually recreational.

I have been keeping track of the work hours I spend for about 20 years. It has become a habit for me, and has provided me many insights. On our house project I also tracked Elaine's hours. This is how we spent the combined total:

Planning:	700 hours
Electric work:	800 hours
Other trades:	300 hours
On-site supervision:	1,200 hours
Total:	3,000 hours

We saved nearly $150,000 on the house, which works out to $50 an hour saved. But we only saved $20,000 on the trade work, or about $20 per hour expended. The other $130,000 is attributable to planning and on-site supervision. Site time is valuable, particularly in preventing mistakes and rework, but not as valuable as planning. I would say planning is three times as valuable as site time. Therefore, I would attribute $120 per hour in savings to the planning and $40 per hour in savings to the site time.

Task	Time	Value	Total
Planning:	700 hours	$120/hr.	$84,000
Electric work:	800 hours	$6/hr.	$5,000
Other trades:	300 hours	$50/hr.*	$15,000
On-site supervision:	1,200 hours	$40/hr	$48,000
Total:	**3,000 hours**		

(*The hourly return for doing other trades is distorted by a factor of three because of time spent after we occupied the house. Considering that time, the return works out to $15/hr.)

It takes a thousand hours to plan because there are so many requisite, high-yield tasks to perform. A thousand hours is a lot, but people in our country watch an average of more than 25 hours of TV a week, so just by eliminating TV-watching, a married couple can open up 1,000 hours in 20 weeks. That's only five months. If you consider that hour is worth more than $100, what's a few missed reruns of "Seinfeld"?

Is 1,000 hours too much? It's only half a year of work for one person. You have to figure that you are trying to do the work of a contractor better than he does it. That contractor may have learned his trade over many years, even decades, he or she might have gone to school for additional training, and you are going to replace him. This naturally takes some effort.

By comparison, remember that saving $100,000 on a custom home could cut ten years off the necessary working life of a person making $100,000 a year — not a bad exchange for a few months of planning.

But the good news is that the effort is enjoyable.

What do you do with your 1,000 hours? On page 38 are the combined recommendations of ourselves and the owner-builders we interviewed along with the suggestions of lenders, house designers, and inspectors. Most of the ideas are explained further in this book. Others are self-explanatory. Use it as a checklist to see that you have worked the suggested areas. Take them in the order that works out for you. Keep track of your time. If you address each area and spend 1,000 hours, you will have an easy project and a quality house. You will beat the system and save more than $100,000 on your custom home.

Each of the planning steps is explained and illustrated in our DVD series, "The Ten Commandments of Owner-Builders" (See page 264)

These planning steps are available on a spreadsheet on our free Resource CD-ROM (See page 270)

When I wrote my first marketing plan for a client 20 years ago, it took me 1,000 hours to complete. After some years, my tenth plan took about 200 hours. Any general contractor would laugh at the expenditure of 1,000 hours to plan your first owner-built home. It wouldn't be considered efficient. But you're not concerned with efficiency, only that you succeed. On your tenth house, you will be able to knock out the prep work in, say, 200 hours.

There are 85 items on our list of planning suggestions. If you or your spouse spent an average of a day and a half on each of them, it would add up to 1,000 hours well-spent, and well-rewarded. Of course, some of the activities will take many days, some a few hours. Henry Kissinger, former U.S. Secretary of State, said of his time in office that "...all you can do is spend the intellectual capital you have accumulated in advance." If you are tempted to short yourself on planning, consider that each hour you forego may cost you $100. Once you start construction you will have no more chances to prepare.

How to Use the Planning Steps Worksheet

Use the Worksheet on page 38 as your notes of planning activities and chart your progress. There is a progress bar provided with each step that you can color with a pencil to see at a glance your level of completion. On the right of each step is a tally of hours to allow you to track the extent of your effort.

Act Like You're a Business

If you plan, organize, integrate, measure, and motivate, you are performing the intended functions of a contractor or developer in building your house. For the duration of the project, you are performing business functions. You are a business and should be recognized as such.

To reinforce your role, make the effort to resemble the existing businesses in the industry. Name your business, (you don't have to incorporate) and get business cards. You can be a consultant or a developer for the duration of your project. Register with your state or province to buy at wholesale and pay sales taxes when you use your purchases on your own project. This is called a sales tax or resale number. There is no charge for this privilege in my state. Get a business license, sometimes called a DBA license, from the city or county where you live. Print the license numbers on your business card along with your phone and fax number.

If you don't have a fax machine, you can use the fax number of your local quick printing establishment. Treat it as if it were your own number. If you receive faxes, they will call you and you can pick up the fax when you pay the charge. You can even put a toll-free number on your card. It is not expensive to set up this service with your long distance carrier.

Sources Say

The Complete Guide to Contracting Your Home
Recommends spending 6 months planning and 6 months building.

(See page 260)

"Form a separate corporation if you want to set your enterprise off from your personal affairs. This may give you a better standing among members of the building trades if they feel that they're dealing with a company instead of an individual."

From ***The Complete Guide to Contracting Your Home***
(See page 260)

Bob Vila? Bob, Norm, and Steve from ***This Old House***? "Sorry, folks, this type of skilled building is seen only on television. Real life means building crews who are more like Larry, Curly, and Moe – bumbling idiots who couldn't tell their butts from a two-by-four. The only thing these guys ruminate on endlessly is which bar they'll hit at quitting time."

From ***Your New House***
(See page 260)

"One of life's greatest satisfactions can come from starting from scratch and ending up with a home that's the result of your ideas and decisions. You can even be your own general contractor! This may seem ridiculous to you right now, but it's not that difficult with the help of companies formed specifically to help you make decisions that general contractors make and to help you save part of the money that a contractor needs for overhead and profit."

From ***Build It Right!***
(See page 258)

Planning Steps

Task	Notes

Create or add to a dream home notebook.

25%	50%	75%	100%

✳ Start and add to a written list of questions.

25%	50%	75%	100%

✳ List the resources you bring to the project.

25%	50%	75%	100%

As a couple, resolve differences and work on your relationship.

25%	50%	75%	100%

Clarify your household budget in writing so you know how much you can contribute while building.

25%	50%	75%	100%

Generate personal financial statements and supporting documentation.

25%	50%	75%	100%

Obtain a copy of your credit report and clear up any errors.

25%	50%	75%	100%

Develop a file of house pictures you like.

25%	50%	75%	100%

Make seasonal observations at your property.

25%	50%	75%	100%

Go out to projects and watch homes go up, talk to foremen.

25%	50%	75%	100%

Scan the classified ads for constuction-related offerings regularly.

25%	50%	75%	100%

Read books about self-contracting.

25%	50%	75%	100%

Network with other Owner-Builders through our on-line Forums or O-B Connections.

25%	50%	75%	100%

Tour the "Parade of Homes" in your area and take notes.

25%	50%	75%	100%

Notes	Tally of Hours

Task	Notes

List and refine your house ideas.

25%	50%	75%	100%

Measure rooms you like in other houses.

25%	50%	75%	100%

Do extra research on kitchens and baths.

25%	50%	75%	100%

Develop lists of features room by room.

25%	50%	75%	100%

Write up specs for each trade.

25%	50%	75%	100%

Interview subcontractors. Try for five in each category.

25%	50%	75%	100%

Background visits with lenders.

25%	50%	75%	100%

Develop preliminary construction budget.

25%	50%	75%	100%

Interview general contractors.

25%	50%	75%	100%

Get estimates from general contractors.

25%	50%	75%	100%

Develop preliminary drawings with architect or designer.

25%	50%	75%	100%

Develop materials lists.

25%	50%	75%	100%

Meet with suppliers to get recommendations and prices.

25%	50%	75%	100%

Visit construction supply outlets regularly. Track prices on items you will need and take advantage of specials.

25%	50%	75%	100%

Open "builder" accounts at lumberyards and distributors.

25%	50%	75%	100%

Notes   **Tally of Hours**

Task	Notes

Confer with each utility. (Includes gas, water, electric, sewer, phone, cable TV, and trash removal.)

25%	50%	75%	100%

Identify and talk with other "team members".

25%	50%	75%	100%

Get lumber package estimates.

25%	50%	75%	100%

Shop for plumbing and electrical fixtures.

25%	50%	75%	100%

Shop for bargains on all other materials.

25%	50%	75%	100%

Read about trades you will supply.

25%	50%	75%	100%

Go to do-it-yourself classes for trades you will supply.

25%	50%	75%	100%

Develop a written plan for your self-work.

25%	50%	75%	100%

List your tools; clean, sharpen and lubricate.

25%	50%	75%	100%

Select and purchase any tools or cleaning materials you'll need.

25%	50%	75%	100%

Buy a generous supply of common fasteners to keep on hand.

25%	50%	75%	100%

Shop for trim materials.

25%	50%	75%	100%

Inspect the work of subcontractors you may use.

25%	50%	75%	100%

Attend home and garden shows or a professional construction convention.

25%	50%	75%	100%

Meet and talk with your municipal inspector.

25%	50%	75%	100%

Notes   **Tally of Hours**

Task	Notes

Interview and select an independent inspector.

| 25% | 50% | 75% | 100% |

Select ceramic tile.

| 25% | 50% | 75% | 100% |

Select hardwood flooring and find source.

| 25% | 50% | 75% | 100% |

Find carpet source.

| 25% | 50% | 75% | 100% |

Study and select cabinets.

| 25% | 50% | 75% | 100% |

Select bathroom and kitchen fixtures.

| 25% | 50% | 75% | 100% |

Shop for towel bars and wall fixtures.

| 25% | 50% | 75% | 100% |

Shop and compare window sources and windows.

| 25% | 50% | 75% | 100% |

Make revisions to drawings with architect or designer.

| 25% | 50% | 75% | 100% |

Share and discuss drawings with selected subcontractors for input and estimates.

| 25% | 50% | 75% | 100% |

Get three bids from selected subcontractors in each category.

| 25% | 50% | 75% | 100% |

Get more bids in categories where you feel uncomfortable.

| 25% | 50% | 75% | 100% |

Get three bids from selected suppliers needed.

| 25% | 50% | 75% | 100% |

Build a file of sub and supplier estimates.

| 25% | 50% | 75% | 100% |

Review the bids down to the line items. Enter on a spreadsheet.

| 25% | 50% | 75% | 100% |

Notes   **Tally of Hours**

Task	Notes

Refine your budget.

25%	50%	75%	100%

Talk with past customers of selected subs.

25%	50%	75%	100%

Write letters to selected subs to indicate their selection.

25%	50%	75%	100%

Watch construction videos, planning DVD's, and TV shows.

25%	50%	75%	100%

Read builder magazines.

25%	50%	75%	100%

Dream.

25%	50%	75%	100%

Check with your state or province about insurance coverages required.

25%	50%	75%	100%

Shop for coverage.

25%	50%	75%	100%

Learn how to use a computer spreadsheet.

25%	50%	75%	100%

Build your budget on computer.

25%	50%	75%	100%

Review your budget with several people.

25%	50%	75%	100%

Build your calendar on computer.

25%	50%	75%	100%

Review your calendar with several people.

25%	50%	75%	100%

Make revisions to budget and calendar.

25%	50%	75%	100%

Develop loan proposal and presentation for lender.

25%	50%	75%	100%

Notes   **Tally of Hours**

Task				**Notes**

Apply for loan.

25%	50%	75%	100%

Develop final drawings with architect or designer.

25%	50%	75%	100%

Study your plans thoroughly, review them with other people.

25%	50%	75%	100%

Take out builder's risk insurance policy.

25%	50%	75%	100%

Set up clear property boundary markets.

25%	50%	75%	100%

Get your permits, laminate a copy for on-site.

25%	50%	75%	100%

Go to Zoning if you need to pursue any variances.

25%	50%	75%	100%

Set up economical cell phone plan, program team member phone numbers into phone.

25%	50%	75%	100%

Preliminary clearing and rough staking.

25%	50%	75%	100%

Call your local underground utility locator service for underground utility flagging.

25%	50%	75%	100%

Make construction sign with street adress and laminated permit copy.

25%	50%	75%	100%

Other:

25%	50%	75%	100%

Other:

25%	50%	75%	100%

25%	50%	75%	100%

25%	50%	75%	100%

Notes   **Tally of Hours**

Project Notes

Chapter 5: You Will Profit By Building a True Custom Home

Time line: Nine months before groundbreaking

Starter, Step up, Custom, Dream house

According to a recent survey of custom builders in Custom Builder Magazine, the average U.S. custom home was 3,950 finished square feet in size. The average total value of a new custom home was $761,000 including land. Factoring out land at 25% of total cost, custom home construction prices were then $144 per finished foot, on average. The average contractor-built custom home construction budget in this survey was $570,750.

By contrast, the average house built in the U.S. in 2001 was 2,324 square feet in size and has a value with land of $200,600 according to the U.S. Census Bureau. Factoring out land at 20%, the average construction cost of a new house in this country was then $160,500, or $69 per square foot.

Traditionally, single-family homes are classed roughly into three groups, by size and cost: "starter", "step-up" and "custom" or luxury homes. To these groups, I

Sources Say

"Getting a custom home is well within just about everyone's ability. But there is work involved. You'll have to figure out just what you want, not as a nebulous dream, but as something that can be put onto paper and then built."

From **Build It Right!** (See page 258)

would add a high-end classification of "Dream Home". The starter homes are at the bottom of the market in scope, the step-up homes are in the middle, and the custom homes occupy the high position. A dream home is a highly customized custom home that the owner personalizes to his tastes without major concerns over its appeal to a subsequent buyer.

With custom (and dream) homes averaging over $700,000 and the average house at $200,000, there is a great distance separating the categories of construction. Factoring out dream homes which can run into the millions of dollars, the custom home category would likely start in the $400,000 bracket currently. Step-up homes would generally start in the $200,000 to $300,000 bracket and starter homes in the $100's.

The issue for you when you set out to build a custom home is that it will be recognized by the market in the custom category, and priced accordingly at resale. The starter and step-up categories hold much slimmer profit potential at resale than does a custom home in total dollars. At the same time, a custom home can bring a disappointing return if it falls into the dream home category and is too customized to attract a solid price.

For example, if you build a high-end custom home of 10,000 square feet with large rooms, but only two bedrooms, as one owner did, you may find very few prospective buyers at resale and attract a very small profit on your costly original investment.

Four Ways to Make Money

Traditionally your house adds to your wealth in two ways. The most important way is through appreciation, which has averaged 5.5% per year in the U.S. for the past 20 years. This is a valuable source of gain, much better than a savings account. If you have a $200,000 house, and made a typical down payment of $20,000 to buy it, your 5.5% gain is measured against your $20,000 down payment. That returns $11,000 per year on $20,000 or 55%. Your savings account pays five percent or less on average.

The second way your home adds to your wealth is through retiring your mortgage. For most of us this is a small but steady gain. If you hold a $200,000 mortgage, and you make $2,000 payments, you reduce the mortgage by only $1,000 or $2,000 per year in the early years.

A house I bought in 1980 gained $67,000 of appreciation in twelve years, or $6,000 a year. I had paid down my mortgage by more than $10,000 or about $1,000 a year during the period. Compared to savings this was a superior gain for us, but small compared to the gain afforded by owner-building.

Owner-building opens up two additional areas of gain. The first is keeping the costs down, and the second is pushing the value up. The latter is done by building a house with market appeal, one which sells better and for more money. This is where selected, researched features come in.

We added $140,000 to our net worth in the eight months it took to build our custom home. And the special features we managed to incorporate will enhance the price at sale. We built the house which was estimated at $90 a foot for $50 a foot using the techniques described in this book. But because of the strategic features we incorporated, we were told that the house is currently worth $150 a foot in some markets.

One architect told me that the right design and features will add 15% to the value of a house. Well-chosen features rank with budgeting and scheduling as your core tools in making money by owner-building your home. The four ways of increasing your wealth through your home rank as:

1. Reduce cost of construction.
2. Improve resale with right features.
3. Derive appreciation.
4. Pay down mortgage.

Your Dream Home Notebook

One important source for feature and design ideas is your personal thoughts and observations. The planning you do in this area need not be confined to the year before you build — it can span a lifetime. I started with a notebook, later included a photo album, and then went to a word processing file that I could keep forever updated and complete.

My first home was just a thrill that wore off slowly. It was such an improvement from married student living conditions that I thought it was perfect. It wasn't until a few years into my second home, around twenty years ago, that I began to write down ideas for improvement.

Some of the thoughts I entered into that first dream home notebook were:

- Guest complex with own bath — privacy.
- Have a dinner party with other couples who have built and tape record the session for ideas.
- Make the place as low maintenance as possible.
- Water filtration system at point of origin.
- Big storage bin or deep freestanding shelves for seasonal items like Halloween costumes, Christmas decorations, camping gear, sports equipment.

It took many years, but eventually all of those thoughts were implemented. Samples from our current idea file include:

- Wider flutes on woodwork.
- Have a probe wire to outside of house for outside temperature reading.
- Use slag for base under garage and basement floor, not pea gravel.
- Basement floor drain within ten feet of hot water heaters.
- Next time, do solid-core interior doors. Choose oak or birch for stainability and solidity.
- Insist that all ceramic tile grouts be mixed with latex additive instead of water.

Our current idea file runs to 100 pages, and we add to it all the time. When you notice something that could be improved for your comfort, enjoyment, or convenience, add it to your file.

Jim Stark, a veteran owner-builder from Nebraska, has built four times. He says: "Building a house will stress any marital relationship. Making choices is a strain. We put together a notebook of what it will look like before we even start. We get most of the arguing out of the way. We take pictures as we build and turn it into an album. We use the album to develop specs."

Before our marriage, Elaine often cut floor plans and pictures out of magazines and placed them in a file. By the time we began to owner-build she was unusually competent at reading blueprints and visualizing the final product. She was a good owner-builder because she had come to a clear idea of what she wanted.

We arrived at common ground as a couple by visiting many "Parade of Homes" houses and noting features that we both liked.

You or the Market?

In marketing, we say there are two orientations: product-driven and market-driven. You may be in love with a product (a house feature), and not find a market for it. In residential construction, hot tubs and swimming pools are notorious product-driven examples. They cost more than they return on resale in many markets. If your thinking is market-driven, you may not particularly care about a feature, but you might incorporate it into your house for the sake of resale. In our case, market-driven features included open floor design and high ceilings.

Owner-builder Gary Ziser stresses this point:

"Be really careful how you design the house. This is extremely important. When laying out a floor plan, you have to know when to back off your personal taste if it falls too far outside the norm. Unless you are wealthy, you want to keep "resale" in mind. Don't overdo quality. You can spend a lot of money that's not recoupable. Remember, if you are an average family, you won't live in the house more than seven years."

To get a feel for the market, Elaine and I made a study of the "Parade" homes we visited in the year before we built. We noted features and the work of craftsmen that we liked in each home we visited, as this sample shows:

"Parade of Homes" Example

Features We Liked

Parade House #2 Robert Nelson Construction
285 S. Main St. Salem

Total Sq. Footage	5,554
Finished Square Footage	5,554
Base Price	$499,860
Cost per total square foot	$90
Cost per finished square foot	$90

Features Noted:

✓ Trex® front porch
✓ Brick borders in front walk
✓ Leaded glass lites and transom front door
✓ Courtesy lights in front steps
✓ Oak entry floor
✓ Sports court
✓ Low, middle, and high molding in office
✓ Wider than normal doors
✓ Brass grab bars in bath
✓ Pedestal sink
✓ Marble bath floor and splashes
✓ Footed tub with heat lamps above
✓ Fireplace in master bedroom
✓ Crown molding in master bath
✓ Outdoor drinking fountain
✓ Swinging door to dining room
✓ Turret room with leaded lites over double hung windows
✓ Porcelain tub in guest bedroom upstairs
✓ Walk-in closet off bath in guest suite
✓ Nine-foot ceilings, wall painting, ceiling fans

- ✓ Fancy crown molding throughout
- ✓ Window seats, individual walk-in closets
- ✓ Wooden wainscoting
- ✓ Verdi Foresta granite countertops ← *quartz*
- ✓ Six burner countertop gas range
- ✓ Tile backsplashes by Terry Robertson *?*
- ✓ Mirrored exercise room in basement
- ✓ Immense plumbing manifold system
- ✓ Shared bath downstairs with urinal
- ✓ Formica™ countertops downstairs
- ✓ Tile bath floor
- ✓ Concrete window wells
- ✓ Home theater in basement
- ✓ Mud and laundry room with tile
- ✓ Breezeway
- ✓ Fluorescents and shelves in back of garage

To check our thinking against the market we enlisted the help of an enterprising Realtor we found. This Realtor pulled Multiple Listing Service® examples from his computer to show the features of houses that had sold recently in our target price range. The examples showed the prices paid and the features included for each house.

We used the Multiple Listing Service® as a checklist to compare against "Parade" homes that we liked. The home in the previous example looked like this on our checklist:

Multiple Listing Features

Parade House #2
(Numbers in parentheses are MLS codes)

Feature	Quantity or ✓ if present
Bedrooms (MLS 9)	5
Baths (MLS 10)	5
Size of garage (MLS 11)	4
Main floor bedrooms (MLS 35)	1
Main floor baths (MLS 35)	2
Main floor square footage	
Levels	
Upper level bedrooms (MLS 34)	2
Upper level baths	2
Upper level square footage	
Lower level bedrooms (MLS 36)	4
Lower level baths	2

Lower level square footage	
Brick construction	✓
Metal siding	
Stucco	
Rock	
Cedar shakes	
Composition shingles	✓
Gas heat	✓
Electric heat pump	
Formal entry	✓
Formal dining	✓
Window coverings	
Water softener	
Garage door opener	✓
Wet bar	
Humidifier	
Jetted tub	
Electronic air filter	
Unfinished basement	
Walk-out basement	✓
Gas fireplaces	3
Wood stove	
Second kitchen	✓
Vaulted ceiling	✓
Cable TV	
RV parking	✓
Satellite dish	
Dishwasher	✓
Food disposal	✓
Refrigerator	✓
Complete range	
Countertop range	✓
Range hood	
Trash compactor	
Microwave	✓
Wall ovens	2
Gas water heaters	2
Electric water heater	
Landscaping	✓

Readers Say

"We have in-floor radiant heating. We're using a hot water heater to drive the basement heat only. Has zones, and has closed loop. Closed system keeps the life of the hot water heater double the usual fifteen year life."

Brad & Jalayne P.
Bluffdale, UT

Sources Say

"You can save money by purchasing your own electrical fixtures. The markup is incredible."

From *The Complete Guide to Contracting Your Home* (See page 260)

Sources Say

"What I learned from my experiences is that traditional approaches to building were often smarter than they appeared. What seems ordinary at first may prove elegant and wise after a few years. Innovation is important, but even new methods that seem well engineered and brilliant may have hidden costs, maintenance problems, or unintended consequences."

From *Independent Builder* (See page 259)

Feature	
Fenced	✓
Sprinkler system	✓
Tile flooring	✓
Vinyl flooring	
Wall to wall carpet	✓
Hardwood flooring	✓
Patio	✓
Deck	✓
Covered deck	
Storm windows	
Storm door	
Double pane windows	✓
Ceiling fans	✓
Central air conditioning	✓
Swamp cooler	
Laundry room	
Nine-foot ceilings	✓
Vaulted ceiling	✓
Family room	✓
Main floor master	✓

Real Estate Survey

Gradually we arrived at a list of features that we liked and the market seemed to like, as well. By looking at the Home Builders Association "Parade of Homes" we got the ideas that local builders seemed to favor. There is a risk that builder ideas are simply personal preferences and represent "product-driven" thinking. By using MLS listings of recent sales we tried to get a "market-driven" perspective. We decided to test the resulting ideas with active Realtors.

We took our planned list of features and made a telephone survey of ten Realtors with agencies that sell custom homes in our area. The Realtors were happy to talk and seemed to enjoy our survey. We asked them to rate from 1 to 10 each feature in terms of its saleability in the price range we intended to build.

The following were the features that scored 5 out of 10 or higher:

A sample list of features from the Riverbottoms house is available for computer on our free Resource CD-ROM (See page 270)

Realtor Survey

Score	Feature
9	Jetted tub
9	Large master bedroom
9	Large walk-in closet
9	Closet systems
9	Formal dining room
9	Walk-in pantry
9	Solid-surface countertops
8	Light, open look *can lights*
8	Hardwood kitchen floor
8	Extensive exterior utilities
8	Office
8	Removable windows for cleaning
8	Water softener
8	Whole-house vacuum system
8	Gas fireplace
8	Tile or hardwood entry
8	Spacious kitchen cabinets
7	Whole-house air filter
7	Sitting room off master bedroom
7	Bonus room over garage
6	Vegetable sink in kitchen island *?*
6	Telephone in bathroom
6	Courtesy footlighting on stairs
6	French doors to master bedroom
5	Whole house sound system
5	Home theater
5	Hot water in garage
5	Center meet closet doors
5	Recycling center

Readers Say

"I had a physician in my law class who built 8,000 square feet for $39 a foot for a construction budget of $350,000. It appraised for $800,000 afterward."

Blaine L.
New Orleans, LA

Sources Say

"If you can, use underground drainpipes instead of simple splash-blocks. Care must be taken that they are not completely buried during the backfill stage. A Heavy PVC black tubing should be used."

From *The Complete Guide to Contracting Your Home*
(See page 260)

Sub and Supplier Input

To the Realtor input we added input from subs and suppliers that we interviewed. (See "How to Interview Subs" on page 87.) The idea is to balance what is desirable with what is doable. The subs helped to explain the costs of doing things and alternative approaches to consider.

Our wish list of features eventually filled several pages. We decided to incorporate features on three levels:

1. Crucial to quality, must accept costs.

Examples were:

dramatic design and good layout
dual furnaces, air conditioners, and water heaters
custom windows
high-end cabinets
jetted tub
closet systems
hardwood and tile

2. Helpful to resale, if costs not out of line.

For example:

pre-wire for "future-proof" house technology
telephone jacks in every room
home theater
courtesy footlighting on stairs
vacuum system
French doors

3. Personal preferences if costs are low or opportunities arise.

For example:

ceiling fans
bedside light controls
whole house air and water filters
solid vinyl deck
indoor sports court
granite and marble countertops *quartz*

Features of a Custom Home

Owner-builders I interviewed from around the country offered their views of important features to include in a custom home. The following list of their suggestions is ranked from most mentioned to least.

High and vaulted ceilings
Upgraded and crown molding
Energy-efficiency
Large, functional kitchen
Large, scenic decks
Spacious custom cabinets
Jetted tub
Ceramic or marble tile
Openness, light
Custom layout
Large bedrooms
Large bathrooms
Walk-in closets
Hardwood floor
Central vac
Well-chosen appliances
Dining room
Island breakfast bar
Countertops of Corian™ and granite
Oversized showers
Master on main floor
Large custom windows
Two water heaters or point of use water heaters
Three tone paint
Gas fireplaces
Decorator touches
Recessed lighting
Spectacular views
Multiple separate bathrooms
Large stone fireplace
Custom ceiling lines
Two furnaces and A/C units or multi-zoned system
Master bath johnny room with reading rack and telephone
Smart House wiring
Full brick
Custom concrete
Curb appeal
Loft with ladder and banisters
Three compartment kitchen sink
Plant shelves
Laundry chutes
Ceiling fans
All upgrades

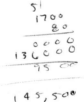

Good idea

Good idea

- Insulated garage doors
- Sitting rooms
- Altered roof line
- Custom plumbing fixtures
- French doors
- Study
- High basement ceiling
- Hot tub
- Steam showers
- Family room
- Good acoustics
- Air-to-air heat exchanger
- Wood blinds
- Two ovens
- Pantry with pull-out organizers _walk in_
- Appliance garages on countertop
- Undercabinet lighting
- Alarm system
- Double vanity
- Hardwood trim
- Bonus space over garage
- Sinks in youth bedrooms
- Whole-house audio
- Location
- Features that appeal to average buyer
- Stucco
- Walk-out basement

A House that Works

"A house that works" is my theme in building a house. My impression after touring hundreds of houses is that they lack imagination. Most houses are tremendously dull concepts involving little more than boxes stacked on top of each other. You can change this. By forethought, you can put all kinds of things into the design and inside the walls that will make your house more useable and comfortable.

I found Don Aslett's book, _Make Your House Do the Housework_ (see page 259) refreshing and interesting. This housecleaning expert found that much recurring drudgery can be obviated by good design. As an owner-builder you have the unique opportunity — I consider it a stewardship — to make your home into a facilitative environment for better living. Winston Churchill captured the thought when he said, "We shape our buildings, and our buildings shape us."

Your house has a job to do, and that is to facilitate your life and those of your successors in the house. Some ideas to put your house to work:

1. Let it process the water with which you will cook, clean and drink. This can be through water filtration, water softening, water distillation, or a combination.

2. Let your house improve the air you breathe. Through a variety of air filtration systems, humidifiers, and air-to-air heat exchangers you can improve the healthfulness of your inside environment, and the cleanliness of your surroundings. House wraps reduce dust infiltration.

3. Let your house feed you. Through forethought, you can simplify the process of preparing and storing food in your new house. You can landscape for a place to grow food and herbs; you can provide a root cellar or fruit room to store the produce.

4. Let your house give you a workout. You can build a sports court into your design as we did. You can adapt a room into a workout room by providing appropriate soundproofing and electrical service and cable or satellite TV to facilitate the use.

5. Let your house stimulate your mind. Provide spaces conducive to two person conversations. Create libraries and reading spots with natural and artificial light and privacy. Pre-wire for electronic internet and computer sharing pathways from room to room. Locate student desks in bedrooms. Pre-wire for telephone and data access to many points.

6. Let your house clean itself. Build in a dust-free whole-house vacuum system. Bring wash facilities to points of use. Avoid designs and surfaces that catch dust. Use scrubbable, cleanable, renewable finish materials.

7. Let your house warm and cool itself. Provide for air flow, orient your structure to capture morning and winter sun, design to shade from the high sun of summer. Provide means of thermal storage and insulate to protect your found resource.

8. Let your house care for you. Make provisions for handicap access if you have immediate need or if you will stay long enough to experience the ravages of unexpected injury or advancing age. See that your hallways are wider, your baths, laundry and entrances are accessible, and your kitchen is open and adaptable. Design in considerations for children and for pets. Make play spaces, gathering spots, and storage for toys and personal articles.

9. Let your house entertain you. Pre-wire for whole house audio and home theater video. Provide for internet, satellite, and computer connections to televisions. Create spaces for guests and gatherings. Design your house to separate activities and permit privacy. Provide for musical performances and instruments, for formal meals and holiday celebrations. Facilitate your hobbies thoughtfully.

10. Let your house make a living. Create and equip space for shop or office, craft or livelihood. Anticipate the necessary utilities and facilities. See that storage, display, delivery, and communication flexibility are built in whether you choose to activate them later or not.

Sources Say

"Simple doorways can be obstacles. In accessible design, the "net clear opening" has to be 32 inches. Since an open door itself uses some of the doorway space, doors should be 36 inches wide or at least 34 inches."

From *Independent Builder* (See page 259)

Sources Say

"In a good layout, you often enter an area between zones via a distinct entry. For example, you come in to a hall; go left to the master suite, right to the public area, or directly up the stairs to the bedrooms. People can come and go without making a ruckus. Very little space has been set aside for circulation, but it gets a lot done."

From *Independent Builder* (See page 259)

Quality Considerations

In Chapter 6 we will talk about bringing your ideas to an architect or designer who will incorporate them into a professional design. Before you see your design professional you should give consideration to the quality you expect to build into your custom house.

As an owner-builder you have the cafeteria-style privilege of selecting the elements and philosophies that go into your home. My interviews with general contractors showed a surprising ignorance on their part of the quality that should go into a high-end home. Designers and architects, on the other hand, proved to be very fluent in issues of quality. As O-B you will consider the issues and assure that your design addresses all the quality possible on your construction budget.

Consider:

1. Noise reduction.

2. Clean air and water.

3. Energy and water conservation.

4. Ease of maintenance and cleaning.

5. Suitable illumination.

6. Longevity of design and materials.

7. Preservation of investment value.

8. Comfort and convenience.

9. Safety and security.

10. Economies of forethought.

Number ten means that you design quality in before you break ground, and that potential conflicts of design are worked out in advance and without the cost of rework and change orders.

Consider the uses to which your house will be put and make sure the design accommodates those uses. Even common activities like food storage and musical performance can raise questions. Inspector Beryl Ford of Tulsa, Oklahoma explains:

"People may think they are okay with minimum requirements. A refrigerator alone weighs 300 pounds. Most residential floors are designed for 30 pounds per square foot of weight, and the fridge exceeds it. Then you load it with food, and a heavy person walks up, the floor sags and squeaks due to concentrated load.

A grand piano weighs 1,200 pounds, and has three legs, that's 400 pounds on each of three square feet. Then a big guy comes over to play. Several people lean on the piano to sing, and the floor shakes."

The thoughtful observations in your dream house notebook, conversations with subs and suppliers, the care invested with the designer, and the on-site efforts of you and your inspector during construction will all impact the quality of your house. Ultimately you are responsible for quality — it won't happen on its own:

"Quality is never an accident; it is always the result of intelligent effort."

John Ruskin
Seven Lamps of Architecture

Comfort and Convenience Considerations

Over the past few years Elaine and I have visited the homes in seven "Parade of Homes". I always look for the same little conveniences: bedside shelves, ceiling fans, lighted house numbers, closet organizers, water softeners, gas fireplaces with thermostat controls. One favorite convenience of mine is bedside light and fan controls. Out of seven "Parades" with more than 100 houses, only one house had dual bedside controls in the master bedroom. Everybody probably reads in bed once in a while, but builders must figure you can take a walk when it's time to turn out the light.

In our house we made sure that there were two individual reading lights over the master bed with separate bedside controls. There are separate switches at bedside to control the ceiling fan and the fan light. These are in constant use and a great convenience. One owner-builder I talked to pushed this convenience further. South Carolinian Ernie Gerdts added deck lights and exterior floodlights to the bedside array of switches. He floods the property with light if he hears a noise in the night.

I have never seen a gas fireplace with a conventional thermostat control in a "Parade" home, although with a gas fireplace the thermostat is a no-brainer. You can maintain a constant temperature in one room throughout a cold night with this simple convenience. Even comfortable features like carpet in the master bath, or an overhead heat lamp are almost never in evidence.

You are the judge of your comfort and convenience, and many small things that you can add to your design are negligible in cost. You can make your home much more livable with features like:

dual pane low-E window glass
house wrap
outlets in roof soffits for holiday lights or snow melt cables
whirly roof vents in warm climates
whole house fan
central vacuum
hot & cold water outlet in garage for car washing
gas and electric outlets for choice at stove and laundry
programmable electronic thermostats
operable bathroom window
porthole window in master closet or laundry
aluminum drip edge on roof
silent floor joists
glued and screwed sub flooring
anti-scald shower valves
lawn sprinklers with line drains
nook storage
pull-out spray faucet in kitchen
no-maintenance siding and deck
seat and grab bars in shower
extra countertop outlets in kitchen and baths
in-wall blocking for hand rails, towel bars, shelves, drapes and cabinets
reading light over tub
light over shower
courtesy footlights on stairs

Pay attention to the fatigue you may feel while standing on your kitchen floor, to drafts or cold surfaces in your bathroom in winter, to noise, and to lighting in work, reading, and viewing areas. Notice when you must stoop or stretch to reach something you need. Notice the little things.

Professional builders are notorious for ignoring comfort factors in building custom homes. Writing in "The Brevard Builder", a home building association news-letter, Tom Luce says:

> "Occasionally a builder will come up with things that are real head scratchers, like an open ended shower in a bath with ten-foot ceilings (that must be a chilling experience), four-and-one half foot bathtubs..."

You will do better than that because it's your house.

Energy-Saving Features

One of the reasons your new home will automatically be more valuable than existing homes is the advances in energy-saving technology that you can exploit. Our new home uses a monthly average of just under 1,000 kilowatt hours of electricity during the summer. My records of 11 years ago show that my former home in Columbus, Ohio used over 2,000 kilowatt hours a month during the summer. That home is a single story house that is 30% smaller than our Utah two-story.

There are newer, more efficient furnaces, heat pumps, and air conditioners on the market now, along with better insulations, glazing systems and air infiltration barriers. New Styrofoam insulated panel sheathing systems (SIP's or "Stress-skin Panels") offer bonuses to the new home builder in energy savings.

The placement of your house on the lot can save energy. Author Robert Roy says: "The orientation of a house — any house, energy-efficient or inefficient — can mean up to a 35% difference in the cost of heating and cooling." You can begin your energy savings strategy by taking advantage of building orientation, and you can take advantage of every strategy of design to exploit your savings, such as deciduous shade trees and lawn around the house for air-cooling perimeter moisture and heat absorption. Place coniferous trees on the north side of your house in cold climates as a winter wind break. Economize the use of water by limiting grassy areas in the design of your landscaping.

Owner-builders relate additional energy savings through the use of hot water radiant floor heat, electric heat strips under tile, heat pumps, sealed top stoves, masonry exteriors, gas-filled insulated windows, low-E glass, dual furnace and A/C systems, dual hot water heaters, setback thermostats, gas fireplaces, ceiling fans, computer-calculated heating and cooling capacities, roof overhangs to shade in summer and admit warmth in winter, tree plantings for shade or to block winter wind, gas appliances, compact fluorescent lighting, and the lower resistance of 12-gauge house wiring.

Readers Say

"My friend owner-built last year, and his house was estimated at $180,000 by a contractor, but he built the house as O-B for $100,000."

Brian C.
Naples, FL

Readers Say

"Where roof truss crosses wall plate, there is usually a cold strip. With SIP panels, however, you can use an SIP truss, using the same material you use for the walls. Then there is no void. SIP's can be premade, with window openings, headers, etc. Also, run pipes under the foundation before you pour the floor."

Jay H.
Draper, UT

Sample Thread from the Forums on our web site:

Message: 1

Date: 02/05/2002 02:09 PM

Author: Jeanne Davison

Message: I have had one builder tell me I shouldn't have to spend $10K to maybe $15K on a foundation for 2,588 sq. ft. and I had one builder tell me that I should spend $24K to $25K... anyone out there want to address this?... Have you built with a similar foundation and what was the cost?... Help!!... I have been told not to waste my money on a soil sample by some and told to get it by others, quoting, it will cost me about $500 for soil sample and $500 for engineer to design my foundation... Any comment?... Thank you... Jeanne

Message: 2

Date: 02/06/2002 11:22 AM

Author: Don Schloeder

Message: There are huge variables that have to be considered: your soil condition, your location, frost lines, basement, drainage, etc. Talk around to people who are homeowners; see what problems they have after a couple years in a house. Visit subdivisions still under construction to see what's being done; and visit custom sites. Ask questions. Your estimates of $10K to $25K are too far spread to have any validity for comparison purposes. I wouldn't bypass a soil test; the saving will be infinitesimal compared to the cost involved if there are problems that aren't addressed upfront.

Message: 3

Date: 02/06/2002 03:59 PM

Author: Jeanne Davison

Message: Don... Thanks for the feedback... I am in Texas... Just North of Houston... About 30 minutes... We don't have basements and frost lines...

Message: 4

Date: 02/14/2002 06:57 AM

Author: Tony Vu

Message: It also depend on your local city/county building official, they want everything here in San Diego and it cost us $2,500 for soil test. Check with the city if you need it, and don't bypass them, it will cost you more.

Message: 5

Date: 02/14/2002 07:52 AM

Author: Jeanne Davison

Message: WOW!!! Only $500 for soil test here in Texas.

Message: 6

Date: 02/14/2002 12:09 PM

Author: Jeff Lewis

Message: And here in Utah, I didn't even need one, though some excavators would have had me believe otherwise. So make sure to check with your local authorities.

Message: 7

Date: 02/14/2002 12:48 PM

Author: Jeanne Davison

Message: Jeff... That is great... I was only saying the LOWEST cost I got... BUT, the builder that is going to install my SIP's told me that the guy, Mervin, that will be doing my foundation has been doing it for 40 years and will give me great piers...etc to Not waste the money having a soil sample and I shan't altho EVERYONE says you SHOULD...its called having faith... Jeanne

Message: 8

Date: 02/14/2002 01:53 PM

Author: Don Schloeder

Message: I can't let this go without a parting shot. $500 is peanuts - your front door will probably cost more. If you have expansive soils, you'll pay forever . . .

Message: 9

Date: 02/14/2002 05:39 PM

Author: Jeanne Davison

Message: I understand exactly what you are saying... I think 8 foot piers should cover it.

Message: 10

Date: 02/18/2002 09:23 PM

Author: Jim Gobel

Message: Jeanne D., BEFORE you make the mistake of trusting your excavator/foundation contractor, ...

Chapter 6: Conquer Details Room By Room and Save 20%

Time line: Eight months before groundbreaking

Change Orders are Costly

A change order is an agreement to modify an original contract with a builder at an added cost. The term applies generically to those changes in the course of your project that change your original plans and increase your cost.

You don't want change orders. You want to get it right the first time because change orders are costly for these reasons:

1. Do—Undo—Redo.

Many change orders result in three times the work. You do the design as planned. That's the first cost. You decide you don't like it. You undo what you did, destroying materials and running up labor. That's the second cost. You redo the work in a different way. That's the third cost. You've paid for the same item — family room, driveway, shower enclosure, whatever — three times.

2. Short Notice.

The affected item must be changed right now. It stands in the way of other work. The interest clock is ticking. The schedules of the subs are on hold and beckoning. You've got to move now. You can't give the item adequate competitive bidding or shopping time. You have no recourse but to pay top dollar.

3. Tip of the Iceberg.

Once an owner starts doing change orders, it's just the tip of the iceberg. If one thing needs to be changed now that the owner thinks about it, other things also need to be changed. The change orders are a sign that planning was weak on the project overall. There is dissatisfaction with many items. But the impatience of the subs and the unavailability of new and different materials or craftsmen to effect the change limits the process. The result is that many desired changes are foregone. And the owner is unhappy with the house, the greatest single investment of his or her lifetime.

Some changes are too late to be done right, as with the master bathroom in one house in the Midwest. The owner decided belatedly to add marbled walls and mirrored ceilings to a sumptuous master bath. The weight of the room became tremendous, and out of proportion to the footings and foundations already in place. The house sagged, the walls cracked, and a legal fight over responsibility ensued.

For many general contractors, change orders are a way of life, and a steady source of income. This group gives short shrift to planning, and hurries to break ground for their customer. When the change orders arise, they are "the customer's fault". The contractor gets the business because he bid it lower than a competitor who included everything and who provided for some planning time. But he ends up at a higher cost than the "up-front" competitor. And the customer winds up stressed and dissatisfied.

In my survey, most of the contractors admitted that change orders arise on all of their projects. The average of all contractors surveyed was a five percent increase in original estimate.

Industry expert Ron Horne says that change orders actually add 20% to the cost of a custom home. When contractors only admit to going over by five percent, who is right?

By the time a project goes over budget by five percent, all the "slop" in the budget has been consumed. Suppose there is a ten percent contingency budgeted for the unforeseen. That's used up. Say that everything from concrete to roofing was estimated a little conservatively, maybe five percent over. That's used up. The owner loses any remaining flexibility to divert unspent funds to upgrades and extras. The project is over budget and nobody's happy, except possibly the contractor.

The contractor still makes his planned profit. If the project is getting a little tight and his profits are threatened, he can make it back with interest on the change orders. The profit margin on change orders is widely regarded to be more than on the original estimate. You are under the gun, everything is rushed, and there's a real potential for contractor profiteering.

This is one of the places where the value of owner-building becomes clear. You control the planning, and thus control the change orders. You use the slop in your budget for extras or you keep your savings. You have the satisfaction of getting exactly what you know you want in your house, all at fully competitive prices.

Custom Builder Magazine reported that custom homes go over original budget by an average of 12% to 19%. On a $200,000 project, five percent is $10,000; 20% is $40,000. If your planning saves $40,000 on your house by averting change orders, you get the "Dime Saved is a Dollar Earned" equivalent of $400,000 in salary for your effort.

How Specs Save You Money and Get You a Better House

A "spec" or specification is a comprehensive written advance description of the details of your project. Let's look at the components of the definition:

1. Written.

Because specs are written they force you to think. As Anne Morrow Lindbergh has said, "Writing is thinking." Once the spec is in writing, you can engage others in the process of that thinking. For instance, you can photocopy the spec and mail it to different vendors for suggestions or prices. If you have the written spec on your computer, you can fax from the computer or word process excerpts from the spec to vendors, subs, designers — anyone involved in your process.

2. In advance.

Since specs are created in advance, they provide all kinds of opportunities to save. With written specs and time to respond, subs can produce far better estimated bids. The sub can be more accurate and more thorough, and can take advantage of the power of planning. You can engage the sub in the process of "thinking through" a better house.

Say you specify higher foundation walls than usual in your concrete spec because you want a nice high basement ceiling. One of your selected concrete subs calls while preparing the bid and says that he will have to rent oversized forms to do it, at a much higher cost than usual. Are you sure you want the high walls?

You assure him you do, and he asks if you have considered an insulated concrete forming system. It would cost a bit more, but the walls could be poured to any height, with a stay-in-place form that is made of rigid foam insulation. The insulation means you will save on heating bills for the life of the house. You take the suggestion, make adjustments to the budget, and rejoice over the improvement in design.

The detailed specifications make the work go smoothly once construction begins. The subs have the right tools and right materials to get the specified job done. There are no false starts and no disappearing subs due to inability to complete. There are fewer questions and delays. The sub knows this and you get lower bids. You save money during construction because there is no rework, there are no changes, and the job is finished surprisingly fast. You attract good subs because they prefer planned projects like yours.

Another benefit of advance specifications is that it permits you to separate materials from labor on your project. This helps in two ways. First, you get the privilege of choosing the materials and components you want rather than those that are standard or the sub happens to like. Second, you have the opportunity to hunt for bargains. You have plenty of time to reflect on the advice of suppliers and find the chosen items at the best prices. You don't miss out on good deals that may have long lead times.

3. Comprehensive.

Your spec incorporates all the aspects of your project, including those which could clash with each other. No decision is made on its own basis alone, or "in a vacuum". I call this "systems thinking". Each aspect of the project is made to complement the other aspects of the whole system.

For example, if you know in advance that you want elaborate crown molding in certain rooms, the framers can provide the proper backing for the molding before the sheetrock is hung. The finish carpenters install the crown molding easily and well and it stays perfectly in place. It is easy to caulk and paint, and no microcracking occurs. You enjoy a better product for years to come.

How to Develop Room by Room Specifications

When you apply for a construction loan, your lender will want to see written specifications for your project. (See Chapter 11.) The ones furnished by your house designer may not be sufficient or in the format the bank uses. Bankers have various forms for specifications. Following are three examples of foundation concrete specification forms that bankers use.

Sample 1

Foundations:

Footings: concrete mix _____; strength:psi _____ reinforcing _____

Foundation wall: material _____ reinforcing _____

Interior foundation wall: material _____ Party foundation wall _____

Columns: material and sizes _____

Piers: material and reinforcing _____

Girders: material and sizes_____ Sills: material_____

Basement entrance areaway _____ Window areaways _____

Waterproofing _____ Footing drains _____

Termite   protection_____

Basementless space: ground cover _____; insulation _____;

foundation vents _____

Special foundations: _____

Additional information: _____

Readers Say

"Our budget is $250,000 for construction and $75,000 for the land. This is a half million dollar neighborhood. It will be a classy house, equal in value to the others around it."

Laurie & Ron R. Kernersville, NC

Sample 2

Concrete Footings:

Concrete footings for walls and piers shall be mixed in the proportion of one part cement, _____ parts sand and _____ parts gravel. Pit run gravel may be used if its proportions of sand and gravel are as called for. All aggregate shall be clean and sharp and free from organic matter. Coarse aggregate to pass 1 1/4-inch screen and to be retained upon a 1/4-inch screen.

Footings for walls shall be _____ inches thick and _____ inches wider than wall on each side: pier footings shall be not less than _____inches square and_____inches thick.

Basement Walls:

Shall be of _____ construction, straight, plumb and level, and as shown on plans. All joints shall be struck flush on both sides. Beam fill as shown on plans. Basement wall will or will not be waterproofed with _____ coats of _____

Sources Say

"...engineers often overdesign like crazy. They hate the thought of lawsuits, and who can blame them?"

From *The Well-Built House* (See page 260)

Readers Say

"Why not get 20 amp fuses, it's only a little more money, and you have more amperage per fuse. Now I don't have to worry with power surges, and don't pop the fuse. Whole house fan you should have because it will suck the hot air out of your house in a hurry."

John P.
Chicago, IL

Sample 3

Foundation

Type: ( ) Full; ( ) partial_____X_____; ( ) crawl space; ( ) pilings; ( ) slab; ( ) other_____

Footer: Depth_____; thickness_____

French Drains: ( ) Yes; ( ) No; material_____

Basement: Walls_____concrete block_____; poured concrete; ( ) reinforced; ( ) other ( ) outside entrance

Basement Floor: Concrete; ( ) reinforced; other_____

Basement Drains: ( ) Yes; ( ) No;_____number; ( ) sump pump

All of the lender specifications I have seen differ in degree of detail, ease of use, definition of categories and scope. Some of them are daunting for an owner-builder (like me) to complete. You can get help filling out a standard specification like one of these if your lender requires them by calling any subcontractor and asking him how to interpret and fill out the banker's form. They will help you and you get exposure to a possible choice of a sub for your project.

Most of the technical specs for your project will be provided by your architect or designer as part of your house plans. While the major technical details are covered by specs like these, it is insufficient in terms of explaining how to build the house you are hoping for.

For this purpose, your dream home notebook works in concert with the technical specs. Compare the following typical standard specifications for a bathroom with my own dream home notes on bathrooms:

Sources Say

Independent Builder describes elements of 'mundane sustainability' in ecologically sound building: Durability, Ordinariness, Accessibility, Small, and Cheap."

(See page 259)

Bathrooms Specifications

Total Baths:	No.____	full_____	three-quarter ____	half _____	
Sinks:	No.____	Type_____	Make_____	Color & Finish_____	
Spigots:	No.____	Type_____	Make_____	Color & Finish_____	
Toilets:	No.____	Type_____	Make_____	Color & Finish_____	
Bathtubs:	No.____	Type_____	Make_____	Color & Finish_____	
Stall Shower:	No.____	Type_____	Make_____	Color & Finish _____	
Medicine Cabinets:	No.____	Type_____	Make_____		
Vanities:	No____	Type_____	Make_____		
Heater-Light-Fan Units:	No.____	Type_____	Make_____		

Excerpt from Dream Home Notebook

Bathrooms:

Put blocking behind all the walls where towel racks and grab bars will go. Also in the wall where tub will need bracing. 2x12" remnants from stairs are good for this and for drapery locations over windows.

Telephone in bathroom.
Steam shower.

Extra electrical outlets in bathroom.

European bathroom fixtures that can be used as hand-held. One knob controls.

Built-in dispensers for liquid shampoo, conditioner, moisturizing cream.

A place in shower to put towel so you don't have to open door to get dry.

Light fixture in shower that won't rust and is vapor proof.

Have linen and bath supply closet in the bathrooms, oversized, floor to ceiling.

Have a deep, wide sink to accommodate the splash of washing your face.

Have the "fountain-type" fixture in the sink that makes it easy to rinse your mouth after you brush, and converts to rinse your face after you wash or shave.

Ceramic tile around tub.

Provide access to shower and tub drains

for cleaning them out.
Antique brass fixtures.

Build double joists under tubs for support. Insulate the open parts of the tub underneath to make it more comfortable and conservative of heat.

Have reading lights over the tub, angled for reading in the tub.

Have plate glass mirror over the sinks in the bathrooms, and use vanities with both drawers and cabinets for storage.

Use quiet-flush toilets with 1.6 gallon water-saver flushes. Have plumbing bids use simple white fixtures to compare apples to apples.

Cable TV hookup plus telephone jack because of possible internet connection through television. Have a GFI outlet nearby.

Separated sinks and vanities in master bath with angles and height changes.

Use exterior door-type opening for an interior door with frosted side lites and transom to master bath.

Have a gas fireplace in the bathroom, shared with the bedroom.

Have a hot water radiant heat system in the basement, and forced air on the other two floors. We can bring the piping up and at least do a staple up system under the kitchen floor, bath floors, and main floor areas of tile.

Have a way to warm your towels in the bathroom, and to pre-warm the clothes you are going to put on first thing in the morning. Could use a radiant wall unit in bathroom like the "Runtal" brand that doubles as a towel bar.

Have the HVAC installer do all the vents, including bathrooms, laundry room, clothes dryer, stove and range hood.

Outside window in johnny room. Insulation around bath vent fans for noise, or use remote fan location.

How about a steam free mirror in the shower? There is a barrier-free sink arrangement available for the master bath sinks. And these are extra wide sinks. Make all towel bars function as grab bars by specifying a rugged type of bar, and providing adequate blocking in the wall.

From the notes you develop for each room and portion of the project, you can extract notes for each trade (plumber, electrician, mason, ceramic tiler, etc.) that will bid on your project. You ultimately have two lists: (1) Descriptions by room, and (2) Descriptions by trade.

Architect vs. Designer

You need more than a design from a plan book when you build a home. In most municipalities, the plans must be adapted to local codes and engineering standards. You can bring sample plans to a local professional to have them adapted to local codes. Sometimes your design professional has a library of stock plans from which you can choose at a reduced cost over custom plans.

Most owner-built homes rely on the plans of a house designer or "architectural draftsman" who is not a registered architect. Most high-end custom homes rely on the plans of a certified architect. You are an owner-builder and you plan to build a high-end custom home. Which way will you go?

Traditionally you would go to an architect for more creativity and more artistry. The designers are known for more practicality, buildability, and construction cost savings. The architects cost five times as much as the designers. (Average: 7.5% of construction cost versus 1.5% of construction cost in my survey.) They spend more time on a project and charge higher per hour fees because of their additional training. They also must cover the cost of the additional liability insurance they carry in some states.

If you are well-prepared for your project, you have browsed plan books to find floor plans and elevations (exterior appearance) that you like. You have considered your needs and preferences and have a well-developed dream home notebook with room by room descriptions and sketches of your ideas. You have earned your first cash payoff for your planning work. As one architect told me: "If you come in and know what you want, you don't need me that much." You can use a designer and save about six percent of your construction budget.

In our case, we used a designer with stunning results. Elaine had a very good eye for what she wanted. The result was a good dialogue which drew on the designer's skill and his considerable experience to produce a special house. The cost for this service was less than $1,200 — about seven tenths of one percent of construction costs.

The next time we build, however, and step up again to a very high-end house, I think we will use an architect. In the process of telephone interviews with architects we found one that was both brilliant and economical, an irresistible combination. This architect is at a distance of 500 miles from our community, but the savings are so great that we plan to fly to his location for meetings.

There are subtle design factors that mean more in a high-end home. Consider the interview comments of architect Douglas Long, AIA:

"A trained architect has a better sense of perspective and design balance than a designer. We are more concerned about the psychological effect of the confined space. Sociologically, it can be shown that environment has an effect on our behavior, like the effect of the beach, the woods, running water, etc. We spend a lot of time in our houses. It should be taken into consideration. Owners should spend as much time thinking about their house as they do about their car. Some of us like to go into our shells, and don't feel comfortable doing that out in public. There should be a single space that is theirs. You can do it with change of ceiling height, a change of furniture, designate your corner in some way. Changes in the feeling of space. Some tight and you feel secure, some wide open and you feel loose."

How To Find a Good Designer

1. The best source is referrals from other owner-builders or from general contractors.

2. You can look up designers in the Yellow Pages under "Drafting Services", "Home Planning Services", or "Home Designers". Some designers will not be listed. You can call blueprint printing services, they will know some appropriate designers in your area.

3. Call and make the acquaintance of the designer or architect on the phone. Ask for references.

4. Ask the references about cost to construct, liveability of design, resale value — any of your concerns.

5. Go to the designers or architects and view their portfolios of past projects. Ask about costs and time involved and current availability.

Architect and Designer Comparison

ARCHITECT	DESIGNER
• Average 7.5% of budget.	• Average 1.5% of budget.
• Involved in details of construction.	• Doesn't visit construction site.
• Assumes some liability — carries "errors and omissions" coverage.	• Assumes no liability.
• Develops a written "program" of your needs and preferences.	• Relies on your preparation.
• Designs special spaces and creative structures.	• Works from floor plans and elevations you like.
• More artistic.	• More technical.
• Doesn't want you to have preconceived notions.	• The more prepared you are, the better.
• More training.	• More field experience.
• Required to "seal" your plans in some states.	• Not authorized to "seal" plans in some states.
• More attention to aesthetics.	• More attention to buildability.
• Higher construction costs.	• Lower construction costs.

Sources Say

"The premise of this book is that people can design their own homes. Many people have been thinking about their house plan for years, and the freedom to design may be a primary motive for the project. It is one of life's great learning opportunities. Since this whole book is made up of advice on how to do this, I'll only add one point here: always get your design checked over by people who have designed many houses."

From *Independent Builder* (See page 259)

You Are Ready to See Your Designer

If you use an architect, you will pay for his attention to details. One architect explained: "You make 20 or 30 decisions for just one interior door. If I make all of those you could spend lots of money. But you can make many of the decisions."

If you are following the recommendations in this book, you will be very prepared to work with a designer. Architects ask for very little preparation. A woman architect told me that if you bring a favorite article of clothing to the session, or a favorite personal object, she can determine your preferences and design from there.

You can save the additional cost and go to a designer if you have done your homework. Bring as many of the following items as you can to the first session. Each one saves time or enriches the design product.

Items to Bring to Your Designer

1. Your dream house notebook and album including photos of houses and details you like – or dislike. Label your photos with explanations.

2. Site survey or a plot plan of your property.

3. Ideas on size of house.

4. Rooms to include, their size and description.

5. Idea of your budget.

6. Idea of level of finish: builder-type, spec home, or custom with high-end finishes.

7. Pictures or video of the lot with depictions of orientation, relation to neighbors, view.

8. Sketches of floor plans or layouts you like.

9. Any item preferences you have that may be non-standard. For instance, a two-sided kitchen sink is 36 inches wide. If you want a "three-sided" sink with the food disposal in the center bowl, it takes 42 inches. A standard kitchen range is 30 inches wide, but if you want a commercial-type range, the designer has to allow 36 to 42 inches, depending on the model.

10. Stock plan books with design selections you have made.

Good Design Saves Money in Four Ways

Work with your designer to ensure that your custom home meets your needs. Good design can give you everything you want and save you money doing it. The first way that design can save is on construction cost.

1. Savings in Construction Costs

•Enable proper bidding. Work the quirks out on paper rather than in the field.

•Keep walls simple and lined up.

•Ensure that the design is easy to construct.

•Organize spaces. A good design can organize the floor plans of a house in a way that the maximum use can come from the minimum space.

•Stay compatible with conventional construction techniques.

•Use cost-effective and environmentally friendly materials. Use local materials and labor.

•Provide easy to understand construction documents.

•Keep floor heights consistent through choice of materials, tile thicknesses, and underlayments.

•Take into consideration standard material dimensions. Plywood, sheetrock, framing, trims and components come in two-foot increments.

•Eliminate change orders and additional work. Provide detailed specs to reduce the unknowns, and assure quality control and craftsman-like workmanship.

•Assure site position is best for lot, reduces excavation and fill.

•Use trusses where possible to save labor over stick-built roof framing.

•Take carpet widths into consideration so you don't have a lot of seaming.

•Orient rooms and spaces to minimize hallways and maximize the borrowed spaces from room to room, as in an open plan. This could reduce the necessary size of your home.

•Place stairways in two story homes to limit hallways and reduce wasted space.

•Reduce insulation cost by wrapping the inside of the walls with plastic sheeting, instead of using insulation faced with a vapor barrier.

•Use cantilevering (suspended support for parts of floor area) versus having the foundation follow every jog to save on foundations and excavation.

•Keep roof pitch below 7/12, (seven inches of drop for every running foot) to make for lower cost and faster roof work.

The second area in which good design can save you money is in the operating costs of the house, including, but not limited to energy conservation.

2. Savings in Operating Costs

- Save up to 35% in energy bills through optimum orientation on the site.

- Place deciduous trees for summer shade and winter sun. Design window openings to permit breeze to flow through.

- Use good quality windows to reduce air infiltration and improve insulation.

- Choose maintenance-free materials and reduced-maintenance mechanical systems.

- Reduce cleaning costs with cleaner mechanical systems, reduction of dust-catching surfaces, and use of low maintenance interior finishes.

- Choose exterior of brick, stucco, vinyl or aluminum siding to reduce painting expense.

- Use natural light to save lighting cost, for example in bathrooms or master closet.

- Use fill with high organic content to save on lawn watering costs.

- Save on hot water by efficient plumbing layout and equip-ment choices.

- Save electricity by using efficient light fixtures such as compact fluorescents and halogens.

- Select higher efficiency HVAC systems (heating, ventilation and air conditioning).

- Lay out multiple furnaces and air conditioners or use zoned system to provide room by room control and save energy.

- Design wall and attic spaces to accommodate optimum insulation for energy savings.

3. Savings in Life-Cycle Costs

A third area of savings furnished by good design is "life-cycle" savings. These are savings that stem from eliminating or slowing down the need to replace the structure or its components. For example, you can pay 50% more for a premium food disposal and extend its warranty from two to ten years over a standard model. Another example is ceramic tile versus carpet. Installed carpet costs about $2 per square foot ($18 per square yard). The expected life is 10 years. Ceramic tile costs about $5 per square foot and will last over 50 years.

100 Year Life-Cycle Costs in Current Dollars

Carpet	Ceramic Tile
Initial cost per foot = $2	Initial cost per foot = $5
$2 X nine replacements = $18/foot	$5 X one replacement = $5
Life-cycle cost = $20/foot	Life-cycle cost = $10/foot

•Anticipate and avoid structural and layout deficiencies to promote long-term viability of house.

•Seek durability and timeliness in concept and aesthetics.

•Choose upgraded equipment and materials for durability.

•Coordinate electrical and mechanical systems for future flexibility.

•Choose features and design conveniences that will meet your needs for the long term.

•Plan the space carefully to avoid the need to add on as your family changes.

4. Lifestyle Savings:

The fourth area of savings that stem from thoughtful house design are savings in your lifestyle expenses. Examples are:

•Plan rooms and doorways to accommodate your furniture so you have no need to replace furniture.

•If you use a health club, design in features like a home gym or steam shower that offer the same facilities at home. Save on club fees.

•Design a convenient and capable gourmet kitchen and spend less on restaurant bills.

•Design a large, well-organized pantry. Buy in quantity at the grocery store and save on food purchases.

•Organize and equip your garage to wash your car and lubricate your vehicles there instead of commercially.

Sources Say

The Complete Guide to Contracting Your Home gives mathematical formulas to figure how much home you can afford.

(See page 260)

•Equip your house with a natural gas concentrator pump that fuels a car adapted to natural gas at about half the cost of gasoline. Or provide the necessary connections to recharge an electric car.

•Provide kitchen facilities for canning and freezing garden produce to save on groceries.

•Allow for a cool basement fruit room or root cellar to extend the use of garden produce.

•Design a home office that meets current or anticipated work-at-home needs to save you from renting elsewhere to run your business.

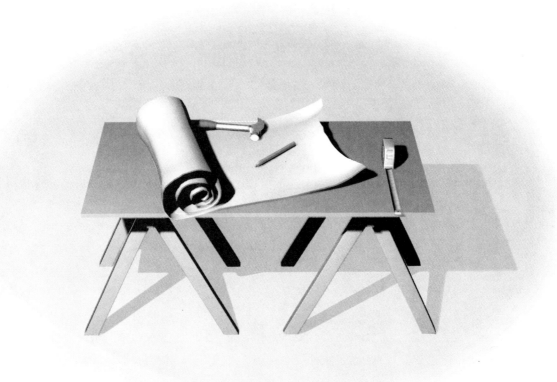

Chapter 7: How to Get the Subs on Your Side

Time line: Four months before groundbreaking

How to Find Good Subs

One of the benefits of owner-building is assembling a team of outstanding subs of your own choosing. To do that you will need to start with a list of candidate subs for your project.

Here is where the buyer must beware. You will want to deal with reputable subs who have something to contribute. There is a risk that you might wind up with a very bad apple. One O-B told me:

> "You can get ripped off easily. Some subs are like animals. They live from week to week for beer money and their hands are rough and cut. One guy gave me a medium price on my septic system. He said he would save me money on materials if he could pay cash for them. He showed me a lower price than I could get, and I gave him the money. He disappeared after he got it."

On the other hand, some of the subs are unbelievably honest and professional. A woman owner-builder told me:

"When you have a really good sub, you really appreciate them. Our marble guy, concrete crew, and finish guys were superb. The tile guy was the most respectful of all. Some of them can get crude. When they are businesslike, you appreciate it. He said it was a pleasure to have had the opportunity to work for us. I will recommend him to everyone. We had many wonderful craftsmen. They kept their music low, and would notice a woman was there, and they were being nice to each other, no foul language. That made me feel comfortable."

Your job is to preselect candidates for each of the team members you will need. Depending on your design, you will use a few or many of the team members on this list:

Potential Team Members

1.	Attorney	24.	Drywall finisher
2.	Lender	25.	Painter
3.	Independent inspector	26.	Carpet and linoleum contractor
4.	Insurance agent	27.	Hardwood flooring contractor
5.	rebar	28.	Cabinet installer
6.	Appraiser	29.	Finish carpenter
7.	House designer or architect	30.	Countertop contractor
8.	Surveyor	31.	Ceramic tiler
9.	Excavator	32.	Construction clean-up
10.	Footings contractor	33.	Asphalt contractor
11.	Foundation contractor	34.	Sprinkler and landscape contractor
12.	Concrete flatwork finisher	35.	Gutter and downspout contractor
13.	Framer	36.	Foundation plasterer
14.	Waterproofing contractor	37.	Trash hauler
15.	Brick, siding, or stucco contractor	38.	Portable restroom vendor
16.	Electrician	39.	Security service
17.	Sound, alarm, and video contractor	40.	Fencing contractor
18.	Whole house vacuum installer	41.	Window well contractor
19.	Plumber	42.	Structural engineer
20.	HVAC contractor	43.	Concrete sawing
21.	Roofer	44.	Water well or geothermal driller
22.	Insulator	45.	Septic system installer
23.	Drywall hanger	46.	Landscape designer

Consider this list in tandem with the list of suppliers on page 124. You may also wish to include an interior decorator on your team. You may have specialty trades like ceiling specialties, stained glass, wrought iron, conveying systems, custom stair rail installer, steel erection, lighting or low voltage system design, and others.

Suggestions for Finding Subs

1. Do not use the Yellow Pages.

2. Drive around to subdivisions near where you want to build, go in and ask who did any job you like. You find small builders very willing to lend out their subs. That way they keep the sub busy, because you are only doing one house.

3. Attend home and garden shows where you may meet subs that impress you. Some have booths at shows, particularly if they are pushing a new product.

4. Ask people whose houses are recent and exemplary who performed the trades.

5. Ask owner-builders in your community which subs they respect.

6. Join the local Home Builders Association as an associate member. Attend HBA functions. Ask generals who they recommend. Get acquainted with subs who participate in the HBA. If you don't join, use the Association directory of members.

7. Seek out the subs who did the work on "Parade of Homes" houses you liked. Their names may be listed in the "Parade" program. You can also call the general contractors who entered the "Parade", and ask for the participating subs.

8. Ask the salespeople at the local lumberyard which tradesmen have good reputations.

9. Ask each reputable sub you talk to who he respects in the other trades. Framers know good foundation people. Footings guys know good excavators. Finish guys know good framers and so on.

10. Check your names with your state's registrar of contractors and the Better Business Bureau. Begin with several names and find the complaints lodged against them. They all have them. Pre-select the ones with the fewest complaints per year of operation.

How to Interview Subs

Before you lock in your plans and specifications with the designer, it is good to have input from the subs you interview. This helps as a "reality check" on your plans and sometimes introduces you to new ideas and technologies. At the same time, you prepare the groundwork for selecting the subs who will bid your work.

Readers Say

"Some framers don't set windows in the basement. We have lost two days trying to get that done. We should have asked first. But my framers have frankly done a crummy job. When you hire someone you think they are great, you need to find out if they are the one who actually does the labor, or do they use a crew."

Lucy & Ivan B.
Provo, UT

Sources Say

"Ask painters for names of good drywall subs. They paint over it and know good finishing work."

From *The Complete Guide to Contracting Your Home*
(See page 260)

Readers Say

"I'm having a great time wandering around. Very few lots left. Some will buy and take house off and start a new one. We found roofers, cleanup guys, and a pool contractor, all from site visits. I introduce myself as a home builder, ask my questions, get their cards, and the names of people they recommend."

Gerry R.
Austin, TX

To interview subs, I recommend using a word processor so you can capture ideas and phone numbers easily and move those ideas to other files as needed to keep your project organized. I interviewed over the phone and used a speakerphone so that I could type. Later, I bought an inexpensive telephone headset at an office supply store for convenience. I surprised the people I interviewed by faxing them a copy of their interview direct from the computer after we finished. None of them forgot me, and we both had a confirming record of their suggestions.

Don't be afraid to interview subs in advance — they are going to become like employees to you, and they know that. It is free marketing to them when someone calls in. Your call serves them notice that you are a conscientious builder. At the same time, feel free to admit your ignorance to a knowledgeable pro. Subs appreciate that, and you will grow in your ability to make educated decisions.

Create your own questions, or adapt the suggested questions on the next page. Call in the early morning and early evening, or if you interview larger firms, during business hours.

Detailed, Accurate Bidding

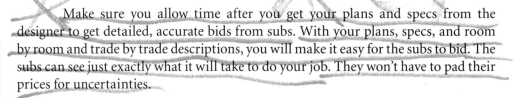

Make sure you allow time after you get your plans and specs from the designer to get detailed, accurate bids from subs. With your plans, specs, and room by room and trade by trade descriptions, you will make it easy for the subs to bid. The subs can see just exactly what it will take to do your job. They won't have to pad their prices for uncertainties.

You will ask for detailed bids that provide breakdowns of approaches, materials, and labor steps involved. You want this kind of detail so that you can compare one sub to another. If two subs come back with one sentence bids that say "Concrete: $3,200", you don't have much to go on when you make your choice. You want to know how many yards of concrete at what price are included. You want to know how they are going to form the concrete, what reinforcing is included, and how long it will take. Will they commit to a start date?

Ask the subs if they usually supply the materials. Then have them make estimates with materials and labor broken out separately. You need to compare their material costs with what you can get them for yourself. You have to be careful of what they are including, and what level of quality each component is.

You ask for further suggestions. This allows you to turn up those that really want work, and those willing to work for O-B's.

Suggested Questions for Subs

Name: _____ Phone: _____ Date: _____

Q: What do you suggest for a good job?

A: _____

Q: What do you do that is better than other subs?

A: _____

Q: What do you need to do a bid for me?

A: _____

Q: Can you give me an idea about cost?

A: _____

Q: What can be done to save money?

A: _____

Q: Is there anything we can do in the way of labor or in purchasing our own materials to save money?

A: _____

Q: What coordination is needed between this and other trades?

A: _____

Q: What do I need to do to make it easier for you?

A: _____

Q: What are your scheduling requirements?

A: _____

Q. How big a crew would you put on a job like mine?

A. _____

Q. Do you personally do the work?

A. _____

A word processor template for sub interviews is provided on our free Resource CD-ROM

(See page 270)

Readers Say

"I pick up bits and pieces from contractors. It's a matter of listening. It's all free knowledge. If they are willing to talk about it, grab it and run with it."

Ron & Diane B.
San Rafael, CA

Our subcontractor interviews for the Riverbottoms house are included in our Special Reports Set.

(See page 252)

Q. How experienced are those who will work on my job?

A: _____

Q. How long will it take to complete your work?

A: _____

Q. Will you guarantee your price and schedule for me?

A: _____

Q: Do you carry Workmen's Compensation?

A: _____

Q: What about errors and omissions liability insurance?

A: _____

Q: Right now we are projecting breaking ground Sept. 25th. Is this good for you?

A: _____

Q: Do you have any other suggestions?

A: _____

Q: How can I contact you? Work, Home, Mobile Phones, E-mail, Fax number, address for sending plans?

A: _____

You can isolate those who are willing to do labor-only deals. You can ask them some of the things you asked in the interview, such as, who do they recommend for other subs, and particularly who would they prefer to work with that affects their trade. Are there alternate approaches, new technologies, ways to save time or money they might suggest?

Give them lots of time to prepare detailed bids — you get the benefit of their thoughtful consideration this way. Allow yourself plenty of time so you can follow up with them and continue refining your plans and tightening your budget: "Why are you approaching it this way?" "Why are you charging so much more for this item than the other sub?" "Can you suggest a place to get good prices on this or that?" "If I pay you quickly can I get a discount on your bid?"

You want detailed, specific bids. This makes them think, which you want, and it reduces your vulnerability to change orders because of items they have forgotten or you haven't considered in the beginning.

Get Three Bids from Subs on Each Item

I was shocked when I started to gather bids from framing subcontractors for our house. I had a preconceived notion from interviews and research that framing should come in around eight percent of our construction budget, or $12,000. The first bid I got was $17,500. The second was $15,400. Better, but far from fitting our budget. The third bid came in at $25,000.

Now I was worried. I decided to look harder. The local lumberyard recommended two people I had not checked, and the first one came back with a bid of $11,350. I had to be honest with myself and admit that this framer was inexperienced and probably not qualified to handle our house. Then the second bid came in, from a very qualified and bright framer. I interviewed him and had more confidence in him than any of the others. His bid was $12,250. He turned out to be possibly the best sub I found.

Your first defense against paying too much is to have an educated guess about what the cost will be. Then you know if you are hearing baloney from your bidders. The second is to have several bidders. In this case, I sought five bids. If my top choice had bailed out, I would have had a back-up plan. I think I would have taken the bid of $11,350 and watched the framer closely rather than pay exorbitant prices.

It is usually wisdom, however, not to take the low bid. You must examine it carefully because of the tendency of some to "lowball" a project and extract change orders from the owner later, resulting in much higher costs. Some of these contractors also do poor work and expose you to the potential of rework to make it right.

I learned something else from those five framing bids. The differences can be huge. In this example, the low bid of $11,350 was 55% less than the high bid of $25,000. If you only get one or two bids, you may never turn up the potential discounts that are available.

Owner-builders I interviewed gave me many examples of the range between low and high bids on identical specifications. For instance: "Plumbing, one at $5,400 up to another bid at $9,200." "Concrete was from $7,000 up to $10,000, and all the bidders were licensed contractors." "Siding: $4,500 versus $9,000." "Air conditioning: $6,000, $9,000 and $10,000 bids for the very same thing." "Electrical: $5,200, $8,000 and $9,000. I took the $8,000 bid because the $5,200 bidder didn't have good references."

The examples furnished me by other owner-builders showed the low bids to be an average of 34% less than the high bids. These examples, however, came from exceptional owner-builders, because the typical O-B I interviewed got very few bids, around two bids for each specialty, on average.

Readers Say

"I put together different bids, three for each section. Last time we didn't get everything in writing. Like sidewalks bid for $900 and the bill came in at $1,500 on the last house. Make sure you get prices from more than one person also. HVAC and plumbing was $15,000 on one bid and $8,500 on a second one. Both reputable companies for the exact same thing. I always added extra to everything, and added 5% at the end. Linoleum was $12.99 a square yard, and when they installed it, it came back at $12.99 a square foot. Because we didn't have it in writing, and the girl we dealt with was gone. We got plush carpet in bedrooms, and berber for heavily trafficked areas. We they came out to install they had it reversed. You need a couple of Valiums when you build. But we saved so much money."

Melissa & Brad D.
Hanover, PA

Why don't owner-builders take advantage of potential discounts and get more bids? One reason is the human tendency to rush to judgement. We like the first price we hear, especially if we aren't equipped with an educated guess of what it should cost. A second reason is that some owner-builders are in a hurry. They leave only a few days to gather bids in their haste to break ground on the project.

I discovered a third reason when talking to a construction industry veteran: "Subs make a habit of keeping you from getting more bids." They can do this by making the process awkward and time-consuming. Each sub wants a full set of your plans and keeps them for a week. If you have 30 trades on your project, as I did, and you get three bids on each trade, that's 90 bidders. To get it done in a month, you would need more than 20 full sets of plans. This makes it simply too daunting for most people, and they settle for the first thing they hear.

How To Get Bids

1. Allow a full month to gather bids, and a second month to evaluate and negotiate.

2. Use the Plan Room concept. Set aside a spot at your home or office where the plans are available for review. Provide a table where the plans can be spread out, and the sub can take notes and do calculations. Rather than run yourself ragged trying to meet subs and drop off plans all over town, have the subs come to your "plan room". Have on hand your dream home notebook for examination. Answer questions and make clarifications on the spot. This way you will rarely have to loan out a set of plans.

3. Do what you can by fax and mail. We have an inexpensive fax modem ($100) attached to our computer. We can send and receive faxes direct to the computer, and view the fax on the computer screen. We took advantage of this by faxing portions of our plans to our home computer from an instant copy center downtown. We then had electronic images of our floor plans on computer. We faxed the needed portions to certain subs along with the written description we developed for their trades. They were able to bid from this.

4. Use an "RFQ" (a Request For Quotation) that summarizes the specs the subs will have to meet for a given category and provides the essential information. The RFQ instructs the sub to itemize material costs and descriptions of components along with the estimate of labor cost in detail. It asks for estimated time to complete, for references, and for any suggestions the sub may have. Send it out in lieu of a set of plans to a large number of potential subs. Using this technique, some O-B's have been able to get as many as ten bids on items.

The ability to buy "cafeteria-style" and select your own subs and suppliers is the greatest leverage the owner-builder has for savings. You can't take advantage of it unless you get three or more bids on each item. After you make your selection, your additional bids become back-ups to the chosen sub. If the first sub can't start or finish the work for any reason, you can often plug in a replacement sub quickly. Lenders look for this kind of back-up.

Having multiple bids can have unexpected benefits. One second-time owner-builder asked the plumber from his first house to bid the next project. The plumber decided he was too busy to do it. The O-B got three bids from other plumbers. Then the original plumber called to say, "I don't have time to bid your project, but I would like to do the work. Give me the lowest plumbing bid you got, and I will match it, and throw in a free water softener."

Readers Say

"My cousin has built several houses. He got estimates on everything last time, and came in within $1,000 of his budget."

Chuck & Kris C.
Lake Charles, LA

Follow Up Your Bids

After you see the estimates, study them carefully. This is very valuable and instructive. Summarize the line items of the comparable bids on paper or on a computer spreadsheet as I did with the two insulation bids I received. I like to use a computer spreadsheet because it will automatically add numbers in a column for you and because it can be laid out much wider than on a single sheet of paper. In the following example I have laid out two bids side by side for comparison. With a spreadsheet, you could place ten or any number of bids side by side for your examination.

Item	Insulation Contractor A Description:	Insulation Contractor B Description:
Attic	R-38 blown fiberglass	R-38 blown fiberglass
Exterior Walls	R-19 Batt and poly	R-19 Batt and poly
Inaccessible attic	R-30 Batt	R-30 Batt
Vaulted ceiling	R-30 Batt	R-30 blown and batt
Rim Joist	R-19 Batt	R-19 Batt
Crawl space	R-11 drape foundation	R-11 drape foundation w/ poly on ground
Attic vents	Cardboard baffles	
Air penetrations	Hilti foam	Foam
Garage Walls		R-11 Batt w/poly
Garage Attic		R-19 Batt w/poly
Total:	$1,997	$1,878

Contractor A: Add: Options or upgrades:	
Insulate garage	$350
R-38 Batt in vaulted	$75
Net and blow fiberglass	$559
Sound insulation in master and bath	$88
Wet spray cellulose	$799
R-11 floor	$98
R-19 floor	$157

Readers Say

"The hardest thing is forcing yourself to get three bids. We all seem to know somebody in each area, and the easiest thing is just go with them. My husband is afraid he'll offend his friends by getting a bid from one of their competitors."

Melanie & Jeremy T.
Riverton, UT

It was easy to select subcontractor B because he included everything that A did at a price that was $119 under A's price. B also included garage insulation in his bid, at no extra charge. This meant that B's bid was $119 plus $350 or $469 under

A's bid. B's bid was also better because it included putting polyethylene sheeting as a vapor barrier on the ground in the crawl space.

Subcontractor B had not included anything for sound insulation in his bid. Subcontractor A explained to me the value of insulating the master bedroom and bathroom from the sounds of the living room and to keep bathroom sounds from traveling to the living room. Since he had a price of $88 for the two rooms, I called and asked Contractor B if he would match the price and add a third room for $44. This brought my total cost to $2,000, the number I had initially budgeted for insulation.

The insulation bids had worried us because there were only a couple of good subcontractor choices in town for insulation. I budgeted $2,000 and when B made his original estimate off the plans, he came in at $3,038. From interviews and research, I thought it could be done for $2,000. I called him and told him so. He said that he would rebid it when the framing was mostly complete so that he could better gauge the size of the job.

After I received A's bid for $1,997 I called B back and said that I only had $2,000 budgeted, that I had a bid for that amount, and could he do it for that? He rebid it after measuring the framing, and met the price I wanted. What amazed me was that he also included garage insulation at that price.

It pays to follow up your bids and negotiate. One industry veteran pointed out to me that "this is a negotiated business". He recommended the same formula that I used:

1. Compare bids line by line.

2. Choose your preferred subcontractor.

3. Call and tell him that he is your choice but that you only have so much available for his item.

4. Ask "Can you do it for that?"

When I got bids for concrete work, I noticed that the subs figured differently the amount of concrete needed for footings. I spoke to my preferred sub and told him, "One of the other foundation men says that only eight yards of concrete are needed, and you say 13 on your bid. Would you mind if we just pay for whatever it turns out to be after you're finished?" He agreed and we saved $350.

The Frank R. Walker Co. publishes Walker's Pocket Estimator (see page 261), a pocket guide that provides you costing information on each trade and component of home construction. This is the construction industry's version of the "Blue Book" that sets used car prices. It can be useful in comparing with the cost estimates you receive from subs and vendors.

Chapter 8: How to Build a Budget That Is a Powerful Miracle Tool

Time line: Three months before groundbreaking

Start with Your Bids from General Contractors

Even though you plan to act as the general contractor, there is nothing to prevent you from asking licensed general contractors to estimate your project. In a slow market, you may find a real bargain and decide to let a general build it. You may be forced by the unforeseen, say sickness or accident, to have a general build or finish your project. You may find a general that you use for a future project or recommend to someone else. For these reasons it is more than fair to take advantage of the free service that general contractors perform of bidding potential work.

Your bid from a general contractor can be tremendously helpful in planning your approach to the work, but only if the bid is thorough and professional. I insisted that generals who bid my project include the following information:

Sources Say

"The 'Achilles heel' of every construction project is always the cost estimating. The shear number of items that go into the house is staggering. A computer can help tremendously with this problem. Don't even think of starting a homebuilding project without a complete and accurate estimate. The bank will be impressed with a well organized printout of costs."

From *The Complete Guide to Contracting Your Home*
(See page 260)

Sources Say

"The process of budgeting exerts a positive force. Many owner-built or architect-built homes express wonderful ideas. The budget encourages everyone on the project to refine all these ideas into an integrated, tight, complete design, a better design."

From *Independent Builder*
(See page 259)

1. Written cost breakdown or budget. You want to see each line item separately with its cost.

2. Who would likely perform each line item. You need this to compare with other generals.

3. Written calendar of completion. Tell them that you want to be sure that they can complete within your six month deadline, so you want to see how long they will take on each line item.

Challenge the generals who bid your project. Tell them that you will either defer building, or you will build it yourself if his prices aren't good enough. Let them do the homework they are trained to do. This is an opportunity for the general contractors to try to "talk you out of it".

Lay out the bids from the generals on a spreadsheet by line item. This is the first big step to building a budget that will save you a great deal of money on your project.

You will be able to use the written line by line estimates that the general supplies you in your subsequent dealings with subcontractors. If you don't go to the same subs that a general proposes to you, you nonetheless can cite the prices he offered you when dealing with other subs: "Thanks for your bid of $3,800. I want to use you but I have another bid here for $3,000. My budget is for $3,200. Could you do it for that?"

Spreadsheet Budgeting

If you lay out the bids you receive from general contractors on a computer spreadsheet, you have the best template you can find for your construction budget. It is specific to your plans and prepared by a person familiar with your local market and with current conditions. If you have several bids you have the advantage of multiple counselors. If one general says that footings are $4,000, one says $5,500, and one says $3,200, you have the average of their wisdom at $4,200. Your footings shouldn't turn out higher than that. And you have a possible $3,200 to contemplate. Maybe his sub will do it for that on your project. Maybe another sub will match it or beat it. And if you get a bid for $2,700 from a sub, you know you are looking at a low price.

Using a spreadsheet can be magical fun. A computer spreadsheet organizes items in rows and columns and keeps a running tally of anything you like. If you make a change, the totals recalculate instantly.

Say you have a list of construction costs like this:

EXTERIOR FINISH

Roofing	$3,650
Vinyl siding/soffit mat'l. & labor	$9,500
Gutter mat'l./labor	$600
Deck mat'l./labor	$1,500

PAINTING

Interior painting	$1,326

FLOORING

Ceramic tile	$1,477
Carpeting	$4,314
Wood Flooring	$1,423
Total:	$23,790
Other costs:	$150,000
Appraised Value of Plans:	$250,000
Overall Total:	$173,790
Equity:	$76,210

Readers Say

"There is a lot of disparity in the bids I'm getting. One guy came back for framing at $27,000 then another came at $22,000 and another at $15,000."

Aaron & Daylene S.
Heber City, UT

Readers Say

"We are scheduling the duplexes one after another so we get a price not for just one but for two. I separated labor and materials and the trades were surprised, but they agreed when I persisted."

Donald D.
Lewisville, NC

Readers Say

"I figure it's better to cut out the middle man, which I learned in business."

Sean O.
Kansas City, MO

You see that your costs amount to $23,790 for the selected items, and $173,790 overall. With your house plans appraising at $250,000 you see that your equity in the project will be $76,210.

When you make a change, the whole calculation changes instantly. Suppose you are expecting to pay $9,500 for siding, but you find a sub you like at $8,000. You correct one entry and the picture changes:

Sources Say

"Except in rare cases, the cost of the process of restoration, rehabilitation, or remodeling plus the cost of the old structure should not exceed the cost of a comparable new structure."

From *Be Your Own Home Renovation Contractor*
(See page 258)

Sources Say

"I do my estimating on a computer, using a spreadsheet program. If you are a good spreadsheet user, you may want to try it for your project. The spreadsheet allows you to easily update the estimate to reflect design changes or costs. And it allows you to track your progress by "zeroing out" the items completed."

From *Independent Builder*
(See page 259)

Sources Say

"Builders try to keep their land costs to no more than 20 percent of the total appraised value of the finished product."

From *Build Your Dream Home for Less*
(See page 259)

EXTERIOR FINISH

Roofing	$3,650
Vinyl siding/soffit mat'l. & labor	$8,000
Gutter mat'l./labor	$600
Deck mat'l./labor	$1,500

PAINTING

Interior painting	$1,326

FLOORING

Ceramic tile	$1,477
Carpeting	$4,314
Wood Flooring	$1,423
Total:	**$22,290**

Other costs:	$150,000
Overall Total:	$172,290
Appraised Value of Plans:	$250,000
Equity:	**$77,710**

Now your list adds up to $22,290 and your equity moves to $77,710. In this sense, the spreadsheet becomes an electronic window on your wealth. As you develop your project and plug various numbers into your budget, you see the effects immediately.

I have worked with various spreadsheets since 1982. After learning my first one, a product called Lotus 1-2-3™, I used various others with little or no change in technique. We used Excel™ for our construction project, and I have used Apple-Works™ and Quattro Pro™ spreadsheets with equal facility.

The spreadsheet is a magical tool that I estimate will save you five percent on your project all by itself. It serves you as a project budgeting tool in the beginning, then a tracking tool on actual expenses, as well as a construction shopping tool that makes the implications of comparative bids and estimates become clear. The same benefit would apply to the use of an old fashioned paper spreadsheet with your numbers laid out in rows and columns.

A five percent savings could be worth ten or twenty thousand dollars to your project. When you consider the savings in DSDE dollars, using a spreadsheet could have the effect of $100,000 of salary on your net worth. It's clearly worth it to learn how to use one. Most people can walk into a computer lab in a local community college and with a little help lay out a simple spreadsheet in a couple of hours. You could take a class, buy and study a manual, or learn through trial and error. If you don't have a computer, you could probably develop a budget spreadsheet on computer facilities at a nearby school or library and save it on a personal computer diskette. You could return to make adjustments and revisions to your budget as you go.

Riverbottoms House Budget

A century ago writer Henry David Thoreau owner-built a home in the country. He recorded his budget for posterity:

Boards	$8.03 1/2
Refuse shingles for roof and sides	$4.00
Laths	$1.25
Two second-hand windows with glass	$2.43
One thousand old brick	$4.00
Two casks of lime	$2.40
Hair	$ .31
Mantle-tree iron	$ .15
Nails	$3.90
Hinges and screws	$ .14
Latch	$ .10
Chalk	$ .01
Transportation	$1.40
In all	$28.12 1/2

We're still doing construction budgets today, though they grow more complex with the passage of time. Elaine and I developed a budget (shown on the next page) for our custom home through trial and error. We started with a bid from a general contractor which we entered onto a spreadsheet. We continued to refine our "guesstimates" of individual costs as we gathered bids from subs.

The keys to a good budget are:

1. easily updatable on computer
2. accurate estimates of items based on detailed specifications
3. no major items omitted
4. includes a contingency fund for overruns

Riverbottoms House Budget

Description	Percent %	Amount Spent	Notes
BUDGET LIMIT:	100.0%	$166,000	
INDIRECT CONSTRUCTION COSTS			
Bldg. permit/fees	2.3%	$3,818	
Setup short-term financing	1.4%	$2,324	
Interest charges	3.0%	$4,980	
Plans and specs.	0.7%	$1,162	
Structural engineering	0.2%	$332	
Survey review	0.1%	$166	
Building lot			
Course of construction insurance	0.2%	$332	
Supervision/overhead	0.2%	$332	
Misc. equipment rental	0.5%	$830	
Temporary/mobile phone	0.1%	$166	
Trash pickup	0.1%	$166	
Clean-up	0.1%	$166	
Temporary power	0.1%	$166	
Title insurance	0.5%	$830	
Other:			
EXCAVATION/SITE WORK			
Foundation excavation	0.2%	$332	
Finish grading	0.3%	$498	
Backfill	0.2%	$332	
Sewer/Water Trench	0.2%	$332	
Electric Trench	0.0%	$50	
Drain tile and gravel			
Other:			
MASONRY			
Footings/labor & materials	2.5%	$4,150	
Foundation/labor & materials	2.0%	$3,320	
Rebar & steel			
Waterproofing			
Termite protection			
Sand or gravel & placement	0.4%	$664	
Basement floor			
Garage floor/labor & materials	0.6%	$996	
Walks and patios	0.1%	$166	
Driveway & other ext. flatwork	0.5%	$830	
Stoop, steps & ramps			

Riverbottoms House Budget

Description	Percent %	Amount Spent	Notes
Fireplace brick			
Other:			
SEPTIC SYSTEM			
Well			
ROUGH CARPENTRY			
Framing lumber	13.2%	$21,912	
Trusses			
Framing labor	6.9%	$11,454	
Crane service			
Windows & screens	2.2%	$3,652	
Skylights			
Exterior doors	1.7%	$2,822	
Garage doors & openers	1.4%	$2,324	
Decks & porches	1.4%	$2,324	
Steel beams and posts			
Other:			
PLUMBING			
Rough plumbing	5.4%	$8,964	
Fixtures & trim	1.8%	$2,988	
Other:			
HVAC			
Heating & air conditioning	6.1%	$10,126	
Other:			
ELECTRICAL			
Rough electrical	2.4%	$3,984	
Finish electrical			
Fixtures	0.6%	$996	
Vacuum system	0.5%	$830	
Alarm system			
Television pre-wire			
Telephone pre-wire			
Audio pre-wire			
Other:			
INSULATION			
Wall & attic insulation	1.3%	$2,158	

Riverbottoms House Budget

Description	Percent %	Amount Spent	Notes
Other:			
DRYWALL			
Drywall materials & labor	4.9%	$8,134	
Other:			
FINISH CARPENTRY			
Interior doors	0.9%	$1,494	
Moldings/stair rail/columns	1.6%	$2,656	
Finish carpentry	2.1%	$3,486	
Fireplace equipment	1.3%	$2,158	
Hearth and mantel	0.2%	$332	
Closet organizers	0.6%	$996	
Finish hardware	0.3%	$498	
Other:			
EXTERIOR FINISH			
Roofing	2.2%	$3,652	
Housewrap			
Siding	5.7%	$9,462	
Stucco			
Brick			
Stone work			
Exterior trim			
Soffit & facia			
Gutter mat'l/labor	0.4%	$664	
Chimneys			
Wrought iron			
Other:			
PAINTING			
Interior painting	0.8%	$1,328	
Exterior painting			
Wallpaper			
Other:			
FLOORING			
Ceramic tile	0.9%	$1,494	
Carpeting	2.6%	$4,316	
Wood flooring	0.9%	$1,494	
Vinyl flooring			

Riverbottoms House Budget

Description	Percent %	Amount Spent	Notes
Stone work			
Other:			
MARBLE, TILE & GLASS			
tubs surrounds	0.7%	$1,162	
Shower doors, mirrors & glass	0.9%	$1,494	
Other:			
LANDSCAPING			
Sprinkler system	0.7%	$1,162	
Fill and topsoil			
Seed or sod	0.2%	$332	
Trees and plantings			
Retaining walls			
Fencing			
Other:			
CABINET, COUNTER & APPLIANCE			
Kitchen and bath cabinets	6.5%	$10,790	
Counter & vanity tops	2.8%	$4,648	
Medicine chests			
Laundry cabinets			
Entertainment center/built-ins			
Kitchen appliances	1.6%	$2,656	
Other:			
MISCELLANEOUS			
Smoke alarms			
Doorbell			
Dryer vent			
Foundation plaster			
Attic fan			
ON-SITE SUPERVISION			
CONTINGENCY			
Other:			
Total Cost of House:			
Building Costs:		$166,382	
Unspent Amount:			

The recommended contingency fund for a first time owner-builder is ten percent. This is the "slop" you allow for spending more than you estimated on the project. If you have done it before, use five percent. On the previous page you can see that there is no amount shown for contingency. This budget is our "as-built" budget - what we actually spent after the dust had settled on our completed project. We had started the Riverbottoms house with a contingency fund of $5,000. That was used up quickly, and overall, we ran over our intended budget by about $20,000. We managed to scare up the needed shortfall from cash and by a loan increase from the bank. Far better to allow sufficient for contingency in the beginning. On a $150,000 construction budget the recommended contingency amount for a first time owner-builder would be $15,000.

How to Read the Riverbottoms Budget

Compare what we spent on our house to your own plans. Every plan is different, so adjust your thinking to your circumstances. When planning for excavation, for example, note on the Riverbottoms House Budget on page 100 that we spent only $332 to dig our foundation. That amounted to .2% of overall costs of $166,000.

Say you had a construction budget of $200,000. Could you assign .2% or $400 to digging a foundation? You'll find out quickly when you interview excavators on the phone how far off that might be. In our case, the hole for the house was very shallow because we have no basement, only a four-foot crawl space under the house. The overall footprint of our 3,500 square foot house was small because it was a two story, so the breadth of the hole was modest, as well.

Reasonably, you can compare your excavation to ours by knowing the depth and breadth of the hole you will dig, and what prices are like for digging in your area. We found prices of around $75 an hour for this work. I was present for every minute of the process, and the digger charged me an accurate number of hours calculated to the tenth of an hour. With a clear lot and easy access, he was in and out in a short time.

Some of the other factors that will help your comparison are that we did four of the trades ourselves, shrinking the amounts needed for electrical, tile, painting, and landscaping. For example, painting is shown on page 102 at $1,328, just the cost of materials purchased carefully. The professional cost to paint the house with three paint tones and elaborate woodwork to prepare would be over $10,000.

Here's an interesting one caught by some of our sharp-eyed workshop attendees: look at the bottom of the first page of the budget on page 100 under the line item "Walks and patios". We got our sidewalks, patio and driveway for $166. This was a case of a relative repaying a loan by providing all the concrete flatwork at his own expense, a cost of $4,300 to him, but no cost on our budget. The $166 was just to pour pads for the air conditioning units at the side of the house, an item we forgot until the last minute.

Don't let your eyes glaze over while reading the Riverbottoms House Budget. Many people think that budgets are complicated and sterile. I did, when I started planning our house. But the budget proved to be a living thing with lots of meaning when we built. You live or die by your construction budget. It's fun to get it right and to get it down through your astute planning and shopping.

Budget Worksheet

You can use the budget worksheet starting on page 100 to build your budget. Make photocopies of the form for your trial runs. At an early point, you should transfer your figures to a computer spreadsheet and use the spreadsheet to revise and update your estimates of cost as you select subcontractor bids and shop for material and equipment prices.

How To Use the Budget Worksheet

First, enter the very important number of what you can spend on your new house, remodel, or addition. This goes on the top of the Worksheet on page 108 in the third column, "Budget Amount". This amount is the key to your project. This is the amount you can qualify to borrow, or know you can afford. Everything depends on staying to this amount. For most people, missing this amount by much means the project dies. If you need to build for $200,000 and discover by building a budget carefully that it will take $300,000 the options are to change the plan and scope of the house, or to skip building entirely.

So this becomes "decision time". It may take several months to lay out your budget and verify all the numbers - don't rush it. But until you are done with this part of planning, you won't know whether your project is indeed feasible.

Second, go to the bottom of page 116 and take 10% of your budgeted amount and set it aside for contingency. From this point on, you will work with the remainder of your budgeted amount, 90% of the whole, to provide for all the parts of the project. Now, revise the "Budget Amount" number you put on the top of page 108 accordingly.

Third, allow a percentage for each line item you'll need in the second column of the Worksheet (These percentage amounts must add up to 100%) If your budget is $200,000, and you have set aside $20,000 for contingency, then you are allocating shares of $180,000 to each category. If you allocate 5% for drywall as we did in the Riverbottoms Budget, you have $9,000 for that category.

Fourth, fill in all the dollar amounts that apply to your project in the third column of the Worksheet. This is an exercise that takes participants less than fifteen minutes in our workshop. When you are done - behold! - you have developed a preliminary written budget for your project. You need to congratulate yourself, because a written budget is something even some contractors cannot claim to have ever done.

Your written budget is not perfect yet, but it is a great key to bringing a dream to life. Now begins the long process of checking and improving each number in the quest for accuracy and cost-savings. Through your preliminary interviews with subs and suppliers and through competitive bidding, you will check and verify until you have a solid number for your project.

"Shop" Your Budget For a While

After you have a budget worksheet filled out with actual bids, price quotations, and "guesstimates", take it around to others who can offer suggestions. In the process of bidding and shopping for materials, you will meet people in the business with a good knowledge of street prices and available bargains.

Often a lender is knowledgeable and helpful. Even if you haven't selected your lender, you can get appointments to talk with experienced construction lenders. The estimator at the local lumberyard could review your budget. Sometimes the "help counter" workers at home center stores are qualified to help. You could speak to several house designers about your budget. Fax or mail a copy to anyone who could review your numbers and call or meet to discuss them.

Most of the owner-builders I interviewed found three or four significant bargains in the process of building their house. If you can locate other O-B's in your area, they can be very helpful in confirming your numbers and in suggesting alternate sources or approaches to save money. If each O-B you consult has several bargains to suggest, you may be able to line up a large collective list of exceptional sources for savings.

Sometimes a retired general contractor in your locale is a good advisor. Some owner-builders have used high school shop or construction class teachers as advisors. If you will be using an independent building inspector, ask him to review your budget. You don't want to: 1) overpay for anything, 2) underestimate anything, or 3) forget anything.

You and your successors will live in the house you build for many decades, possibly centuries. Take time now while you are in the planning stage to shop your budget for a few weeks. The harder you work this planning step, the more money you will ultimately save.

Project Notes

Budget Worksheet

Description	Percent %	Budget Amount
BUDGET LIMIT:	100%	
INDIRECT CONSTRUCTION COSTS		
Bldg. permit/fees		
Setup short-term financing		
Interest charges		
Plans and specs.		
Structural engineering		
Survey review		
Building lot		
Course of construction insurance		
Supervision/overhead		
Misc. equipment rental		
Temporary/mobile phone		
Trash pickup		
Clean-up		
Temporary power		
Title insurance		
Other:		
EXCAVATION/SITE WORK		
Site clearing		
Foundation excavation		
Finish grading		
Backfill		
Sewer/water trench		
Electric trench		
Drain tile and gravel		
Other:		
MASONRY		
Footings/labor & materials		
Foundation/labor & materials		

Expenditures	Final Cost	Sub/Supplier	Phone Number

Budget Worksheet

Description	Percent %	Budget Amount
Rebar & steel		
Waterproofing		
Termite protection		
Sand or gravel & placement		
Basement floor		
Garage floor/labor & materials		
Walks and patios		
Driveway & other ext. flatwork		
Stoop, steps & ramps		
Fireplace brick		
Other:		
SEPTIC SYSTEM		
Well		
STEEL BEAMS AND POSTS		
ROUGH CARPENTRY		
Framing lumber		
Trusses		
Framing labor		
Crane service		
Windows & screens		
Skylights		
Exterior doors		
Garage doors & openers		
Decks & porches		
Other:		
PLUMBING		
Rough plumbing		
Fixtures & trim		
Other:		

Expenditures	Final Cost	Sub/Supplier	Phone Number

Budget Worksheet

Description	Percent %	Budget Amount
HVAC		
Heating & air conditioning		
Other:		
ELECTRICAL		
Rough electrical		
Finish electrical		
Fixtures		
Vacuum system		
Alarm system		
Television pre-wire		
Telephone pre-wire		
Audio pre-wire		
Other:		
INSULATION		
Wall & attic insulation		
Other:		
DRYWALL		
Hang drywall materials & labor		
Tape & texture		
Other:		
FINISH CARPENTRY		
Interior doors		
Moldings/stair rail/columns		
Finish carpentry		
Fireplace equipment		
Hearth and mantel		
Closet organizers		
Finish hardware		
Other:		

Expenditures	Final Cost	Sub/Supplier	Phone Number

Budget Worksheet

Description	Percent %	Budget Amount
EXTERIOR FINISH		
Roofing		
House wrap		
Siding		
Stucco		
Brick		
Stone work		
Exterior trim		
Soffit & facia		
Gutter mat'l./labor		
Chimneys		
Wrought iron		
Other:		
PAINTING		
Interior painting		
Exterior painting		
Wallpaper		
Other:		
FLOORING		
Ceramic tile		
Carpeting		
Wood flooring		
Vinyl flooring		
Other:		
MARBLE, TILE & GLASS		
Tub/shower surrounds		
Shower doors, mirrors & glass		
Other:		

Expenditures	Final Cost	Sub/Supplier	Phone Number

Budget Worksheet

Description	Percent %	Budget Amount
LANDSCAPING		
Sprinkler system		
Fill and topsoil		
Seed or sod		
Trees and plantings		
Retaining walls		
Fencing		
Other:		
CABINET, COUNTER & APPLIANCE		
Kitchen and bath cabinets		
Counter & vanity tops		
Medicine chests		
Laundry cabinets		
Entertainment center/built-ins		
Kitchen appliances		
Other:		
MISCELLANEOUS		
Smoke alarms		
Doorbell		
Dryer vent		
Foundation plaster		
Attic fan		
On-site supervision		
CONTINGENCY		
Other:		
Total Cost of House:		
Building Costs:		
Unspent Amount:		

Expenditures	Final Cost	Sub/Supplier	Phone Number

Sample Links from our Web Site

(Web addresses change frequently, and we update the hundreds of links provided on our site regularly. See our web site for the updates to links mentioned in this book.)

Shopping:

Access Carpets
http://www.accesscarpets.com/
Carpet and flooring for home.

Amazing Deals Daily
http://pdadeals.net/
New deals on many items including computer, coupons, clothes and many more items updated daily.

Atrium Furniture Mall
http://www.theatrium.com/
Atrium Furniture Mall is located in North Carolina's furniture valley. Save loads of money on furniture from brand name furniture manufacturers with furnishings to fit any room in your home. Settle down at Atrium Furniture Mall in High Point North Carolina for the best priced furniture all around.

Closets Central
http://www.rta-products.com/
Ready to assemble closet organizers and closet systems. Design your closet organizer on line.

Decorate Today
http://www.decoratetoday.com/
All home decorating products available from decoratetoday

Faucet Outlet
http://www.faucetoutlet.com/
Online outlet retailer of faucets, sinks, toilets, and other accessories for your bathroom and kitchen. Clearance items available.

Faucet.com - Your Premier Faucet Source
http://faucet.com/
Faucet.com offers a large selection of kitchen and bathroom faucets, sinks, fixtures, tubs, whirlpools, and toilets. We carry top brands including Delta, Moen, Grohe, Elkay, and American Standard. You can get a quote online.

Furniture Store
http://www.furniturefan.com/
Shop online for office and home furniture

FyHome.com
http://www.fyhome.com/
FyHome.com is a licensed distributors for wallpaper, window treatments, area rugs, and many other home decor items.

Georgia Carpet Industries
http://www.georgiacarpet.com/
Wholesale carpet mill featuring carpet, vinyl, laminate, direct from the source in Dalton, GA Save 50-70% off retail

Home Outlet
http://www.homeoutlet.com/
Your Complete Home Product Source for Online Stores, Contractors, Home Loans, New Products, Product Information and more! ...

Chapter 9: Commando Shopping Techniques

Time line: Three months before groundbreaking

The Price of Marshmallows

Elaine and I have been avid grocery shoppers for years. It's a science and a sport with us. We follow good rules of comparison shopping, we read labels, we check product sizes for comparability. When we buy a larger size of a product, say breakfast cereal or olive oil, we make sure that the price per ounce is lower than for a smaller size.

We took the level of shopping up a notch some years ago in an effort to save money to build a house. Using a computer spreadsheet, we listed and totaled all the products, brands, and sizes that we use. We discovered that all of the items we buy regularly, from applesauce to light bulbs, add up to less than 300 products. On the spreadsheet we listed the usual price of the item: ("one pound bag marshmallows: $.99") and the lowest price we have found for that item: ("one pound bag marshmallows: $.44, Storehouse Market, March, 1996").

When we find a price that comes close to the "lowest ever" price we buy that item in bulk. By organizing our grocery shopping we have reduced our monthly

Readers Say

"I'm an interior designer by trade. Prices in my area are twice what they are elsewhere in California, and the only way around it is to be an owner-builder. I have always known about the cabinets and cute stuff, but the rest has eluded me until now."

Toni F.
Carmel, CA

grocery bill from $400 to $175 while still getting the exact brands and products we prefer.

When we were developing early plans to build our home we took a vacation trip in the car. Elaine brought up the idea of owner-building the house, and I expressed real hesitation. While on the road we stopped at a convenience store for gas. I browsed the shelves idly and noticed marshmallows were selling for $2.59. As an organized shopper, I mentally compared that price to the $.44 we had paid when we last stocked up. It was more than five times as much. As I looked closer I discovered that the convenience store product was in a small 12 ounce size. That made it almost eight times as expensive.

I began to wonder whether the products we needed to build a house — lumber, wiring, plumbing fixtures — also could be had at much lower prices than you see in the first place you look. Would the simple shopping and bargain-hunting skills of any householder apply to building a house? The answer turned out to be a resounding "yes".

The marshmallows were available at a convenience store for a high price, but they were convenient. The store was open long hours, and was situated to be a quick stop for the customer. Lines at the cash register were short. Customers paid the high prices there in exchange for convenience.

Professional builders follow a convenience ethic much more than owner-builders do because they are in a production mode. They have a volume business to do that depends on consistent, repeatable production methods and procurement. Since time is of the essence, a contractor won't mess with a convenient established arrangement to buy something he needs to build your home. But an owner-builder can and will shop for hours to save money on a single item. Your issue is not convenience, but savings.

Much of the 1,000 hours of owner-builder preparation we advocate has to do with finding better values than you first see on every item for your home. It takes time and effort to do the research involved, and a general contractor wouldn't dream of spending the time that you would. As long as his price is competitive with other builders, and the builder makes a customary profit, he sees no need to do it differently.

The builder will tend to use the same subs and suppliers for every project. Often, no bidding is done. It's more comfortable and convenient for a builder to use the same people. If the builder has found a good sub, he will not rock the boat by looking for better values. He wouldn't want to risk alienating good help, and he makes only token efforts to get the prices down.

If a builder handles a $200,000 project in 100 hours of management time, and earns a clear profit of $20,000 he has been well enough paid at $200 per hour for his trouble. Even though he could make more profit by shopping, it would eat up time, and builders are in a production mode. In a 2,000 hour work year, a small custom builder would hope to do three or four houses. He doesn't want to spend more than 100 hours on managing any one house. With administration and marketing, the builder only has about a thousand work hours a year to spend on actual projects.

Since custom builders have found they can make more profit by doing more of the trade work on each house with their own forces — over 50% of the trade work on average — much more of their time is consumed in direct supervision and labor. Though a very hands-on builder might spend 300 hours on a luxury home project, very little of that time will be spent on finding bargains. The key to his profit will be reducing his hours per project.

Bargains

You can and will find bargains that contractors can't match. The savings may not match those we found on marshmallows, though they occasionally do. The reward for your bargain hunting is that you will save much more money in total dollars on a single custom home than you can in a lifetime of grocery shopping. The savings are superior to those from other kinds of shopping, because they mainline to your net worth.

When we built our house we stumbled across terrific savings on a number of items. One was the balusters for our staircase. They were available at more than $10 each from a contractors supply house. We saw them in a lumberyard newspaper ad on close-out for $3.30 each. We sourced most of our stair parts from that lumberyard, and negotiated an additional ten percent discount for doing so. This made the balusters $2.97 each. Our savings on 120 of them was $895.

We found a bargain on solid granite for our countertops by poking around in the "boneyard" of a stone and tile operation where returns and discontinued species of stone were stored. We paid $4,300 for a more than $10,000 value.

Every owner-builder I interviewed told me stories of savings they had found. Here are some examples:

"We have septic tanks here. I learned that the guy doing my grading was trying to get into the business of septic tank installation. I was his first customer, but I wasn't worried because he was a competent digger, and the system gets a thorough official inspection anyway. He did it for $3,000. The inspector told him it should have been $10,000."

"We have a big home center store close by, and we often buy on sale. With our photo album of ideas, we have our shopping list. Every weekend we look for sales. Appliances work well that way. Carpet was another example. We told them the yardage, and they came back with a low price factory deal. On windows, we had a local supply yard that had just taken on a high-end national window line. We negotiated a $7,800 price on what would be $12,000 worth of wood windows at contractor prices."

"I picked up my windows from a contractor who ordered them and the customer didn't want them. They were brand new triple glazed windows worth about $5,000. I paid $1,200 for all of them."

"We found our appliances on a close-out and saved $2,500 on a fridge, dishwasher and range. On flooring, we shopped heavily, and saved $3,000 on carpet. On ceramic tile, we shopped subs and got leads, and saved $2 a foot. On cabinets, we used an independent guy who was a dealer for factory cabinets, and saved $6,000 versus a custom cabinet maker."

"Our kitchen cupboards we found discontinued at a local cabinet shop, and we got them before we even broke ground because they were such a good value at 25% off. We stored them in my brother's garage. We did well on light fixtures by picking up the ones we wanted whenever there was a sale."

"We went to one home center store and saw the Jacuzzi tub we wanted for $1,700. I started talking with the salesman, and he told me that another store down the street had that model for less. We went down the street and bought it for $1,000. We had a friend in the import business who got granite for our countertops and saved us $6,000. We had a section of copper roof and when we called around, we found it cost twice as much here as what it was in the bigger city 50 miles away. We saved $900, even though they came from that far away. We installed beautiful marble floors after we found what a good price we could get."

"Our siding was quoted at $7,000-$10,000 and we got it for $4,500. We found the guy by word of mouth. A good sub will tell you things. You can shop for the right sub right up until you schedule it. You are not obligated until you sign. We did a lot of shopping on our windows, and got a bargain on custom made ones. We bought direct from a factory that makes and sells windows to distributors. We went to their showroom and saved. If you walk into a wholesaler and find a slightly damaged version of the countertop you want, you save. Look out for things. When Hurricane Andrew came through, I had a bid on my lumber just before the storm. So I hurried down and made a deposit to lock it in. Contractor prices on lumber went up 20% right after that."

"My plan of attack is to find a subcontractor on a site, find his best person, and offer that person an after-hours job. I offer him a couple of bucks more than he makes per hour. I did it with some of the framing. Also painting — I hired a guy for $8 per hour to work with me. He did some taping, spraying, etc.. Remember that a sub is a contractor, he adds something to the costs in every category too. Go to other jobs and pick up workers. It's really easy. You ask questions, and you say, 'Do you know anyone who wants to make a little extra on the side?' Their wage is the smallest part of the job. Don't hesitate to use skilled laborers. Electric work is more tricky. Just use them as consultants, or it gets expensive. It helps to know somebody on that one. On plumbing you will nearly always find a subcontractor who has crews. The crew leader is making $10 an hour, you offer $12."

"Since I wasn't looking for a specific color, I got carpet for $4 a yard, a Shaw 40 oz., in a discontinued shade. It was a taupe, a good color for resale. The flooring contractor sent out their guy to install it at $.50 for pad, $1 for installation. They agreed to charge the regular installation price with no profit applied. The package would have been $30 a yard at retail."

"Buy in bulk and always watch for sales. It does pay to shop around. You need to watch as they select materials, so you get straight wood, etc.. Be there when they load it. I selected a tub and shower unit for the bathroom. I saw it for $420. Then I saw it at another store for $280. Don't be in too big of a rush."

"I went to a door shop looking for a value on a high-end front door for the house. They often make ones which are ordered with the wrong swing and I got a perfect one from the door shop for $600. I saved $1,200."

"You can save an incredible amount of money just buying doors at one of these wrecking or salvage yards. I got a mahogany entry door worth $2,000 for $40. I got doors with leaded glass, restored them to new condition so they were acceptable to the inspector, and put them in front rooms."

"When I got bids in the beginning, I ran into a local building supply company. They were not the cheapest, but the salesman was the most helpful person, and I could bounce ideas off him. I had 3'x6' windows, 15 of them, across the back of the house in the design. He told me about these wood windows that went out on a job, and were sent back. He sold them to me for $100 each. They were worth $400 each. I actually altered the design to take advantage of the deal."

"I only had one true contractor, the plumber, the rest were all moonlighters. It takes longer that way, but it is smooth. You have to use weekends. If a portion isn't done by Sunday, you may lose a week. But sometimes their other jobs die, and they come full-time. I saved about half this way."

A woman who is an experienced construction lender from Florida told me that people who build with general contractors don't save money like owner-builders do:

"I have seen people pay too much for what they are getting. They are not knowledgeable consumers and good negotiators. They make emotional purchases. They buy on impulse. People lose some detachment and objectivity. Paint, carpet, tile, appliances, toilets, hardware, fixtures. That's where builders make some of their best money. People never seem to pick out what the house comes with. Builders count on people going a little crazy with select items. They will make 30% on select items."

Identify Your Suppliers

Over the course of construction of our home, in addition to about 30 separate subcontractors, we used more than a dozen specialty suppliers. It is important to get three or more bids or "take-offs" from each category of supplier, just as it is with subcontractors. Subcontractor bids vary widely, but supplier prices can vary

---

Readers Say

"We are doing a custom log home for $60 a foot. It's 2,650 s.f. with 2,000 s.f. of porch around it. We did six years of homework. Bought 40 acres with a lake for $32,000, an old dairy farm. We've made it look like a state park. First did a well, driveway, septic system, so now we just have to tie into it. That was $15,000-$20,000. And we got a lot of the support beams from large cedar trees that blew down. We justpeeled the bark off. They are 12-14 inches in diameter. We have a story tree where those who help carve their initials."

Sharon & Tom S.
Bradford, TN

Sources Say

The Complete Guide to Contracting Your Home has a master plan, project schedule, sub reference sheet, plan analysis, lighting appliance order, cost estimating summary and checklist, subcontractor bid control log, purchase order, change order, sub agreement, sub affidavit, loan draw schedule, building contract, and building checklist in its appendix.

(See page 260)

even more. Because subcontracting involves direct labor, there is a limit to available discounts. Materials are inventoried, and thus have a carrying cost to the supplier.

Suppliers sometimes discontinue items because of changes in style or features, or due to lack of demand. The result can be a bargain for you. Suppliers frequently must take back return items, and often discount them deeply. Damaged items, overstocks, and discounts for quantity purchases are reasons you can save. Identify suppliers who can meet your needs, and check prices on everything you buy. You will be able to buy some or all of the items on this list directly:

Potential Suppliers

1. Sand and gravel
2. Brick and block
3. Concrete supply
4. Lumber
5. Floor coverings
6. Electrical supplies
7. Paints and wallpapers
8. Appliances
9. Windows
10. Tile
11. Drywall
12. Cabinets
13. Doors
14. Trims and mill work
15. Stone
16. Sealed fireplaces
17. Trusses
18. Wrought iron
19. Closet organizers
20. Blinds
21. Cultured marble
22. Mirrors and shower doors
23. Finish hardware
24. Plumbing supplies
25. Lighting fixtures
26. Window wells
27. Skylights
28. Plumbing fixtures
29. Vacuum system components
30. Roll roofing supplies and shingles
31. Fasteners
32. Insurance
33. Tools
34. Specialty supplies
35. Door knobs and locks
36. Heating and air conditioning components
37. Wood flooring
38. Sprinkler supplies
39. Fencing
40. Decking and siding
41. Title insurance
42. Stair rail parts
43. Telephone, alarm, audio and cable components
44. Gutters and downspouts
45. Countertops
46. Computer software
47. Built-in sports equipment
48. Topsoil
49. Plants and landscape supplies
50. Steel and rebar

When You Pay for Materials Separately You Save

Sources Say

Chapter 7 of *Be Your Own House Contractor* lists 13 suppliers you as a contractor most likely will be using.

(See page 258)

One of the ways that general contractors improve their profits is by buying materials separately from labor on the trades that go into a house. The contractor can establish regular sources of supply with consistent discounts for volume purchase and favorable credit terms. He increases his profits by passing along the materials to his customer at marked-up prices.

Owner-builders can enjoy the same privilege. 85% of those I interviewed bought materials separately from labor on the trades. I found out dramatically how much this can save when I shopped for the stair rail system for our house.

The subs who do custom stair rail work in our region use a formula for bidding that takes the prices for stair rail parts (newel posts, balusters, rosettes, hand rail, anchors, and so forth) and adds an equal amount for labor to build the system. The parts for ours were bid at $2,000 and labor was an additional $2,000. The carpenter assured me that I couldn't get better prices on materials. I decided to find out.

With the discounts I got on balusters (the vertical spindles running from floor to handrail) I got all the parts for $1,000. Then I looked for a carpenter who was willing to do labor only. The one I found preferred avoiding the hassle of selecting and sourcing materials and handling the costs. He wanted $650 for labor only. I offered cash, and he agreed to $600. The total cost came to $1,600.

Generals tell me they have the most difficulty getting labor-only deals on the mechanical trades: electrical, plumbing, and HVAC (heating, ventilating, and air conditioning). Nonetheless, 50% of them say that they buy all the supplies for the mechanical trades directly except electrical boxes and wire, and plumbing pipe and connectors. You can do the same by having subcontractors who bid your work furnish you with a list of required materials.

Two different owner-builders I know found that they could save by installing the duct work for HVAC themselves. HVAC duct work used to be made of sheet metal and was difficult for do-it-yourselfers to install. Newer technology employs energy-efficient insulated flexible tubing that is easy to install. Savings on both material and labor: $2,000.

Some subcontractors have the attitude that they are entitled to the mark-ups they garner from furnished materials. Contractor John English says so in his book, *The Building Buddy*:

"If you ask a plumber to work on a toilet you bought because it was $25 cheaper than his own bid he may want to charge more for his labor. This is fair because he cannot be expected to be familiar with all installations. You probably won't save much, you will use a lot of your own time, and you may upset an honest man."

You and I are the honest people who are upset by this kind of thinking. First of all, you already have an understanding with the subs about purchased material. They know up front. Next, $25 is a lot to save. It's the net worth equivalent of $250 of your salary, which for most people is more than a day of work. Finally, it doesn't take much of your time to find a bargain. You may work at it for a half-day and establish a way to get $25 off on each of several dozen major plumbing items. You save $500, the DSDE equivalent of $5,000 in salary for four hours of thought and effort.

I saved nearly $2,000 off retail on lawn sprinkler parts alone by buying them directly from the distributor. I saved another $1,000 on faucet fixtures. It would take a year of work for someone making $30,000 per year to set aside that much cash. Your tradesman may or may not charge you more for his labor when you source the parts separately. In many cases, I have found labor-only deals that are actually less than the labor component of a bundled bid.

The benefits of buying materials separately include:

1. You save money on materials.
2. You may save on labor.
3. You know what you are getting.
4. You control the quality of components.
5. You have direct access to warranty information.
6. You can get refunds on any excess material you overestimate.
7. You will discover some components that you can install yourself at a savings.
8. You get contractor pricing you can use on future purchases.
9. You protect yourself against materialmen's liens. (See Chapter 12)

How to Use a Computer to Save

Some of the computer techniques for managing your project have been mentioned in earlier chapters. All can save money on your house project:

• Dream Home Notebook

By keeping your notes in a word processing file, you clarify your thoughts and make design choices early. With your room by room and trade by trade descriptions of your specifications, you can make a ready record to mail or fax to potential bidders.

• Sub and Supplier Interviews

If you use a word processor to capture the interviews you make with specialists, you can make changes and add detail to your trade by trade descriptions. Your bid requests to the trades are more detailed and professional, and you get improved bids.

• Spreadsheet Budget

As you build your budget on a computer spreadsheet you undergo the discipline of obtaining and defining estimates for every cost category for your house. This process always tightens up and reduces overall costs. Once you begin to make expenditures on construction costs, you enter them into your spreadsheet and see the impact on your totals. For instance, you may spend $4,500 for construction permits after budgeting $5,000. You see a reduction of $500 in your overall budget. Or you may learn that the soils on your site are unstable, and you must add concrete pilings at an unanticipated cost of $3,000. As you track each expense, you can make adjustments in future expenditures to stay on target.

• Spreadsheet Shopping Comparisons

Alternative bids by subs and suppliers can be laid out side by side on a spreadsheet in every particular and compared. This helps to understand details and find cost savings. When I laid out my options for plumbing faucets on a spreadsheet, I discovered expensive features that I could do without. I "cost-engineered" the faucet purchases to include only the desired features in the desired locations in the house. This helped us save $1,000.

• Computer Fax

There is tremendous convenience in faxing direct from your computer to a fax machine anywhere in the world. By installing an inexpensive fax modem on our computer we were able to send copies of many documents to those who could help us. (New machines usually include the modem). We sent out descriptions of requirements for many of the trades to various subs with fax machines. This saved much time and brought us more bids than we could get by face to face communication. We were able to find better prices. We sent around our budget to experts for review. We installed a second phone line to handle fax and e-mail traffic. There were occasions when we were having a conversation with a sub or supplier on one phone line and we were sending him a fax of pertinent specifications at the same time on another line. We were able to complete the conversation with the information in the other party's hands.

• CD-ROM Telephone Directory

One of the computer products which has a significant impact on planning is a nationwide directory of phone numbers. These directories, available in computer and bookstores are in a CD format exactly like the discs used in a CD player. ROM means "read-only memory". These computer discs hold volumes of information. The CD-ROM phone directories and Yellow Pages enable you to call vendors of a given product or material in cities anywhere in the U.S. and Canada to compare prices. For instance, some distant lumber dealers have told me that they can beat local prices even with the cost of shipping over 1,000 miles. The same may be true of plumbing suppliers and others. Since there is no threat to local customers for them, they can serve you freely.

Readers Say

"At first had difficulty separating out labor from subs. Now we say, 'We've already selected the stuff, we're just bidding the labor.' For example, 'I need a bid on installing a fireplace, I have it already, and the pipe, and I just need you to install it.' They give a bid, and then I say, 'It's not yet delivered. If you want to beat this number, go ahead, we'd be happy to look at it.'"

Joan L.
West Mountain, UT

Sources Say

The Complete Guide to Contracting Your Home has a good section on computer programs that help the owner-builder, like CAD, spreadsheets, PIM programs as well as internet sites.

(See page 260)

• Computer Schedule

In the next chapter we will show you how to organize your construction schedule on computer. With a schedule on computer, any change to your plans is easily understood. Your computer schedule can be distributed by fax or e-mail to your reviewers or team members. The computer offers you better control and faster completion.

• The Internet

You can use your computer as a gateway to a world of information by subscribing to a service that connects you to the Internet. The Internet provides access to the home sites of individual vendors, or to directories like Sweet's Directory ("Sweets.com") that provide detailed information on the products of selected construction vendors who have paid to be listed. The Thomas Register ("Thomasregister.com") is a site that lists all the manufacturers of given products, but provides less information for each. Hundreds of thousands of sources are available to provide you do-it-yourself information for self-work. You can use the World Wide Web to shop for comparison pricing on almost anything you will purchase during construction. We keep a list of hundreds of useful links updated at our web site.

Owner-Builder Connections helps you find O-B's anywhere. (See page 272)

The Internet also provides an efficient means of communication. Many vendor sites welcome your questions about their products and will send you answers via electronic mail. Using electronic mail ("e-mail"), you can correspond with other owner-builders around the world, without even paying postage for a letter. Our web site (address: "www.OwnerBuilderBook.com") facilitates communication with other O-B's through our Forums and through Owner-Builder Connections. Using e-mail, you can also send your construction budget, schedule, specifications, or other documents direct from your computer to experts and friends for review.

100 Construction Bargain Strategies

1. Start Early

The earlier you start your planning, the more bargains and ideas you find to make a better house. If you start just a month before, you never see the problems or opportunities that begin to emerge after two or three or six months of thought. Your house is built before you even see the key issues.

Suppose you start a month before groundbreaking and just come out with a budget and schedule at the end of that month. Then you have to go with it. But we recommend working and adjusting the budget many times over several months, even a year, before you start to build.

Some bargains take time to shape up, like special seasonal prices on house materials. How do you know what the seasonal prices are until you've checked them over time?

2. Take Time

It takes time to find savings on anything. You need to research your buys. Allocate enough time to get the full benefit of your work. Give the most time to the biggest costs. Our single biggest line item was lumber. I worked on lumber pricing for several days and eventually found a way to get the price down by $5,000.

Once you start to build, you find you have no time for anything else. Take the time to work through problems and questions now. You'll have much better luck later if you get stuck on something.

3. Know What You Want

I recently reviewed 27 pages of electrical components offered at eBay, the Web's biggest on-line auction site. I wondered if I could use some of the fast-disappearing bargains on our next house, but realized I would have no idea until I had a detailed list of components needed for that house.

One reader wrote me: "I could have been better organized by making a proper lay down on materials so I can see what it is." The point came home again when some windows caught my eye at a lumberyard staging a going out of business sale. There were hundreds to choose from at drastically reduced prices. But how many windows of what size and style would be needed for our next house? I had no details and had to pass on the opportunity.

4. Written Budget

All of your construction bargains need to fit within an agreed budget. Unless that budget is in writing, it is a moving target. Say you find a bargain on wood flooring at only three thousand dollars, more than fifty percent off the agreed price. You make an advance purchase only to discover that you can allocate only $1,500 to wood flooring for lots of good reasons. Make the budget decisions first and carry the written budget with you.

Reader Ted Magleby told me: "I will get the best numbers I can from a contractor friend who will break down the budget, and tell me what he pays for everything. Then I will try to beat it. It will be detailed with brand names, and all."

5. Use a Spreadsheet

There are thousands of unique items in a new house. The task of managing them is overwhelming. A spreadsheet on computer solves a problem by keeping the items all in one place with infinite flexibility for organizing, editing, pricing and

Readers Say

"Wenco Windows came in at $14,000 less than Anderson on a $29,000 job."

Nancy F.
Salisbury, NC

Readers Say

"We were surprised to learn that our stress-skin panels were even with the price of conventional framing. We got free shipping and a technical rep for a day, and good competition between vendors. $4.13 a square foot."

Dave & Sheila Anderson
Boone, IA

Readers Say

"I got lumber prices a few months ago, and since then it has gone up $5 a sheet. A lot of framing is happening right now, and that drives up prices quick."

Paul & MaryAnne D.
Pleasant Grove, UT

totaling categories. At a glance you can see how your planned purchases in a category compare to your budget decision for that category.

6. Know What Things Cost

From your interviews you can get many early indications of what things cost. Keep good notes on your planned purchases. If you know prices, you can tell when you find a bargain.

This proved true on the windows for sale at the lumberyard that was going out of business near me. The vinyl double hung windows with grids inside the double panes would probably work for our next house. The three by five foot size was just like the windows in our current house. At $64.95 they were about a third less than the bargain we got for our windows. But my interview notes showed that a friend bought good windows locally for $50 on a special sale. I could wait and look for a better deal.

7. Schedule in Writing

A written schedule does a lot to help you avoid delays when you build, which can save you interest costs. The construction interest on an average home is over $1,000 for the last month before occupancy.

By scheduling in writing you can also anticipate dependencies that very often cause people to pay extra to get something fast. You may see for example that trusses save you time and money in framing, but that they have a six-week lead-time. If you fail to get them ordered on time you have to pay a third more for stick framing, or pay a third more for rush charges.

8. Always Get Three or More Bids

Sometimes you are sure which sub or supplier you will choose for something well in advance. In those cases it seems unnecessary to get a second or third bid. However, those additional bids may bring surprises in prices, valuable information, or negotiating leverage with your chosen source. The key is to be organized to obtain additional bids with very little extra effort.

Force yourself to think of three bids when buying a big-ticket item. This applies to labor, which is the lion's share of new house cost, and it applies to material components as well. The average difference O-B's reported between low and high bids was 34%. Theoretically, a "one-bid" average house could be $68,000 more expensive than one based on two or more bids for each item.

Readers have reported that this is true even when the bidder is your friend. There can be much lower prices out there that you don't know about.

9. Do the Round Robin

Follow up the bids you receive by comparing the line item prices and talking with the sub or vendor about them. Sometimes your preferred vendor will match or beat the lowest price you have received or provide some upgrade free of charge.

You can do the round robin just before you are about to use the trade or material in question. As conditions change there may be a "soft spot" in the industry or with one of the subs or vendors that gives an unexpected savings when needed.

10. Get it in Writing

It's customary for subcontractors to provide written bids with perhaps a 90-day expiration on the stated price. Vendors can do the same thing on material estimates. Even if a vendor estimate is about to expire, you may be able to purchase the order and have it stored at the vendor, often free of charge, until it's needed.

Without written estimates, your own written notes will often suffice. Show the sub or vendor what they told you earlier, and they will frequently match or come close to the number written. Or show the written notes to competitors for a price match, even if the first vendor is no longer interested at that price.

11. Buy Materials Separate from Labor

Naturally, a tradesman who handles materials for customers will add to the cost to provide for overhead and profit. This mark-up could range up to 100% of the tradesman's cost. Since list prices are artificially high, the tradesman can point out that his marked-up price is "still under list price."

However, the mark-up can range to 200% of original cost. And often you can even beat the original cost by making a special, well-researched buy.

12. Be On-Site

By being on-site, you can often discover cost-saving approaches that didn't occur to you in the planning phase. Opportunities for free items, cost engineering, free or low-cost upgrades from subs, and special deals from salesmen often arise. You answer questions for the subs to prevent delays and ensure that materials are provided at prices you choose in a timely fashion. Disasters are averted and costs are controlled.

13. Keep Your Jobsite Clean and Organized

A clean organized site saves money in several ways. You often avoid paying for the same fasteners or tools more than once because you can find them. You can make use of scraps and minimize waste on every trade. Tradesmen can get in and out faster, potentially reducing labor costs and shortening construction time. Mistakes and rework are reduced, and paperwork is protected that assures warranty service when needed at no charge to you.

14. Cost-Engineering

Look at your purchases to be sure that you are not overdesigning your project. Sometimes a lower priced component has all the quality and the important features you are looking for.

As a marketing consultant, I got cost-engineered once by an expert. I presented a planning proposal to Tom Fitzpatrick, a third generation commercial construction man, and president of the oldest construction company in Ohio. Tom cut my proposal from $39,000 to $25,000 and left me feeling good about it. He selected the highest yield activities that he was really interested in and offered me an easier project with a better profit.

Readers have cost-engineered granite slab countertops to granite tile, used brick only on the most visible walls of homes, eliminated rain gutters in arid areas, chosen upgrade woodwork in public areas of homes, but not in youth bedrooms, and installed quality cabinets or faucets without "designer" prices. As they say, the best way to save is to never spend at all.

Reader Ivey Sutton built a 75% panelized home, but customized the front exterior to create additional curb appeal. Two readers installed radiant in-floor tubing to heat their homes and used standard concrete for the floors instead of Gypcrete which is pumped in at a high cost. They specified quarter-inch aggregate in the concrete mix, and got stronger better floors with a smoother surface at a big savings.

15. Trade

You could trade almost anything imaginable to subs and some vendors in lieu of cash. You could even loan something you own, like a tool to someone in trade for something you need. Tradesmen are famous for doing this between themselves. One tradesman, Ron Thorgersen, offered O-B Joanie Low granite countertop for the price of Formica. He got the granite because he had done some trade work with the countertop man. Meanwhile Joanie, an attorney, in turn did legal work for Ron to pay much of the cost of framing, excavation and foundation for her project.

Mike Cambiano told me, "I am doing some trade labor, I have a lot of skills, but I am going to manage my electrician's project for him. My wife also has management, money and accounting skills." O-B Sharmisa Martin says that her husband is an electrician: "We've already started doing trades, one is to a carpenter, where we have $500 credit built up already. This way we'll be able to get our trades accomplished in not too long a time after we build."

If you have something to trade, you could talk to all your subs and vendors, and ask them if you can trade with them. Make it a standard question in your sub and vendor interviews. You could turn up a bargain before you even ask for bids.

16. Join a Barter Club

You could get trade credits with a wide variety of partners by joining a barter exchange. Jon Pfunder, a metal worker, has developed over $10,000 in credits on an exchange. He says that he can get lots of business without marketing cost or effort this way, and always has a waiting list.

One O-B got creative with a barter club and cut special deals with one of the participants to help him build credits. The other participant was a cruise broker who traded the O-B some cruises at 40% off. The O-B then offered cruises to subs and vendors for their workers in the off-season at full value and got big reductions in the amount she had to pay in actual cash to get the work. She also brought a big new customer to the barter club in exchange for a discount in the price she had to pay to buy additional credits. They also agreed to waive her transaction fee for trades.

17. Home Show Discounts

When the building products vendors get together to display at a home and garden show, there is an atmosphere of competition for your attention. At these shows, many vendors offer trade show discounts. We purchased our whole house vacuum unit at a savings of 40% this way.

Where there is no discount or coupon offered, you can ask for "show special" if you use that sub or vendor in the future. Just make a note on the exhibitor's business card, and have them initial the card.

Some exhibitors ship sample products to each show they do and plan to sell them off to avoid return shipping costs. Jane Himes found a $2,100 jetted tub for $300 at a show in Las Vegas. The exhibitor did 84 shows that year and shipped 84 tubs one way.

18. Attend a Contractor Show

It is especially illuminating to attend a show for contractors. We went to the giant JLC Live Show in Las Vegas one year to try the waters. JLC, the Journal of Light Construction, stages the show every September, attracting contractors from all over North America. You can register as an owner-builder, because for the moment you are engaged in contracting. It's easy to register on-line, with a discount for advance payment. (Link provided on our website.)

Many competing construction systems vie for contractor attention, presented by the manufacturers, not third party vendors. There are opportunities for show discounts, coupons, (I got one for $500 off an SIP system) and the sale of floor models of components you may need for your project. Manufacturers would far rather sell a show model of a device like a radiant heat boiler or heat exchanger than ship it back to the plant after the show.

These shows are also a great source of information from national experts on ways to save money or trouble when you build with their products.

19. Buy Direct from Manufacturer

All the middlemen between the manufacturer and you have to be compensated. When you know what you want and where it originates, sometimes you can get a factory deal. Sometimes the programs are well established, like carpet purchased at mill-direct prices. Sometimes you have to go freestyle.

Cameron Gull did this by looking on the store package for a manufacturer name and location for window blinds. He then called the factory and talked his way into a factory direct deal, recording the name of the clerk and the price. When he called back to arrange shipment he had to use his notes to get re-approved because procedures had changed there. He saved two-thirds.

Residential Designer Dale Booth says: "Go to Kohler factory for tubs, sinks, and faucets. Plan a vacation route, call ahead, and get deals en route to bring home." Jeff Roberts, a purchasing agent and O-B told me: "I started calling all the manufacturers rather than hardware stores on the windows. I get a call-out from one, and then I fax it to 18 manufacturers in my state."

20. Special Price in Lieu of Distributor

Some manufacturers have merchant agreements that forbid them from selling direct to the public, but can deal through reps or distributors. O-B Kayla Lamoureaux has learned to work through the factory rep to buy direct: "I look for the manufacturers rep and try to work directly with them buying wholesale."

No distributor in your area? Get the manufacturer to sell to you at distributor prices. (If they want to make a sale.) Ron Barela did this in Arizona with a company from back east.

21. Buy Factory Surplus

You get a double bonus if you manage to buy factory surplus. Even manufacturers with prohibitive sales agreements often can sell off their product overruns, blemishes, overstocks, wrong colors, and at less than the usual factory price. It may pay to look for producers of high value items far from your location. Some of them have outlet stores for the purpose. Reader Barry Munson describes his experience buying cabinets: (Contact information on our web site.)

"I have shopped the Kraftmaid outlet store. What a rat race. You have to get in a line at 5:30 a.m. for a 7:00 a.m. door opening, getting a ticket number as you enter. Really worth it though. We bought our vanities at $70 each. Cabinet bases and wall units are same price. My pots and pans drawer tray pullouts were $2 each. These retail at Home Depot for $60 each."

O-B Don Frick did two surplus deals: "We got a local mill end and discontinued lumber dealer here, and he got us Port Orford Cedar planking for decks, 2X6 normally $.87 a board foot at discount, and we got it for $.41 a foot. This shipment was intended for Asia, and shipment was turned down, so they had overstock. We also got solid foam R-Max insulation manufactured in Nevada, and we got 4X8 sheets of R-36 solid sheet. You use two 2 and a half inch sheets together to get that R-factor. They take your name, and store up their seconds, and you go and pick it up in Fernley, Nevada, 25 miles from Reno. I paid under half of the usual price. I think other factory producers have similar programs. You could probably get shipping, too." (Contact information on our web site.)

Also check for surplus with building suppliers and specialty suppliers, and even subcontractors and general contractors.

22. Check an Unexpected Source

Some O-B's have reported that they found custom cabinets from an independent craftsman at better prices than stock cabinets. Some found materials from subcontractors at better prices than from any independent supplier. If you have pursued one type of source for your item, give a different approach a look before you close off your research.

23. Avoid the Construction Loan

I could have saved $8,000 in loan fees and interest if I paid cash for my project. Some owners have sufficient equity in their current homes to pay cash for their next house. They can sell the previous property before starting the new house and work with the cash proceeds. Or, they can take out home equity loans to finance new construction. Interest rates and origination costs are much lower that way.

Owner-Builder Lynn Hardy says: "Short-term loan for construction saved us $5,000." John Richardson says: "Build one, use it for an equity loan, and get loan for much less to build second one. Live in the first one and get tax savings."

24. Negotiate Your Loan

When you apply for a construction loan or mortgage, get good faith estimates from several eligible lenders. These give all of the costs involved just like a construction bid or estimate. Enter the various costs in a spreadsheet for comparison. Let the lenders compete for your business. O-B Kathy Maggiora says, "There is a list of mortgage guys and their rates in the real estate section of the Sunday paper. We called the lowest guy and it worked great, no surprises."

Remember, too, that the points charged up front are negotiable. I called five or six lenders when we decided to refinance our house. We had several offers on the origination fee of 1/2 a point (one percent of the loan balance.) The best offer was for 3/8 of a point.

25. One-Close Loan

John Norton, an owner-builder whose story is featured on our web site, used a one-close loan to build. The construction loan and the eventual long-term mortgage loan were handled with just one closing, saving considerably in loan fees. The construction loan portion was only one point higher than the mortgage loan. His income and credit rating were sufficient to allow him to bundle the cost of land and construction into one loan, as well.

26. Save on Title Insurance

One unconscionable cost in every real estate loan is title insurance, easily a $1,000 cost on a residence. Although we were told at first that that was necessary and unchangeable, we learned that there is some flexibility for savings here. We called on several bidders for a recent refinance of our home and broke out the competing estimates. Title insurance cost estimates were $935, $505, $410, and $155 (from our original lender.)

You can make the title insurance go away if you pay cash for your project, or use a loan secured by another source, like an equity loan on your current residence. Or you might get a "reissue rate" from a title company if they issued you a policy on the property within the past three years. More than that, title companies have the flexibility to give you a "friend's rate" or an "abbreviated title policy". Worth calling around and trying for the best deal.

The same applies to the appraisal that is part of your loan. Some lenders will let you use a "limited appraisal" at a much smaller charge if you clearly have large equity in the project.

27. Shop at Home Center Stores

The big home center stores, with more than 1,000 stores in a chain, more than 100,000 square feet per store, and more than 100,000 items carried have changed owner-building in North and now South America. They have partially broken the "old boy's network" of "contractor-only" distributors, and brought generally low prices and accessibility to the public.

Owner-builder Earnie Callender told me: "After two hours searching for faucets on the Web, we found the two best deals were three cents different in price, and one of them was at the local Home Depot.

With some creativity you can enhance your savings at the home center store. Jeff Robertson did it this way: "Found a deal through Home Depot, on some returned doors. 25-50% off original. Canceled orders, mistakes. And little outlets also sell them at sharp discounts. My doors were solid wood six panel colonials priced at $180; I got a price for all of them at $112. In addition, they have a yard sale going on, so I will get them close to $100 and they will store them for me."

Dave Mayfield found stores in the same chain differed widely on prices, and at one he picked up on a 'demo buy': "I bought a chop saw, air nailer, and DeWalt battery pack kit at half the price in Utah, than what it costs here in Northern California. Both Home Depot prices. The DeWalt kit I got a demo for."

28. Get a Contractor Discount

One way to increase your savings is to have a hardware store, lumberyard, or home center set you up for an additional discount, as Phil Smith did: "Buy all your own fixtures i.e. toilets to lighting. Utilize Lowes, Home Depot, any of the big names. They will generally all give you a discount if you tell them you'll buy exclusively from them (what you do later is your business). Small independent hardware stores will definitely do the same, generally from 5-10% savings. Nine out of ten times the prices at the chain stores undercut subcontractor prices."

Edmund Moriniere got set up first with a credit account, then asked for a discount: "I opened an account at Lowe's under a construction name, and I think it will give me leverage as a long-term customer when I ask for discount."

29. Work at a Home Center Store

Last year I undertook a project to interview 60 store managers at The Home Depot. Most of them had built their own homes. A few of them had built legitimate mansions. It's no wonder because of their access to materials deals and special discounts, and their relationships with subcontractors. You can do the same by having a member of your family work in a home center store or lumberyard. You get first dibs on contractor returns, specials, discontinueds, and your 10% employee discount, too. You also get to meet all the subs.

O-B Mark Alexander did as much: "My wife took a job at Home Depot so we can know all the bargains coming up. Last weekend we bought marble tiles for $2.64 that are usually $7.00. The guy told me that contractors are buying them by the palette load and putting them in warehouses. Later, when they install them they'll be full price plus all the mark-ups for their customers."

30. Track Prices on Major Budget Items

If you can't work at a home center store, at least you can visit frequently before and during your project. Go to the home center store once a month or more, check prices, and consider current specials on tools and materials. You could do a market basket of representative items on paper, tracking price variations by month. Also save a series of catalogues for later reference. One reader discovered that a sheet of OSB board used in framing varied upward by $5 from November to April of the following year.

31. New Customer Discount

Many of the home center stores take ten percent off your first purchase if you open a credit account with them. Everything you put on the ticket that day gets ten percent off. Save up your major purchases, catch them when they are on sale, and get a ten percent bonus for doing it all at one time.

32. Ask About Upcoming Sales

One of the brickyards in our area has a once a year cash and carry sale for discontinued styles, overstocks, and customer returns. The salesman doesn't bring that up unless you ask. You can schedule your purchase to take advantage.

One appliance vendor has seasonal sales. We asked what was coming up and he told us the upcoming sales prices on our selections. By checking with a manager he was able to offer us the future prices.

33. Store-Wide Sales

Most retail suppliers put selected items on sale each week. Home Depot tries to avoid this by following an "everyday low prices" policy. But they do storewide sales from time to time where everything goes on sale at a percentage discount.

Another good-sized chain did this in our area, and we spent all of one day selecting 65 items we knew we needed for our project at 20% off. We got all of our paint on this occasion. Whenever we weren't certain if the price was the best possible, we walked up to the customer service desk and called the competition to check it. Our receipt at the register was four feet long. We opened a credit account at the same time and got an additional ten percent off the entire amount.

34. Use a Coupon

Some of the home centers send out valuable coupons in mailings or print them in newspaper ads. You may see "10% off your purchase", or "$100 off any purchase of $500 or more." O-B Hilary Checketts shopped for large items amounting to thousands of dollars and found the low price at a store that does not do couponing. However, they matched competitor deals and thus honored her coupon for a savings of more than $500.

35. Price Matching Plus Ten Percent

A very popular promotional policy among home centers and lumberyards is to beat the competition by 10% on an exact item match. Note that this is a safe practice because unless a competitor decides to sacrifice margins, no store in the area needs to get aggressive. They just respond to the occasional foray into price breaks elsewhere. This puts the burden on you to find true good prices.

To take advantage of this policy, save your ad circulars for home center stores in your region. We have three large home center stores in our area that take ten percent off a competitor's price. When you find a 25% discount on something you need and add ten percent to that savings, it can be significant. For this purpose we saved all the ad circulars in a file basket for a year. When we had a major purchase to make from one of them, we reviewed the ads for all of them. On presenting the ad at the cash register we got the discount. It didn't matter that the ads were sometimes months old. They were almost always accepted.

O-B Angela Daniels says: "We know somebody who bought all his materials from Home Depot. He got bids from other places, and Depot matched them all and took an extra 10% off. He also set up with them as a subcontractor because of his trade, and got a pro discount of 10% more."

Jeff Robertson did it: "On my vacation house, I called all the lumber dealers in several states, and got a list of materials, and starred the lowest price on any given item and Home Depot was happy to beat that number by 10%."

36. Do Double Play, Triple Play, or Grand-Slam

The "couponing" industry in books and newsletters touts the idea and game of getting extra leverage from a store coupon. For instance, you might get a triple play at the grocery store by using a coupon on an item that is also on store discount, and is eligible for a mail-in rebate. You might get a grand slam if that store is doubling coupons at the cash register. It's very fun, and couponers have been known to be paid for taking an item home. On that basis Elaine and I once were actually paid one cent for each free jar of mayonnaise that we bought, so we stocked up.

In many instances you can make double and triple plays on your construction expenditures. Say you have a contractor discount, the item is on sale, and you have a coupon as well. You have a triple play. You'll find many creative combinations. I can't explain it, except to say that we have a great country.

37. Store Closings

Sometimes chains go out of business, sometimes they are taken over by other chains and converted, sometimes a single store in a group is closed, and sometimes a just a warehouse is closed or moved. In the last six years there have been four home center or lumberyard closings in my small community.

Greg Rush shopped the going out of business sales at more than one store in the chain: "You could get some outrageous values at Eagle because they were converting to Lowe's. We went to the one near City Center and got toilets for $85 each, regularly $212 with the elongated bowl. The one on the south side didn't have as much."

We are very familiar with the formula now. The prices drop storewide every week to a certain percentage off. You wait for a deep cut and hope that your items are not yet taken. I waited until the bitter end when Home Base went out of business here, and much of my last remaining item, paint, was still on the shelf at 90% off. On the last day of the sale I couldn't make it down. I drove over anyway the day after, and paint was stacked on pallets outside with a sign that it was free for the taking. I got enough to prime our next house.

38. Buy Tools From Pawn Shops

If you are doing self-work, it is very valuable to have high capacity tools to get a job done right. But an O-B doesn't make daily use of the tools, and it's hard to justify paying new prices. We have seen significant construction tools like air compressors and paint sprayers for twenty-five to fifty cents on the retail dollar at local pawnshops.

O-B Toodie West says: "We got a Senco Finish nailer for $200 at a pawn shop. It was $450 new. Try Cash America, they have a network and will call around and find the stuff you want."

39. Share the Cost of Tools

Since good tools are expensive and for many owner-builders rarely needed after the project is done, several strategies can be used to bring the cost into balance:

•Rent a tool and share the cost with someone else in your new neighborhood who is also building.

•Buy and resell.

•Buy and use, and then trade for other services you need.

•Borrow a high-value tool overnight from a tradesman on your job who will expect it to be ready to go in the morning. We borrowed a tile saw from our tile man overnight because we did a portion of the tiling in our house.

•Buy and share the cost of tools with family members. Have a tools lending library.

Steve Orton did this with his brothers for tools like a high-end drill and a reciprocating saw. Karen Morrison's extended family did it with a pressure washer.

40. Shop Discount Tools Store or Catalogue

When we built the Riverbottoms house a friend told us we would need a bolt cutter "for all manner of tasks". There's a lesson in the fact that we only used it twice while building. Men are famous for buying tools they don't need. We searched first at the home center stores and found a 15% swing in prices from the high to the low store. Using the high store we price matched the low store and got the tool for $28. Only years later did a discount tool store open in town and we found a comparable bolt cutter for $12 on special at $6.

That chain, Harbor Freight Tools, has stores in seven western states of the U.S. and sends out a sales circular to a mailing list. (Contact info available at our website.) In the current sales circular, they have a comparable reciprocating saw (sawzall) to the one I bought on a double play for $89, at $35. An 18-volt cordless drill with case is $40. I've seen them recently at around $200 elsewhere.

41. More Tool Tricks

We had a friend who took out a construction loan to build his home that included $5,000 for tools. That seems ill advised for a non-tradesman, since the tools now ride on his 30-year mortgage, and will cost him $15,000 with interest over that period. It also seems ill advised because there are so many ways to save on tools:

•Prepare the task you need to do so that you can make immediate use of a rental tool and rent for a shorter period. For instance, a half-day rental saves.

•Rent long-term for a lower rate on a major item like scaffolding, and share with another owner-builder or even tradesman.

•Buy at a construction auction, at a favorable price, then resell after use, or trade for other benefit.

•Buy used off classified ads

•Trade for it.

•Find tool bargains on the Internet.

•Keep a spreadsheet or other record of your tools, their cost, and location.

It's hard to keep track of many small items otherwise. Managing tool costs takes some effort.

42. Buy Builder Items

Often readers tell me they are excited about building with a national brand of windows. In shelter and architectural magazines they see sumptuous ads and hear confirmation from others who tap into or profit from consumer sales of such items.

Ads like these are very costly. As a manufacturer of a construction product in the 1980's I paid $25,000 for an insert into the Sweet's architectural catalog for my product. Full page ads in Architectural Digest cost almost as much. Manufacturers with regular marketing costs of that magnitude must charge higher prices to compensate. But that doesn't make the windows better.

Left to their own devices, custom builders would not offer heavily marketed products like these to their customers, as it increases cost and cuts builder margins. Builders have sources for products that are of good quality without all the marketing. Usually they involve a good-better-best array of choices, and you can get all the quality you want for a bit more money.

We once saw a heated towel bar apparatus in a prestige consumer catalog for $3,000. Later we saw a similar item in a trade catalog for $175. On reflection we came up with a way to warm towels in our next home by running heated water tubes through a bathroom wall at very little extra cost.

Like windows, faucets, carpets, appliances, paints, light fixtures, and many other items are sold by creating consumer demand for designer versions. Be sure you check builder sources for such items before paying for the marketing.

43. Piggyback

A great way to get a bargain is to pool your purchase with a larger volume customer. Elaine and I did this with the friendly general contractor who bought $250,000 in lumber annually from our lumber-yard. We also did this when we bought under the plumbing account of our school custodian, and under the HVAC account of our heating man.

44. Buy at Construction Auctions

Some of our readers have attended construction auctions where brand new components such as doors, windows, and countertops were sold as surplus. Sometimes new tools are sold this way. Check in the phone book, with tradesmen, or in the classified ads for one in your area.

Reader Piper Holloway describes them: "We used to go to auctions where construction people sell their surplus products. As an electrician and a security system installer my husband met a lot of people with nice houses. One homeowner called him about the auctions. They had brand new stuff, doors that were pre-hung, steps, windows, countertops, interior doors, and tools in boxes. You bid on items you want."

John Wolf "…went to a molding and millwork auction last year before I was really planning to build. A local manufacturer puts all their inventory on sale once a year to reduce inventory."

45. On-line Auctions

Auction sites like eBay handle very well the function of displaying materials, collecting bids which you can see, and notifying you by e-mail when bids are placed or new items come up. Such services provide a convenient place for you to resell excess materials or tools as well. Check our web site for links to specialized construction materials auction sites.

46. Buy Salvage Material

There is a salvage dealer in our area that we found in the newspaper. He sells lumber, roofing material, and other supplies and components that have been fire or water damaged. One O-B told me bought salvaged lumber that was damaged in a transport crash and fire. Some of the edges of the lumber were singed, but he paid less than 20 cents on the dollar.

Owner-builder Kevin Waller said: "I built a house for a relative with salvage wood from semi wrecks, 2X12's, plywood, etc. A lumberyard caught on fire, and a local salvage dealer handled the sale. We heard about him by word of mouth. We did a $230,000 house for $80,000. We also used furnaces and hot water heaters that were water damaged."

You can use salvage materials if you self-finance. Even if you must undergo bank inspections the risk of hang-up over recycled material is small, O-B's tell me. Municipal building inspectors have discretion under the new code to inspect and approve used materials for new construction.

O-B Phil Smith has used salvage materials: "Remodeling contractors sell the stuff or there are salvage yards. Salvage tile, bricks, windows, (but don't skimp on energy savings, - very important in a window) doors, lumber, old beams, perimeter fence stone (broken concrete), light fixtures, block for fence wall or basement wall, make fireplaces out of salvage brick. Salvage cabinets. Bone yard countertop. Some barn wood floor from falling down barns. Plank floors. If over an inch thick, you can eliminate some OSB boards in the floor."

47. Use Recycled Materials

• Demolition contractors run recycle yards. Check the phone book.

• Use builders' materials yards. Check the phone book.

• Starbright Foundation in Phoenix accepts and recycles building materials for a charitable purpose.

• Governmentsales.com has recycled "glass" tile and recycled office furniture. (Updated links on our web site.)

Designer Dale Booth says: "Go to an area where they are building a lot of houses and ask if you can scavenge through their scrap piles. You can probably get $200-$300 of nails and hangers. Also scavenge for lumber. Stuff over 16 inches is useful for fire blocking, backing behind cabinets and towel bars." O-B Preston Heiselt procured recycled 1" plywood from the Blue Bird Bus factory in Ohio that was used as flooring in school buses. He used it as extra strong flooring and wall sheathing in his custom home.

48. Items from Remodeling Jobs.

Real estate broker Vickie Bischoff told us: "One of my real estate clients was remodeling her new place before moving in, and she gave lots of fixtures and things away. I finally talked her into selling them, and she sold all the kitchen cabinets (oak) for $150, the dishwasher for $25, and the stove for $25. If you want used bath vanities, toilets, cabinets, etc., you can talk to renovation contractors, or sometimes Realtors know."

Dennis Stoutsenberger says, "A lady remodeled near me and tore out nearly new carpet that she didn't like, and I could have taken it all, a good sized lot in light green. You can find the kitchen and bath remodelers that work in the nice part of town, and give them some cash for some nice things they pull out of million dollar houses, like cabinets."

49. Thrift Stores

Elaine and I volunteered as intake workers one Saturday at a huge local thrift store called Deseret Industries. We saw donations of sinks, cabinetry, windows and plumbing fixtures brought in, some in nearly new condition. We saw complete solid surface vanity tops with built in sinks and faucet fixtures priced at $5 for sale there. There were minor surface imperfections, which you can sand out.

50. Sell Your Plans

One reader paid $600 for house plans and sold them after completing her house for $150 in the classified ads.

51. Free Stuff

When we built the Riverbottoms house several free items fell in our lap, worth nearly $10,000. A relative paid an old debt by sending over a concrete man to do our walks and drives. The city sidewalk cracked when the roofing truck wheeled over a corner of it making a delivery. I noted the name of the driver and the date and replaced that part of sidewalk when a crew poured the cement pads for my back stairs and air conditioners. I took the concrete invoice to the roofing supply company and they paid it all, no questions asked, rather than quibble over how much each piece of concrete cost.

After a boundary disagreement, a neighbor sent over 30 loads of topsoil for our yard, valued at $3,000. Another hauler brought me 10 dump truck loads of composted manure at no charge. Our foundation man gave us a free window well. Our siding man gave us free bathroom tile. Someone we had helped build gave us bricks for our brick walk.

O-B Bill Harrington says: "We'll be able to put in top end stuff for a moderate amount of money. I got low voltage quartz halogen spotlights from a friend, like they use in supermarkets to accent displays - they bring the color out. He had them left over from a job and they were going to be thrown away because they were special order, and I can use them in the house to accent sculpture and other art. Also over the kitchen island, and for reading and music lights."

Scan the classified ads or place your own ad for items that you need, offering to haul away and clean up. Be alert for internet promotions involving free stuff, too.

52. Upgrade Inexpensively

As owner-builder you certify that each aspect of your plan and construction are well thought through and upgraded to the best quality possible within budget. Many of these upgrades are possible on forethought rather than money. Little luxuries like a heat lamp in the bathroom or ceiling fans are of very low cost if anticipated by you. We consider well-blocked vinyl doorstops and well anchored stair railings to be quality though cost-free upgrades.

For $20 we put in a conduit pipe from basement to attic that provides a clear electrical path for future changes in the house. For $10 we made sure there was a four-inch pipe under the driveway that made lawn sprinkler installation easy. Our drain tile around the house foundation was not a required item but easy to do and has provided us with perfectly dry crawl space for under $50. The costs are usually minimal investments in materials, not contract labor.

53. Plan-Ahead Items

Since we could do it for low cost as owner-builders, we anticipated many future needs that may never affect us, but improved the house for future owners. These items include stub-ins for water softener, entry chandelier, future lights on garage front, pre-wire for cable or satellite, alarm, audio, sprinkler system, internet, optical fiber, whole-house vacuum, garage hose bib, 3'0 doors and four foot halls throughout for handicapped, and levered doorknobs on interior doors.

One handy item to save money is to stub in for a TV antenna in your attic, and wire it in. Then you'll get you local stations free if you want later. For some homeowners this could save an annual satellite or cable TV cost of $500 or more.

54. Mail Order

Reader Piper Holloway writes: "Also we looked at wholesalers catalogue, where we got our wall to wall carpet, only paid $50 for shipping, North Carolina furniture and everything. Book is called "Wholesale by Mail & Online 2002: The Consumer's Bible to Bargain Shopping". The book and other guides in print offer sources for household items as well as carpet, appliances, electrical and plumbing fixtures and other items of use to owner-builders.

55. Question Each Item

When you can buy a given grocery item for a half or a third of the normal price occasionally, imagine the collective power of buying each item in a construction project at a deep discount. Try to make everything as inexpensive as you can—go item by item and be creative.

A given item may be unnecessary or have potential for unexpected savings. Through design choices, we've eliminated the need for air conditioning in our next house (in Idaho), a huge savings. General contractor Jay Halverson provides another illustration: "Caulk all the joints of your sheathing if you use OSB board. It eliminates need for house wrap, about a $500 item." Reader Ted Magleby says: "I also learned from the book that you have to go down item by item and see where you can save."

56. Do-It-Yourself

Kevin Clausen is typical of O-B's performing self-work on high value items: "The HVAC quote was $8,900; I installed it all for $3,500. The furnace was quoted at $4,000 and I got it for $900." The average savings off quoted subcontractor price for self-work in our survey of owner-builders was 62%.

57. Plan Your Self-Work

Self-work is a potential gold mine of savings with a definite downside. All our observations of owner-builders indicate a universal tendency to overestimate the self-work they can do. In fact, the average owner-builder does around four of the trades out of about 30 potential trades on a whole house project, while usually planning to do more.

John Norton's comment about self-work when owner-building (his job diary is on our web site): "I should never have started this..." is typical of the unprepared owner-builder. Better to be prepared in the first place. The difficulty comes when provision has to be made at the last moment to replace self-work with subcontracted work. Typically this causes an avoidable cost overrun.

You can avoid this overrun by a: choosing self-work you know you can handle, and b: by planning the self-work long before you start.

We recommend that people give a specific 50 hours to each trade they plan to do. This is a big saver of money and effort. Too often people get to the end of the project when they are maybe way overcommitted and beaten down, and they lose it, and say, "I decided to hire that one out." These are the finish steps which are particularly expensive, and at a point when there is little left in the budget to pay for them. They are budget busters. Don't let self-work become your Waterloo.

Everybody drops one or two planned self-work items, at a cost of at least $1,000. On a high value trade, the loss might be $5,000. Plan your effort. Say you budget 1,000 hours for self-work. What can you do? It took me 800 hours to do electric. Now I think I could maybe perform that trade in 250 hours.

You could do a spreadsheet of tasks for say, electrical work, and run it by an electrician who owes you a favor or perhaps over a restaurant dinner. You could estimate how many hours it would take you for each step and what the steps are. He could say "That part there used to take me 10 hours, but I built a jig that cut my time in half. I've got an old one you could have for $50." Or, "No way that should take you that long if you have your wire all spooled up first. The spooling only takes a half a day, let me show you how." Maybe you come away with a time budget of 150 hours (where it takes him 80).

You do this on four trades of 250 hours, and you've saved 400 hours, enough to add maybe three more trades. The consulting on seven trades might be $700; the three extra high value trades save you $15,000 which makes a net savings of $14,300 because of planning.

Money saving strategy:

1. DIY with an overall time budget you can afford, say 1,000 hours
2. Plan your trade by tasks with a time budget.
3. Review plan with an expert for say $100 or in exchange for favor.
4. Refine, save time, and add additional trades for further savings.

58. Unbundle

Bundling requires you to buy a group of items rather than pick and choose among smaller pieces or alternative sources. A classic instance in the housing industry is log home construction.

Reader Gary Bailey told us about the shell package bids he got for his log home of from $42,000 to $90,000. The formula in the industry is four times shell cost as the cost of a turnkey log home. That would make at 4X: $360,000. But he is building it for $160,000 with help from his sons, both mechanical subs, and other goodies up his sleeve. He will save a minimum $90,000 that someone else would indeed pay, because of the effect of the multiplying factor. Whoever goes for a turnkey home with the vendor who quoted $90,000 for the shell will probably pay $360,000 for the equivalent to what Gary is building for $160,000.

59. Avoid the Middleman

The biggest savings from owner-building comes from removing the general contractor middleman from the equation. The contractor has necessary overhead to stay in business, which you eliminate. You then work harder than this middleman to find one of a kind bargains in materials and labor, and adapt your process to optimize your house and resulting net worth.

The same applies to the middlemen in the distribution chain who bring you desired components for your project. Where it's possible to replace the necessary services of the middleman by your own effort, you can pick up greater savings. Lumber, for example, is said to have more than 6 levels of middlemen from mill to consumer.

Middlemen have recently crept into the process of finding subcontractor labor for residential construction. One of the bright ideas people came up with for the Internet was services that match you up with "approved", "quality-checked" subs for your project.

Many such services have proliferated because of the typical aversion tradesmen have to marketing themselves. Thus they pay a fee to be included by these services. Naturally, you absorb the cost of such fees through higher prices. My objection is that there really isn't any quality checking by the middlemen, just fee collecting. By matching yourself up with those subs in your area and on your schedule who fit your needs, you get a better price and a better outcome.

60. Don't Fall for a "Package Plan"

Elaine and I attended a package plan presentation a few years ago at a local hotel. The package or "owner-builder plan" was a format where you are called the contractor, and the service provides materials and offers you subs from an approved list.

After listening for a few minutes we asked a few questions and found ourselves attended to by the owner of the franchise who dealt with us personally to prevent contamination of the rest of the group.

We figured out that the service made money in several ways:

• They bought land in bulk and sold small parcels to participants.

• They charged a fee on your construction budget, which they estimated.

• The bundled the land into the budget and you paid the same 10% fee on the land you just bought and paid for.

• They sold you the materials.

• They provided the subs via an "approved" list. This means they extracted a fee from them, which you absorb through higher prices.

• They provided standard plans, which you change only with an up charge. The standard plans cost very little to produce, and enhance the standardization of materials for greater profit.

• They procure financing for you, and receive commissions from lenders, as well as interest for your funds on deposit.

• They allowed you to choose your own subs, but they had to approve them, which means they extracted a fee from them to continue being "approved".

• They reluctantly specified savings for participants as being in the 15% range versus contractor-built homes. Since we've learned that the average owner-builder saves 35%, there is 20% taken off the table by the package plan. On an average project, more than $40,000 of the owner-builder's equity.

Owner-builder T.J. Cox came to his own conclusions about this: "It would be a decent program for someone that had absolutely no experience in building or project management. They provide lots of material requirements, budgeting, scheduling and so on. For a price of course; their fee was going to be $13K, which would be reasonable, I thought, for all the work they would be doing. I just decided that I could do everything they proposed just as well and would save the $13k."

61. Buy Cafeteria-Style

This is the great privilege and genius of owner-building. You can source each element of your project in your own way. Some trades you may do yourself. For some you may barter, some you modify or eliminate, for some you find special deals that build your equity. This privilege extends to the intangibles like building permits, impact fees and financing costs. All is under your control for potential advantage.

62. Buy a Fax Machine

Buy a fax machine. It helps with bids, as vendors and subs are accustomed to receiving requests for bids by fax and answering the same way. You can use an inexpensive computer fax program in lieu of a fax machine, or just provide the fax number of the local office supply store as your fax number and send from there, paying by the page to send and receive.

63. Build in the Off-Season

The law of supply and demand really does work, and most parts North America have a low season when more tradesmen are available for immediate work then at other times. Paradoxically, a sun city like Tucson, Arizona even has such a time. In wintertime, they get an influx of framers and carpenters who can't find work in their own climates. Prices fall.

We recommend you take steps to allow you to break ground in the off-season. You can find good advice locally as to the steps you must take to separate yourself from the bulk of projects that start in high season. Lynn and Judy Coy told me: "Building a shop right now, and found material is much cheaper in January, February than later on. Last year the OSB board went over $10, but was $6.30 this past winter. It's worth your time to plan and shop."

64. Build in a Downturn

A different kind of opportunity arises when the economy is down. Not seasonality but cyclicality of the economy is on your side. Materials and labor, even financing, is available usually at a savings that later translates into improved equity when the economy rebounds.

65. Use Moonlighters

Owner-Builder Dan Meserve said: "None of our guys maintain a storefront. They are all moonlighters. I'm the electrician. Drywaller just quit an outfit, and gave us half off the labor rate. We figured we could build 2,700 square feet but we'll finish 4,000 for $200,000 or $50 a foot."

These moonlighters are tradesmen who work for somebody else by day and build for extra money on evenings and weekends. They may work for other subcontractors, or be in an entirely different job. Matt Gerhard told me: "I work in the school district, and I found all my subs as district employees."

The most active occupational group I have seen as owner-builders are firefighters. I have found that many of them have a building trade that they ply on the side. They often trade their services to other firefighters who owner-build in exchange for like assistance.

Using moonlighters is not a path to rapid completion, however, because the work schedule tends to be erratic. Stay in close communication with the tradesmen if you try this.

66. Hire Tradesmen by the Hour

You could pay your tradesmen by the job, or by the hour. In the first case, the sub offers a bid price for the project, and takes the risk of making a profit at that price. In the second, you take the risk that the job will be finished at or below a prevailing bid price for the work.

If you attempt this, you need to know the trade, and need to supervise, or have high trust of the workers. Some readers have paid about a third the bid rate that way. O-B's Kathi and Joe Donato said: "By being there we got away with using some $8 per hour labor, and still got the quality we wanted."

67. Hire the Apprentice at a Lower Rate

John Norton had a busy plumber who wouldn't come out in a timely way. John arranged to have the plumber's apprentice handle the work with occasional check-ups by the journeyman. He paid him at about half the usual rate for the work. Again, check up closely.

One O-B told me he found a plumber's apprentice in the classified ads who did a very satisfactory job on his house, working on nights and weekends. The man was paid a very low hourly rate and said he did it for the experience.

68. Hire So-Called "Illegals"

Immigration lawyer Austin Johnson called to tell us about immigrant tradesmen who are in the process of naturalization or whose legal status has been challenged and who can work legally while their case is pending. There are many skilled ones in need of work. Call a lawyer in the field and ask if he or she has such clients you could use. Check references as usual.

One reader: "...had a painter who was too busy, so he sent us two guys, possibly illegals, who agreed to the work, and a maximum number of hours at $8 an hour. Total job was $1,200 for labor, with us buying the paint, while bids to paint ran about $10,000 for the same job."

69. Use a Designer Rather than an Architect

The usual system of architect fees involves paying a percentage, (up to 10%) of overall project cost to the architect. This creates a conflict of interest, in my view, because if the architect makes choices that increase the budget, the fee also increases. It certainly demotivates the architect to save you money. Many residential designers are in fact degreed architects, and you can get fine creativity from residential designers, degree or not. Check designer portfolios to find the artistry you want when choosing a designer.

We have a beautiful house design, and our total fees to the designer were well under 1% of the job. In addition, we had complete freedom in choice of materials and methods and built quality for far less than if an architect had directed the process. Perhaps 50% less.

70. Try a Buying Group

O-B Chris Clark has a membership in something called the Triad Group that beat the appliance prices he found elsewhere by hundreds of dollars. Check for buying privileges offered at your work or by a membership discount retailer. As always, get multiple bids for your items.

It might also be possible to form an informal buying club with other owner-builders with whom you network. (See Owner-Builder Connections on our web site to find other O-B's in your area.) By buying quantity of almost anything from lumber to appliances you may get a bigger discount on a competitive price, or earn referral fees on say, financing, that you can share with your collaborators.

71. Use Built-ins

Consider built-ins for various fixtures or items of furniture like bookshelves and dressers. They appreciate with the rest of your house, and you can take a tax deduction for the payments you make and then be reimbursed for the whole amount plus interest when you sell. You can eliminate dressers and make bedrooms comfortably smaller as a result.

72. Cabinet Creativity

Since cabinets are costly and don't hold much, use a simple walk-in pantry and fewer cabinets to store much more. The same can be done to reduce bathroom cabinetry, by building in a bathroom supply center and reducing vanities and countertops in favor of simple pedestal sinks.

You may be able to obtain the cabinets you need inexpensively by buying floor models and returns from a custom cabinet vendor. Many owner-builders like Coy and Stephanie Bowman have recycled cabinetry removed from a house being remodeled, at no cost. They refurbished the items and improved them with better knobs, hinges, drawer glides, and finishes. You could get creative and send a mailing to cabinet shops asking if can have their discontinued models, or to remodeling contractors asking for salvage cabinets and other materials.

Dennis Stoutsenberger told me he has: "…a friend who is the local sales rep for Three Day Kitchens and Baths. They have access to various cabinetry they have pulled out of remodel houses. Might also have appliances."

If you make a find on free or inexpensive cabinetry, knowing your configuration, you could plan your kitchen, bath, laundry or entertainment center around your find.

73. Save the Shade Trees

It would be very desirable to find a place to build where there are big shade trees because they have a wonderful capacity to reduce cooling and heating costs. According to residential energy auditor Dan Schuring, you can eliminate air conditioning in many homes with just a few shade trees.

74. Buy Contractor Returns

We have a Builder's Bargains outlet near us that features construction materials "up to 1/2 off." Habitat for Humanity has stores in Tucson, Austin, Charlotte, and other cities that recycle construction materials for sale, including donated contractor returns and store overstocks.

Reader Arvind Nerurkar has found three stores in the Seattle area that feature contractor returns and large rejected orders from major construction projects. He says: "The Ugly Duck and Windsor Plywood have tons of oak doors for $30, maybe $25. They have trim by the mile, overorders by a hotel in Las Vegas for marble, 50 cents a foot. Tormino's is another one; they have deck glass with beveled edges for railings, seven-foot long panels for $25. They're in the newspaper every week."

75. Build Energy Smart

Orientation, insulation, and mass are the three things Melissa Dunning of Denver Colorado says bring her low heating bills. Her mother, the general contractor on Melissa's house, says: "It shouldn't take more than a good argument to heat a home." She was featured on Dream Building on HGTV. She says her heating bills are only $10-$15 a month in winter. She uses insulated curtains over the windows that she puts down after the sun goes down in winter and when it comes up in summer, completely covering the windows.

76. Upgrade for Energy-Savings

Once you begin to upgrade features and systems in your house for energy savings you begin to get a payoff as valuable as the reduction to your house payment that owner-building provides. Take a simple thing like compact fluorescent lights:

We bought the latest compact fluorescents, standard bulb shaped, for only $4 each at the local membership discount store (Costco). They match up to a 60-watt bulb, providing 760 lumens, but only use 13 watts. Over the life (8,000 hours) of the bulb it saves $45 (at 12 cents per KWH). If you factor in the inevitable rise in electricity costs, that might be $60. If you add in the typical cost of regular bulb replacement during the period, you have $8 more. Minus the cost of the compact, you have a $64 savings. And we have about 75 bulbs in the house, so this could be a $4,800 value in eight years for us.

If you install compact fluorescents, you need more can lights than if you use powerful standard recessed lights. Allowing for the additional cans you'd put in, (maybe 25 more at $15 = $375) you have $4,425 saved in eight years. 30/8 = 3.75*$4,425 or $16,594 in thirty years. This assumes you use the lights three hours a day.

One fridge/freezer could cost $10 more a month in energy use than another that costs only $200 more. And you may have it for 15 years or 180 months, an $1,800 difference. Get rid of that old freezer in your garage, it gobbles up juice and costs a fortune over time.

Owner-builder Ted Magleby is planning an active solar house similar to that of his neighbor, Eric Tuft, which saves Eric at least $100 a month in energy costs. That equals with energy cost increases, $1,200 a year, but maybe $15,000 for the decade. Then with cost increases and inflation, maybe $23,000 for the next decade. Then maybe $35,000 for the third decade. Thus, $73,000 for 30 years. Mostly by forethought with some outlay for special features and equipment.

The same kind of economics applies to 12 Seer air conditioning compressors and energy saving versions of appliances like fridge, freezer, and dishwasher. Everything from whole house fan, house orientation, extra insulation, water-saving toilets, house wrap, awnings or overhangs against the sun, or trees for shade or windbreak, and windows facing south or west against the cold.

Look at the money you spend on energy. That constitutes a river of funds that could be altered to pay you for your forethought. In my case, I spend $140 a month on electricity and gas, or $1,700 a year, or with cost increases, $25,000 per ten years. Suppose I could save a part of that amount through planning. Maybe I could save half, or $12,500 in ten years, and with energy cost increases $100,000 of today's dollars in fifty years. We talk about saving $100,000 or more in the construction of your custom home; here's $100,000 just in the operation of the home, and that could be true of even a modest home.

77. Make A Solar Home

Sun tempering (without adding mass to the house) can save up to 30% on heating bills with no increase in construction costs. Adding more mass and glass can save even more. Planning for solar is one of the most cost-effective things you can do to a house, but it must be done in the planning stage to realize its full potential. (We have an updated web link with more information on our web site.)

78. Build Twice

Thirty years ago the Boston Consulting Group found that with every doubling of manufacturing experience, production costs dropped 15%. So a roll of film that cost $1 to manufacture for the first million rolls costs only $.85 after the second million produced. Same with a can of soup or a hammer or any manufactured product. I think a house that you "manufacture" would fall under the same rule.

If you were to build the same house twice, you costs would fall 15%. If you built four times, your costs (adjusted for inflation) would drop 30%. Kathy and Derek Eitreim illustrate: "We went through it once on our own, using a supervisor, and sold that as a spec, and we have three or four more to go. Now we can build the same home more than once, and there is so much less brain damage the second and third time that way. I can see how much tile to order, how to adjust an arch, etc. Each time we build we change the exterior skin so it looks different. We build in the same neighborhood and save commute time, too."

79. Use Student Labor

Owner-builder Vince Miner found all of his tradesmen among his students at the local community college. Many tradespeople are seeking education to further their careers. Their trade skills are on hold while they go to school, though they could perhaps use some extra income. Check the student newspaper for work wanted or register your need with a college employment office.

Even some high school students are sufficiently skilled to perform a trade on their own or with some helpful supervision. Two high schools in our area build entire houses with students each year and sell them for a profit. Some owner-builders have told me that they used a high school student to design their homes with a design teacher looking over their shoulder.

80. Hire a Design Teacher

O-B Gerry Ronga says: "For our house we found a design teacher who does the drawings for 65 cents a foot. Found her by talking to builders about who they use. We called her up, had a cup of coffee, and arranged a schedule of payments. We arranged to take the preliminary drawings to the respective tradesmen; to be sure they are complete enough before we close the book on the drawings. She agreed. It was all AutoCAD. The architects were a minimum of $2.50 a foot for the same service. The back and forth iterations are what particularly helped."

81. Clever Floor Coverings

Very nice carpet in remnant sizes is available from dealers at a reduced price. Not enough to do a whole house, but a bargain for a single bedroom. If you used tile or wood flooring for hallways and entries, where traffic is higher, and remnants for individual rooms, you could save on initial cost and have a longer life flooring combination.

One of our friends had new carpet that was installed three times and ripped out twice. The grain and seams weren't matched to her satisfaction, and she insisted it be redone, twice. A mountain of carpet was taken back to the warehouse. Ask your dealer about special prices on customer returns.

82. Buy in Lots and Divide

Many items are priced sharply lower in quantity. Buying large quantities many permit you to deal with a big distributor or direct with a factory. Suppose you buy an item in quantity, then break it down and resell at a discount to others. Maybe caulk is $1.39 a tube. You buy a palette load for $.50 a tube and sell the remainders to others at $.79. One friend buys items by the case from one web site, and then sells them individually on eBay.com for a profit.

You could buy and split up a big load of, say, lumber to three or more people. In other words, buy with friends. You could advertise for the friends. Or you could buy for yourself and divide later by advertising the items in the newspaper or on the Internet.

83. Do the Same Thing with Land

Many owner-builders have saved on land by investing in a large parcel and dividing it into smaller building lots for sale to others. Naturally this requires a big investment, but you could reduce risk by advertising for a partner who like you is looking for land and dividing the cost up front.

Or you could just buy two lots when you find your land and build on one while allowing the other to appreciate for a future profit. Some owner-builders have bought an existing home on a good-sized piece of land and built on the open portion of land, while living in the home. Later they deeded off the existing house with a smaller yard and sold it to someone else.

Be sure before you invest that local zoning ordinances allow you to subdivide and sell smaller pieces than you initially buy.

84. Take the EPA Exam

One of the hardest places for a civilian owner-builder to do business is the local mechanical distributor where air conditioning and furnace parts are sold to tradesmen. But it's possible. The difficulty is that air conditioning systems contain refrigerants with the potential to damage the ozone layer above the earth and hurt our environment.

You can break the code by taking the test that the U.S. Environmental Protection Agency administers to certify those who service or dispose of refrigerant. Once certified, you can do business with these HVAC supply houses and buy furnaces, boilers, and air conditioning units directly as the mechanical subcontractors do. Yes, a normal person can take this test, and two owner-builders have called me to say they did so.

The test is called the E.P.A. Section 608 Certification Exam. It is administered by thousand of mechanical distributors, community colleges, trade schools and government centers. One large testing service called the ESCO Institute offers a training manual and testing through its 6,000 registered proctors nationwide. The proctors are usually mechanical supply houses where you can sit and take the test for a fee on paper or on-line at their computer to get immediate feedback as to the outcome. (Updated link on our web site.)

I was able to pick up the $12.95 manual at a nearby ESCO proctor for free by agreeing to take the test for $60. I actually got "bidders" on this, too, as another place wanted $75 to test me. The friendliest place for training and testing I found was the local community college. They had a mechanical trades department with a very knowledgeable director. He gave me a 25-page study guide and 100-question practice test at no charge and said he could answer my questions and administer the test at my convenience for $60. Unlike the mechanical distributors, he didn't ask what business I was in.

The first question on the practice test is "Which refrigerants contain the most chlorine?"

> A. HCFC's
> B. HFC's
> C. CFC's
> D. Ammonia

The answer is C. CFC's. (Chlorofluorocarbons) One O-B said: "It's about as hard to pass as the written test for your driver's license." It could be well worth it, because as Kevin Clausen found out, you may be able to get your furnace and air conditioning units for 75% off list price.

85. Use Your Frequent Flyer Card

You might spend $50,000 or $100,000 on your project that could go on a credit card. Not just material suppliers but some subs will accept cards. They get your business with the benefit of immediate payment, and you have 30 days to pay. If you use your card just after the end of a monthly cycle you may have up to 55 days to pay.

You can find bargains on both sides of the equation. Some cards have smaller annual fees than others, or no fee for the first year. Some give a free flight much sooner than others. On the payment end, you may deal with some vendors who give you 10-day terms where you get a discount of 2% if you pay in ten days, and still accept your card. Many more allow you to wait 30 or 45 days before paying and accept the card as payment.

Many owner-builders have used the free flights to get further benefit. (You may get five or ten round trip tickets during the project.) Clinton Brown from Alaska told me: "I can buy a plane ticket for a good tradesman, like my brother, an electrician from Kansas, and save a lot of money. I have a retired framer from Arkansas I'm going to use."

86. On-Site Container

Many owner-builders have indicated the need for on-site storage to protect tools and materials during construction or to store material bargains acquired beforehand. One O-B found out that stolen lumber was not covered by the course of construction insurance he carried on his project. To be covered it had to be under lock and key.

Jeff Robertson solved the storage problem in two steps: "I rented some space from a neighbor to my property for very little money that allows us to keep some of our bargains in storage until I need them. Then, I will get an old tractor-trailer for $1,000 and up. There are always trailers that people have that are not in use, maybe you could rent one, and build up the sides to hold stuff. I will find a friend with a CDL license and pay him a hundred bucks to haul it up there to my site. They are 9 feet wide by 40 feet plus, and 8 feet plus tall. Much cheaper than to build an outbuilding that I would have to pay taxes on. When I'm done with the trailer, I can sell it for a small loss. Put lights and receptacles on the side, and put a table saw in there. CNP (the power company) wanted there to be a structure before they put power in, but I put in a pedestal, very elaborate, and they had to run power to it. I put underground telephone to the house, and pulled a lot of extra back to the trailer for phone service."

Dick Kauffman told me the same thing about a shipping container: "Many companies have these sitting around, and will rent or sell it to you. You can rent a 20 footer for $75 a month or a 40 footer for $125. Just rent for part of the time until your garage is lockable. Or you can buy a 20-footer for $1,300 or a 40-footer for $1,700. You could put a desk and telephone wire in there, too. Use, and sell at the end. Just look in the Yellow Pages under storage."

87. Manage the Impact Fees

Shelter editor Rodger Hardy of the Deseret News told me that we have Proposition 13 to thank for the impact fees all of our municipalities are charging on new construction. California started it as a way to recover from their reduced property taxes, and now our state and many others are imitating it without reducing property taxes.

The fees are a very substantial taxation without representation levied on you, the newcomer to a community. Currently a survey of communities in my state puts the average impact fee at $10,000 for a typical new home. There is a substantial variation between communities as John and Jessica Norton learned when they owner-built. They called all the towns in their target area and chose the lowest one.

Some communities will exempt you from paying an impact fee if you already own a home in town and thus pay taxes. Call city managers or planning departments to find out.

88. Door Smarts

There are half-price door vendors who buy damaged metal or wood doors from manufacturers and repair them as one would a boat or automobile after a wreck. This benefits the door manufacturers, reducing waste, and they should inform you of local shops that recycle the doors, if you ask.

Used doors also interest me because older doors in schools, hospitals and government buildings tended to be solid wood doors that are very pricey today. I intend to use solid-core doors in my next home because they shut off noise far better than hollow-core. Thus a good market in salvaged doors exists. One architect in California told me that she recycled a front entry door for a client that was worth "easily $1,000" which she bought salvaged for $50. Owner-Builder Ron Horne bought very simple solid doors at a savings from a door shop and had his carpenter add moldings to the door face to emulate an expensive door look.

89. Order Over the Border

Many readers living in border states have bought lumber from Canada, and tile from Mexico. Dale Booth lives in Tucson, Arizona: "My uncle goes over the border into Mexico from Arizona, and gets ceramic tiles for $.50 apiece. They were $2.25 each in the U.S. Medication is also only one third the cost there. You can bring in the first $400 free per person."

Peter and Doreen Minkwitz from California said: "We looked at kitchen gear in Vancouver, Canada; high end stoves and dishwashers, and the prices were lower than Kenmore." Clinton Brown from

Alaska said: "And there's not much competition here. Example is Viking appliances; we got them priced for our kitchen at $12,200. On the Internet I found a guy in Canada, in White Horse, a days drive, no duty because made in the U.S., and we can save $3,500 by a day's drive. The trip will cost $500 so there's $3,000 saved on our kitchen before we start."

90. Read the Classifieds

We've seen very interesting classified in our daily paper ranging from maple flooring at $1.75 a foot to free kitchen cabinets from a remodel job. Sometimes a distributor of a given construction material may sell off accumulated samples through a classified ad. One reader found solid maple stair rail balusters valued at $12 each for $2 apiece this way. Check "Appliances", "Building Materials", "Construction", "Equipment, "Services", "Subcontractors", "Tools", and any others that interest you.

Save the classified ads that cover your areas of interest for a year before you build to give you a database of values available. You only need to save one day a week; Sunday is the biggest. After a while of looking you will have a sense for the going price for things. We did this before we bought a piece of land for our house: we went to the local newspaper office where we wanted to build and checked land prices for the past six months in the archives. Then we bought with confidence as to local prices.

The local library has newspapers for cities all around your own, and you can make buys in the region through researching them. The Internet has web sites for every newspaper on the planet, it seems, and they all feature searchable classified sections. They tend not to give you more of a database than a few days or a week past, however.

Another useful format for classified ad buying is a classified ad paper. We have a Thrifty Nickel paper here that is all ads. They have franchises in dozens of states, and competitors everywhere. These are weekly free papers available at convenience stores, bus stops, restaurants, and other public places. These inexpensive advertising mediums tend to have more construction-oriented offerings than the dailies. These are a good vehicle for placing your own ads for materials or services that you are seeking, or surplus you'd like to sell to others.

91. Appliance Bargains

There is a movement in custom homes to restaurant grade kitchen appliances that can be fabulously expensive, up to $10,000 for a kitchen range. Some owner-builders have beaten the cost by shopping restaurant liquidators and scratch and dent sections of appliance dealers. One told me: "You can find used restaurant stoves, built-in fridges. Restaurant supply houses have the used stuff because of guys going out of business. You could buy 60" wide Sub Zero double door fridge for $1,100."

Dennis Stoutsenberger got all the floor models from the local appliance company for next to nothing when they brought in their new models. He sold them to friends. Matt Clifton found high-end appliances at open box buy prices: "Call appliance companies periodically asking for open box buys. We saved $6,500 on high-end appliances that way." Once you have identified the distributors for certain products like the Viking ranges, get on their list for open box, floor models, and scratch and dent availability.

Another U.S. owner-builder found favorable prices shopping over the border in Canada. If retail prices are better there, due to currency translation, perhaps restaurant supply houses, scratch and dent sales, open box buys, and restaurant equipment auctions would yield even better savings.

92. Buy In a Construction-Depressed Community

Dan Meserve found great lumber bargains in a town less than 100 miles away where there had been a major plant closing. Due to unemployment, the bottom fell out of the building materials market there. To get his business, they provided delivery at no charge. He also found window bargains that way: "We priced windows in a glass shop in a town with a dead market - Rawlings, Wyoming. Bought Amsco. They hauled them up for us in the middle of winter. Paid $3,200 for 22 windows. Had bids from $3,200 to $4,800. In most cases, we had a bid range of from X to 2X on many items."

93. Rough-cut Lumber

Phil Smith says: "Could rough-cut be used for framing your home? Rough lumber can be bought at a third of the cost of traditional lumber. I have personally used this lumber for walls and partitions, simply because it costs less and is never seen when sheetrock or other coverings are put over it and it's just as good as traditional methods. Rough-cut lumber, planed to your specs, generally beats big name outfit costs, and behind sheetrocked walls who cares as long as it's straight and dry?"

Ask your lumberyard if rough-cut is available. Bid it like the rest of your lumber package to find if a range of pricing exists on the item.

94. Culled Lumber

There is a bargain rack in the lumber section of all the home center stores where you can get slightly damaged or bowed lumber at a 50% savings or so.

95. Buy Lumber from a Mill

If you succeed in sourcing your lumber direct from a lumber mill, you've eliminated one or more middlemen who increase costs. To pursue this strategy you may need to combine with another owner-builder to increase quantity.

Sometimes lumber prices are very favorable for U.S. buyers in Canada, depending on currency fluctuations and import duties imposed on the category by Congress. I interviewed a U.S. Customs officer who owner-built near the Canadian border. He sourced his lumber from Canadian mills and did a triple play in the process: favorable exchange rate, favorable lumber pricing in Canada, and sourced from a mill instead of a lumberyard.

96. Hot Loads of Concrete

You can call and get on a list for "hot loads" of concrete from a cement plant. These are partial loads that are left over in cement trucks after delivery, or were rejected by builders, etc. It saves money, but you have to be ready, with your forms in place and waiting.

97. Enjoy the Tax Break

Elaine and I are amazed that the 1997 U.S. tax law governing the sale of houses is still in place. How often does the government give us a huge freebie like this? You can sell your principal residence and pay no capital gains tax on the first $500,000 in capital gains for a married couple. And you can get the waiver as many times as you like. You only need to live in the house any two out of the preceding five years. Much more detail is in our Special Report on the Tax Law.

Instead of paying $100,000 in tax on a gain of half a million dollars, as we were once required to do, you can now keep a house for a long time and sell with tax impunity, even if you don't build a similar house to replace the one you sold.

98. Plan Taxable Events

The tax waiver mentioned above is for the gain on a principal residence. It does not cover raw land. We discovered this when we bought our second parcel of land before building the Riverbottoms house. We were trying to decide on which of the two places to build when we learned that if we sold one of them without building on it, we would be taxed on the gain in the value. The tax would be over $5,000. We decided to build in the Riverbottoms and hold the other parcel for future building, to get the waiver on both pieces.

Some owner-builders have built on speculation, and resold a house quickly. If you do this without living in the house first you must pay tax on the gain on the property. If you spend $200,0000 on a project and sell it for $300,000 you must pay capital gains tax on $100,000 – a tax of around $20,000. For a developer with many projects, or housing units, this is a normal cost of doing business. For an owner-builder, the option to live in the house and save the taxes may be feasible.

O-B Bill Stevens told me his plans: "Built home two years ago for $237,000 including land, will sell for $345,000. We own several lots nearby, several near a lake with cost of $75,000 per lot and then lots in one of the largest developments in the U.S. We are in a building boom here with appreciation near 20%. Want to build every two years and take advantage of the capital gains tax breaks."

Another way to avoid taxes on raw land at sale is to do a tax-free exchange for a different piece of property. You can save $10,000 in taxes on a $50,000 piece of land. Kayla Lamoreaux told me: "We have a historic house, paid $218,000 and it is worth over $300,000 now after we have remodeled it. If we sell it earlier than two years as our primary residence, we can do a 1034 tax-free exchange, and pay no capital gains."

99. Tax Deductions

If you have or can start a home-based business you may be able to deduct some of the items you build into your home office. The percentage of your home used for business can be depreciated on your U.S. income taxes. A creative O-B might be able to get a bigger, faster deduction by making a Section 179 election to write off some items pertaining to the home office in one year. Lighting and wiring, carpeting, paint and finishes, woodwork, cabinetry, and other built-ins might be eligible.

Some owner-builders can write off some or all of tools, mobile phone, computer, and other assets involved in construction that can be used and claimed by their own businesses.

If you have leftover materials at completion, consider donating to charity. This can apply to excess materials that you have been ingenious in procuring. You may buy or trade for a thing at a bargain price, and it give to charity at the market price later and claim a tax deduction if you itemize your deductions. Like expenditures on energy, your future taxes are a river of expense you can tap for savings.

More than 100 additional Construction Bargain Strategies are available on our web site, part of a growing database to which many readers have contributed.

100. Tax Credits

Check and see if your state or province gives an income tax credit for a "clean fuel alternative appliance" like a natural gas fireplace or a solar energy collector, wind power device, special insulation or other energy-saving feature. We got a $50 credit from our state for a fireplace when we built the Riverbottoms house.

The U.S. government has an "Energy Star" program offering builders and owner-builders incentives for building to a high standard of energy conservation. A government-approved energy consultant must verify the airtightness and energy features of the home. (See our web site for updated link to government site.) If you build to EPA standards, you may get an upfront state or federal tax credit, or possibly mortgage discounts, or special utility rates, or all three. The EPA can issue you an Energy Star rating which will help to attract a buyer when you sell, as well.

Chapter 10: How to Schedule the Work at a Savings

Time line: Two months before groundbreaking

Another Miracle Tool

Sources Say

"The people you pick to build your house will determine the quality of your home and the cost of that house. Finding the right person at the right price is essential."

From *Everything You Need To Know About Building the Custom Home*
(See page 259)

Like a written budget, a written schedule has a magical effect on your outcome. If you have a deadline, in writing, with written steps that lead up to it, you have a very good chance of coming in on schedule.

Your schedule would be like a calendar with a start date and an end date. The steps for building your house would be indicated along with their durations and sequence.

You need the help of a written schedule because the upcoming construction phase of your project has a way of getting out of hand. One industry expert calls this phase, "Mr. Toad's Wild Ride". The construction phase tends to follow Murphy's Law: "If anything can go wrong, it will. And at the worst possible moment." A written schedule gives you a proven control device on the process.

Only 22% of the owner-builders I interviewed had a written schedule. This is one of the reasons they slipped an average of two months from their original completion dates. I want you to have a written schedule and to take advantage of your planning to make it an exceptionally good one.

The National Association of Home Builders says that the average contractor-built house in the U.S. takes six months to complete. The same group says that owner-builders take an average of 9.5 months to complete. It's hard to know how the NAHB obtains good statistics on owner-builders. My findings are that owner-builders typically get done faster than 9.5 months. One possible explanation for the 9.5 month figure is the "hobby" group of O-B's who poke along at a project, work off personal funds, and do most of the construction themselves.

This group can and will take two or three years to complete a house. I know of examples that took ten years to complete. If these numbers are averaged in, the 9.5 month owner-builder average may be valid.

But your goal should be to finish in six months, the widely accepted middle of the road goal for home building. Through good planning, this goal is more than possible. What slows down a project is indecision on the part of the owner, tardiness on the part of subs, and occasionally, bad weather.

By being organized, you will not be indecisive. By virtue of your planning you will be exceptionally prepared to run a smooth project and bring materials and workers together smoothly. This is the management function of Integration. Remember POIMM in Chapter 4? By planning and organizing thoroughly, you are ready to integrate smoothly. During construction you will practice measuring and motivating.

Try to get the weather on your side by starting the project in a favorable season of the year. Most owner-builders I talked to favored the spring. In our region, I favor the fall. My reason is economy. There is less construction work available in the winter, and more competition for the work, hence lower prices. But in our area you need to start in the early fall to be closed in before harsh weather hits.

Picking the Right People is Half the Battle

I had always thought that picking subs was a price issue. After building a house, I see that what other owner-builders tell me is true. It's just as much an issue of character and fit. The character part is that the sub you choose does what he says he'll do. The fit aspect is that you can work well with this sub, and he can work well with others on your team.

Remember that the first qualification of a successful owner-builder is that the O-B can come to work each day prepared to fire his help. Prevent the need for firing people by making your expectations clear to the sub and seeing that they are met. You will be able to work with some subs more easily than with others. You alone can assess the chemistry, communications, or "fit" you have with the candidate subs.

The process of assessing fit is to: 1) Interview subs in the early stages of planning. Get a feel for the communication you have with each. Ask each who they like to work with in the related trades, and if there is anyone they are unwilling to work with. 2) Seek bids from candidate subs on your detailed specifications. Evaluate their responses to the bidding process. Negotiate with preferred subs after receiving bids. Determine the ease of communication with the sub and the level of understanding of your needs. 3) Check references.

Checking references is a lost art. Consumer Reports found in an actual study that only one percent of the public checked references when making a buying decision. Here's how you do it:

1. Do it.

2. Ask the sub for references of past customers in the bidding process. Call the references. Ask:

   • Did the sub show up and finish on time?
   • Did he do what he promised?
   • Did he do quality work?
   • Were there any surprises?

   Then ask if they know of other past customers. This is important because the sub will have the normal human tendency to refer you to those who like him a lot. Possibly the aunt or cousin he did some work for. You don't want to hear "good things", you want to find out how he will fit with you and your team.

3. Check the other past customers.

4. Look at projects physically that the sub has completed.

5. Call the contractors' licensing division of your state or province to see if there are recorded complaints against your candidates. Check the Better Business Bureau also for complaints. Usually there are some. You just want to avoid someone with an undue proportion of complaints, or unresolved complaints.

Computer Scheduling

Your first step is to use the schedules provided by the generals who estimated your project. These are valuable to you because they reflect the actual construction steps deemed necessary to build your plans. I told the generals who bid my project that I wanted a written schedule with a six month deadline. They responded with very helpful information about the sequence and duration of each trade involved.

From the sample schedules and my interviews, I developed a calendar for construction on the computer. I used a calendar creator program that laid out the tasks on the pages of a calendar. Better still would be a project management program. You can use such a program, or a spreadsheet, or even a word processor program. The important elements are:

- Is dynamically updatable;
- Includes the right tasks;
- Is in about the right sequence (many jobs can and will overlap);
- Shows correct durations for tasks;
- Provides some margin for error between steps.

The schedule on page 164 was constructed using the rows and columns format of a computer spreadsheet. Once you line up your construction steps on the left, and the weeks across the top, you have a very useable format for your schedule. If you pencil in the durations of each task by shading or drawing X's, or type them into your computer version, you will have a clear picture of your schedule. The sample schedule on page 164 provides average durations of typical steps as a comparison for you. Use the durations that bidders provide you to make your calendar accurate.

Live in Your Schedule for a While

Lay out your own schedule carefully. Piece together the tasks, durations, and lead times that have come from your bidders, from your telephone interviews and from the general contractors who estimated your plans. The durations that bidders provide you are particularly important. They are committing to you that their work will be done in four days, or two weeks, or whatever. Enter these commitments accurately on your schedule.

Now walk through the schedule mentally. You will be the genius that will manage this well-planned construction project. This particular bit of planning will make a big difference to your success. As you think through each step with a pencil, telephone, copies of bids you have received, your construction calendar and your own day planner at hand, some important items will pop out for you. For instance, when you see that framing will start in the second or third week, you ask yourself — when do I need to order the framing lumber?

You pick up the phone and call your lumberyard and ask how much lead time they need. Or, you call one of your framing bidders and ask how this is done. You discover that with your lumber estimate on file with the lumberyard, you can call two days before. You make a note right on the framing lumber line of your calendar, or in your day planner.

So far so good. You remember that roof trusses are a part of your framing. You call one of the truss suppliers who bid your plans and ask what the lead times are. You are told that it normally takes a month, but they are backed up and it might be six weeks. Congratulations! You have just dodged a bullet. Because you are still in the planning stage, you will be able to place the order before you get in a bind.

You look on the bid documents for doors or windows and see that your preferred supplier has noted that you need to place the order three weeks before delivery. Or, you notice the information is missing and you call. You find that three weeks are needed, but to be safe they suggest six weeks. Once again, you found out soon enough to protect your future schedule.

Many first-time owner-builders, and even some veterans have found themselves waiting for a crucial delivery while their unfinished project just sat. I know of a two month stoppage caused by delays and misunderstandings on a truss order. Professional builders occasionally slip up as well, especially when dealing with an unfamiliar supplier.

I found that I could sometimes move heaven and earth to get an overlooked item delivered fast, but I wound up feeling that I paid too much or got a less than perfect choice because I didn't have time to shop. The scheduling phase is the time for you to avoid these disappointments.

Once you have thought through your schedule, submit yourself to the discipline of having others review it. Many possible reviewers are available to you. I suggest you think about the subs and suppliers who have just bid your project. You have probably turned up some bright minds and helpful people in the process of bidding. These people in the industry can tell in a flash if you are on the right track.

Fax or e-mail a copy of your work to your reviewers. Or you can phone and carry the documents to your people and talk the schedule through with them. There is strength in multiple opinions. This is a good time to talk to people because you haven't yet broken ground, and as they say, "nothing is set in concrete" yet. You may get new suggestions to save time or money, improve your design, or run a smoother project.

Sample Construction Work Schedule

Task	Duration	1	2	3	4	5	6	7	8	
Site work and excavation	3 days	▬								
Temporary utilities	1 day	▪								
Foundation preparation	1 day		▪							
Underground plumbing	3 days		▬							
Foundation Inspection			✓							
Foundation erection	5 days		▬	▬						
Slab, basement and garage	2 days			▬						
Rough framing	2 weeks				▬	▬				
Windows and exterior doors	2 days						▪			
Rough plumbing	7 days						▬	▬		
Decking and sheathing	5 days						▬			
Rough electrical	7 days							▬	▬	
Cornice trim	2 days							▪		
Roofing	4 days							▬	▬	
Exterior paint	5 days								▬	
Rough HVAC	7 days									▬
Four-way Inspection										✓
Insulation and Inspection	3 days									▬
Brick work or siding	2 weeks									
Hrdwd. floor & underlayment	4 days									
Interior wall finishing	12 days									
Interior trim and doors	1 week									
Cabinetry	3 days									
Interior paint	13 days									
Countertops	2 days									
Vinyl and tile floors	3 days									
Exterior flatwork	2 days									
Plumbing trim	1 week									
Heating trim	1 week									
Electrical trim	1 week									
Appliances	1 day									
Carpeting	4 days									
Clean-up	3 days									
Landscaping	4 days									
Final Inspection										

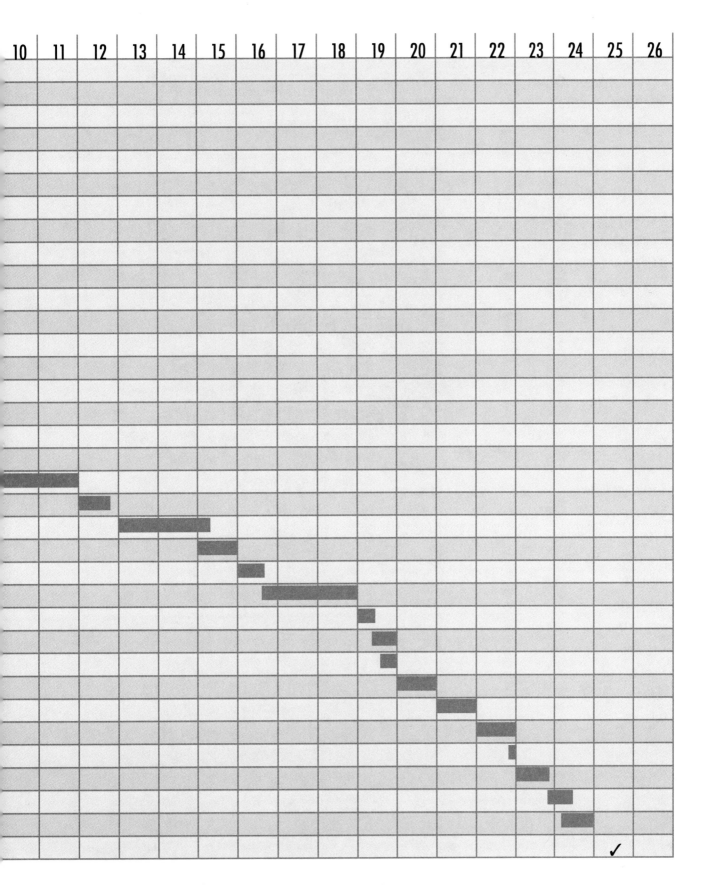

Schedule Worksheet

Weeks from Start:		1	2	3	4	5	6	7	8	9
Site work and excavation	3 days									
Temporary utilities	1 day									
Foundation preparation	1 day									
Underground plumbing	3 days									
Foundation Inspection										
Foundation erection	5 days									
Slab, basement and garage	2 days									
Rough framing	2 weeks									
Windows and exterior doors	2 days									
Rough plumbing	7 days									
Decking and sheathing	5 days									
Rough electrical	7 days									
Cornice trim	2 days									
Roofing	4 days									
Exterior paint	5 days									
Rough HVAC	7 days									
Four-way Inspection										
Insulation and Inspection	3 days									
Brick work or siding	2 weeks									
Hrdwd. floor & underlayment	4 days									
Interior wall finishing	12 days									
Interior trim and doors	1 week									
Cabinetry	3 days									
Interior paint	13 days									
Countertops	2 days									
Vinyl and tile floors	3 days									
Exterior flatwork	2 days									
Plumbing trim	1 week									
Heating trim	1 week									
Electrical trim	1 week									
Appliances	1 day									
Carpeting	4 days									
Clean-up	3 days									
Landscaping	4 days									
Final Inspection										

10	11	12	13	14	15	16	17	18	19	20	21	22	23	24	25	26

Schedule Worksheet

Weeks from Start:		1	2	3	4	5	6	7	8	9
Site work and excavation	3 days									
Temporary utilities	1 day									
Foundation preparation	1 day									
Underground plumbing	3 days									
Foundation Inspection										
Foundation erection	5 days									
Slab, basement and garage	2 days									
Rough framing	2 weeks									
Windows and exterior doors	2 days									
Rough plumbing	7 days									
Decking and sheathing	5 days									
Rough electrical	7 days									
Cornice trim	2 days									
Roofing	4 days									
Exterior paint	5 days									
Rough HVAC	7 days									
Four-way Inspection										
Insulation and Inspection	3 days									
Brick work or siding	2 weeks									
Hrdwd. floor & underlayment	4 days									
Interior wall finishing	12 days									
Interior trim and doors	1 week									
Cabinetry	3 days									
Interior paint	13 days									
Countertops	2 days									
Vinyl and tile floors	3 days									
Exterior flatwork	2 days									
Plumbing trim	1 week									
Heating trim	1 week									
Electrical trim	1 week									
Appliances	1 day									
Carpeting	4 days									
Clean-up	3 days									
Landscaping	4 days									
Final Inspection										

10	11	12	13	14	15	16	17	18	19	20	21	22	23	24	25	26

A schedule worksheet is available on a spreadsheet on our free Resource CD-ROM.

(See page 270)

Back-up Plans to Keep the Work Going

An engineer I know says he is "a belt and suspenders kind of guy". His pants won't fall down because if the belt fails, the suspenders go to work.

Your scheduled plans will in some part go awry. That is Murphy's Law. If you anticipate that possibility, you can "go to Plan B" without a hitch. Your plan B is a back-up plan for all the things that can hurt you on your schedule. Of course, the biggest problem is subs that won't show up.

My footings contractor told me the week before construction that he had broken his back. He was convalescing, and his brother-in-law, an established footings contractor, was covering his work. I called the brother-in-law, and learned that he was scheduled out a month ahead. And he wanted about 1.5 times more money than the injured contractor had agreed to. It was a scramble to find an available sub and a decent price in time to preserve our schedule.

What do you do in a case like this? You go to plan B — if you have a plan B. You do indeed have a plan B if you have gotten multiple bids for all of the trades. Even though you select one bidder to get the work, you should leave the door open for the other subs that bid. I suggest that you write each bidder a note expressing thanks and saying that "perhaps we will do business again some day." To those bidders who were close to being chosen, send a letter or fax saying that they are your alternate or back-up choices for this work. If anything goes wrong with your first (or second) choice, you will contact them immediately and ask them to participate on your project.

To have this luxury, which almost guarantees your schedule, you must get multiple bids in the first place. Having made the effort to get several bids, you can count on back-up. Having as many as ten bids on something is a great comfort, though I erred on this when building our house. I had multiple bids in some categories, but not where people were going to "help me" or "do me a favor". For instance, the construction advisor I used agreed to help me wire the house. I trusted this man implicitly, but my judgement was off. He never came as planned to show me how to wire the house. I had not budgeted for the category, and I felt very inadequate to start without help. I thought or hoped that he would yet show up. I spent some lonely weeks at the site waiting.

Eventually Elaine and I checked out some books on wiring and read them. We then jumped in to fill the void. It took a long time and plenty of paid advice, but we ultimately did a superb job. However, our schedule was shot. I had to make many phone calls moving other subcontractors affected by the delay.

We had an unbelievably hard time getting the helpers who agreed to work with us on painting, cabinetry, deck work, and stair rail work to show up. I was disillusioned. I was new to this part of the country, where Elaine was raised. I thought a person's word was their bond. Elaine explained to me that the local culture is that "'Yes' means 'maybe', and 'maybe' means 'no'."

Readers Say

"The construction loan process ended up taking longer than I thought it should and it put us behind about 2 weeks; all that planning and scheduling put on hold. To those looking into owner building: "DON'T RUSH THINGS!" Stories of custom homes being built in 4 months may be true, but they are the exception, not the standard. Watch the critical path of the process. There are things that must be completed before another can be started. Pencil in the subs that will follow a critical step and don't confirm them until that step has been completed."

Barret R.
Charlotte, NC

The moral of the story is that you should be very sure before relying on volunteer labor. And you should have a back-up plan. I should have bid the volunteer categories just as I did the paid categories. In the paid categories I did fairly well, but I found that almost no subs were precise about their show-up times.

While you are waiting for people to do what they said they would do, the interest clock is ticking. At the end of our project the interest was running $1,000 a month, $50 a day, and $6 per working hour. You need to beat the big, bad interest monster, and back-up plans will allow you to do that in style.

Schedule Reinforcement Program

1. Communicate in writing

By following the planning steps in this book, you have had communication periodically with the subs that will do your work. Be thorough with this communication. Send thank you notes to subs that interview with you — I featuresed them a copy of the interview with my thanks. Follow up with those who bid your project, thanking them or letting them know you have received their bid. After you select your subs, thank the others who bid and let your alternates know that you have chosen them as back-ups.

2. Get written schedule commitment

When you commit to a chosen sub, extract a return commitment of start date, duration and finish date, or at least two of the three. Include the time commitments on the sub's estimate and you and the sub should both initial it.

3. Distribute schedule

When you have refined your written schedule, follow the advice found in the American Institute of Architects Project Checklist. Distribute the written schedule to each member of your team. If you have fax capability, you can do a mass faxing to the group in a very short time. Or make photocopies of your schedule and send it to the participants.

4. Call, call, call

Veteran owner-builder Jim Stark provides the next bit of advice.

"The rule is to call the subs once a month to remind them of your schedule until the month before they are due. Then call them once a week to report progress and verify that they are still on schedule to show up as planned. In the week before their start time, call every other day to confirm and verify that you will have any needed materials on hand. The night before they are to start, call and confirm that they will

---

Readers Say

"I am building 3,400 finished square feet for $291,000. The price is higher than otherwise because the contruction market is very busy here right now. I stopped trying to work over the subs for better prices because everyone is busy and you lose them. It's been more important to get the quality people who will show up. Against contractor prices, we are still saving over $100,000, though."

Chuck C.
Spokane, WA

Sources Say

"You can run the gauntlet of government percolation tests and planning boards and zoning and wetlands acts. Do this in the fall. Perc and soil tests are often the bugaboo, because in some towns they can be done only in certain seasons."

From *The Well-Built House* (See page 260)

be there in the morning. Successful general contractors follow this advice to the letter."

5. Strengthen relationship

To let the sub know that I care and have serious expectations, I made it a point to visit them at their current job site before they started my work. I did this both in the bidding process to assess their workmanship, and later to strengthen communication. If the schedule changed at the last minute, I went to a lot of effort to inform them so that they would not lose a day of work.

In one case, I went to the excavator's home the night before a planned start to inform him that the city had delayed our permit at the last minute. From our meeting when he inspected the lot and bid the job, I remembered that his five year old daughter had a birthday on his planned start date. I apologized and brought a gift for his daughter's birthday. That excavator was very reliable for us over the course of his several contributions to our project. He always informed us if he would be a few hours late, for example. These are the kinds of things you expect on both sides when you have a good relationship with team members.

6. Bonus program

Owner-builder Jay Sevison, who is a manager in a computer software company, used a further technique to strengthen his schedule. He offered $50 to each sub who started on the designated day — he physically handed them a $50 bill. Later, if the work was as hoped and finished on time, he surprised some of his subs with another cash bonus.

This, too, can work both ways. You can negotiate "liquidated damages" with subs in advance which specify that they will pay a penalty — a reduction in your invoice — for each day they miss the agreed deadline.

Chapter 11: How to Make Your Lender Swoon

Time line: Two months before groundbreaking

Your Next Thousand Hour Payoff

By this time in your preparation, you have been rewarded for diligent planning by saving money on house design, by finding good subs, and by pinning down some real construction bargains for your house. You are ready for your next payoff — smooth sailing through the loan application process.

The myth that you can't get a construction loan without a licensed general contractor is widely circulated. You can indeed get the loan, but there are many people who will tell you that you can't.

Of the lenders I surveyed, 45% made owner-builder construction loans routinely. 15% did so on a case by case basis. That's more than half who will make these loans. If your preparation is well-done, you will get a loan from any of the 60% who will consider it. You may come out so prepared that the 40% who don't do it will make an exception for you.

What the Lenders Want

The lenders want what you and I want. They want you to be prepared for a smooth and successful project. Several lenders used the same words with me in interviews: "They have to convince me they can do it."

Lenders are justifiably wary of the typical O-B candidate for a construction loan. Construction lenders find O-B's woefully unprepared on average to control a project and bring it in on budget or on schedule. The owner-builders I interviewed had averaged only 238 hours of preparation before breaking ground. The lenders know that over the course of construction these same candidates will spend much more time than that trying to make things right (average 1,068 hours on-site).

Since it's the bank's money, the lender can't help but wonder why these same candidates can't make the effort to reduce project risk before they take out the loan. Most owner-builders leave too much to chance, and lenders know it. The lender wants to see that this is a no-risk proposition. Which is exactly what you want.

Remember, when you take out a construction loan, it's not your money. The bank lets you use their money in return for your commitment to repay them (with interest). They have to be sure you will repay, and in the event you don't, they want the house you build to have plenty of equity so that they can resell it and recoup their investment.

When you meet with a lender, you should address their concerns decisively. The leading concerns are:

Risk

Prove that you have done the necessary planning to pull off a successful project. Document your financial soundness and financial qualifications. Show that you have secured the necessary insurance coverage to protect the lender from liability.

Quality

Show that your house will meet any and all quality standards, resell easily, and be a good risk for their investment.

Cost Control

Demonstrate that your house will be built for a competitive price, and that you will stay reasonably within budget.

Job Control

Convince the banker that your house will be finished well within average and reasonable time limits.

Your Loan Proposal Book

You can do all this with a loan proposal for the lender. By proposal, I mean a written book or portfolio that documents all of your answers to the lender's concerns.

You should not go in empty-handed. One lender told me that a couple came in to see him and said they were sure they could owner-build at a savings because "all builders make 30% profit." The lender asked them the penetrating question: "Have you built before?" "No." "Have you remodeled a house?" "No." "Do you maybe have relatives in the industry?" "No." "Did you perhaps have a summer job at some point in construction?" "No. But we did read a book about owner-building and we know all about it." The lender declined the loan.

You wouldn't dare tell a lender that he should make you a big construction loan because you read a book, would you? Particularly our book because you know by now how to prepare and this is your moment to show off that preparation. You might say: "I have worked for six months planning this house and I have this proposal to give you."

Your proposal should knock the lender on his or her Fanny Mae. Here's how to put it together:

Before your meeting with the lender, stop into the bank and ask the secretary or loan officer for copies of all the forms you will need to fill out for the eventual loan. Ask for a list of all the documents they will require in evaluating the loan. Ask for a copy of their Lien Release for your records. Ask what insurance coverages they require of borrowers so you can line up the coverage.

Go home and assemble the documents required. The application they provide will undoubtedly ask for your employment and banking history, and your credit references. You will need to bring in copies of your last few tax returns. These are pretty standard requirements for loans. All applicants need to supply the same financial paperwork. The difference in your case is that you will have prepared it thoroughly in advance.

To the financial paperwork you will add the construction and management documents that you have been working on for months. Some of these are also standard, but you will provide some documents that the lender has never seen before.

Make your proposal or portfolio neat and organized. If you are not skilled with paperwork, get help! There are many people who handle these types of documents for a living. Use a copy shop to reproduce original documents that you supply (like subcontractor bids), and shrink or enlarge them to a consistent size. If possible, make a notebook or have a printer do a "GBC" spindle binding of your papers and put a professional looking cover on it.

Not all lenders want the same documents. But, all the suggestions below are pertinent and demonstrate your readiness to bring your project in on time and on budget:

Your plans and specs from the designer

This is standard. Include engineering report and soil conditions report if unusual conditions exist. Include any engineering for non-standard structural design.

Land purchase contract or warranty deed of ownership

A standard requirement.

Copies of bids from subs and suppliers

Having this is rare. This sets you apart and makes the requested loan amount a realistic number.

Your room by room descriptions

This will surprise your lender.

The text of your interviews with subs and suppliers

They've never seen this before. You have become a unique applicant. They will likely say in the loan committee meeting: 'This person has put a lot of thought into this.'

Evidence of the construction insurance the bank requires

You can photocopy the one-page binder the insurance company provides to show you have coverage. If you haven't signed up yet, give the name of your chosen agent, and carrier, and the quoted cost of the policy.

Include a copy of the bank's lien release form

This is the paper that subs will sign, when they are paid, that says they have been paid and will not put a lien on the house. You are showing the banker that you understand the process.

Cost breakdown

Put in the written budget you have developed for your project. Include at least a five percent contingency in the totals. Include any work you are doing yourself at market price. That way they know you can still get the project finished if something happens to you.

Written schedule

They may have never seen one of these before from a candidate.

Qualifications Statement

Give the background on you and your spouse showing what related experiences to construction you have had, even if it's your management experience at work. Indicate how your employment situation will allow you to spend at least three hours of daytime on-site supervision.

Résumé of construction advisor or superintendent

If you or your spouse can't be on-site for three to four hours a day, include the credentials of someone you have arranged to provide this service.

Lenders Want to Put a Copy of the License in the File

Most of the lenders I interviewed said they wanted the candidate to have some construction experience. If you can't prove this experience to the banker's satisfaction, you may have to get creative.

I recently interviewed my own construction lender. He told me that his bank absolutely refused to make construction loans to owner-builders. I said, "What about me?" He answered, "You had a contractor." This amazed me. "He was an advisor — and you know he never did anything!" I said. "I know, but we needed to put a copy of his license in the file," was his response.

Evidently this satisfied the loan committee at the bank. When I was told that my qualifications were insufficient, I found a semi-retired general contractor to help. He provided a photocopy of his license for the file. The bank furnished me a perfunctory "construction agreement" which he signed, although no money changed hands. This satisfied the bank.

It is not hard to set up an arrangement like this. Half of the general contractors I interviewed said they had at some time provided a copy of their license to an owner-builder friend who needed to pass muster with the bank, at no charge. You could call around and even offer a fee for this service. Try semi-retired contractors. Meet with your candidate builder and show them your dream home notebook.

The bank's agreement with my general contractor said that he would be paid a set amount per hour for his services. My advisor agreed to $25 but said that I could help him out on his projects in trade. I never had to spend any money on the arrangement, although it turned out to be a comfort and source of good connections and information.

Sources Say

"To present your best case to the lender know your project. Never say, 'Well, I don't know.'"

From *Everything You Need To Know About Building the Custom Home*
(See page 259)

Readers Say

"Don't be concerned about getting a construction loan. I've been a banker for 20 years. Community banks like the one I work for want to loan money to anybody who will take it."

Bob O.
Santa Fe, NM

On the other hand, your bank may accept your qualifications as an owner-builder without a license for the file. You may have had experiences they will accept if written up in an official-looking way in your loan proposal. Talking with lenders, I found that the remodel I did on my house in 1983 could be acceptable experience, or the months I spent helping a friend finish his house some years ago. I never thought about it, but my consulting assignments to commercial contractors would have been applicable, and most banks would have accepted the time I spent as a vice president of a construction company. They wouldn't have to know it was *marketing* vice president.

You can acquire experience if needed. For instance, you could put in time building a Habitat for Humanity house in your area. Document your experience for your Qualifications Statement. Get a letter from the supervisor or chapter director describing your involvement. You'd be amazed what banks will accept if it's in writing.

Altogether, your loan proposal will overwhelm your construction lender. Your proposal itself is evidence of your qualifications to manage the project. By the time you have spent a thousand hours planning and have documented it for the banker, you are more than half way home — no pun intended!

Don't Budget Self-Work

Suppose you have a construction budget of $190,000 including all of the bids and bargains you've gathered, and including several things you intend to do yourself on the project. Further, say you have a borrowing limit of $200,000. You feel you need to submit the budget as is so that you will qualify for the loan.

Don't do it.

If you flesh out your budget to include bid numbers for items you will do yourself, it will be larger. For example, you may have painting in the budget at $1,000 — the cost of materials, because you intend to do it yourself. But the bid prices you received vary from $5,000 to $8,000. Include the $5,000 in the budget you submit.

This is a very important item with lenders, who all tell stories of people who intended to do some of the work on their homes but didn't. Many reasons exist for the failings, and you might get lucky and do all that you intend to do. But the banker doesn't want to take that risk.

Never before have I had surgery, but two months before I had to start our house, my orthopedic surgeon informed me that the pain I was feeling in my knee was real and it had to be operated on. I was to report in for surgery in two days. I thought maybe I would recover quickly and bounce back like an athlete does. Not this time. I was in bed for a week and got around with crutches or with great caution for several months.

Things like this happen to owner-builders all the time. Sometimes things come up at work that force a change of plans, sometimes they have health problems, sometimes they go through marital difficulties, sometimes they are simply overwhelmed, and just can't do what they thought they could. The lender wants to know if the bank could take over the project in the event of disaster, and finish it for sale without losing money.

If you have budgeted the work fully there is no disaster. The project can stand on its own feet. As long as there is enough equity to protect the lender, you will be approved.

However, you may not qualify for the loan at the larger amount. Suppose your $190,000 budget becomes $225,000 with street prices and a ten percent contingency. If you only qualify for $200,000, what to do? In our case, we didn't see anything we could do, and we presented a skinny budget to the lender and got away with it. But not for long, because although we did the work we intended, volunteer help and favors didn't come through. We went over by about $20,000.

Before we could convert the construction loan to long-term financing, we had to find a co-signer. It was an anxious time, because if we didn't find one, we would lose the house. We found a relative to sign the papers as a co-signer. We qualified and the mortgage loan closed. Later, the relative agreed to quit-claim the deed on the house, surrendering any rights of ownership.

If you confront the possibility of a shortfall in the beginning, and line up a co-signer then, you are spared the grief. Your banker wants to see that you have qualified for the larger amount. If you succeed in doing all the self-work you want, and if all your bargains materialize, you will finish the project under your borrowing limit. You can then take out your long-term mortgage without a co-signer.

⌐ Your Loan Presentation

Most of the lenders I interviewed said that the candidate had to "convince" or "sell" them on their ability to handle construction without a general contractor. You are equipped with a written loan proposal loaded with information. What else do you need to do?

One O-B told me that he got his loan without a contractor by making "the mother of all presentations" to the lender. Give some thought how to present the information you have gathered in a cohesive way. You could "go Hollywood" and make up flip charts or overhead transparencies to convey your main points of preparation and qualification. Or you could simply mark places in your proposal with sticky notes and turn to those pages and describe them to the banker.

This may be a key to commanding the lender's attention in a tight market where O-B loans are generally not made and there are few institutions to choose from.

Sources Say

Everything You Need To Know About Building the Custom Home has a good chapter on getting a loan, coauthored by an attorney.

(See page 259)

Readers Say

"We used a portfolio for the bank like you suggested with all the info, which causes us to get a higher appraisal. It will go through every room, and all the materials. This will go to the appraiser with samples. Like we have a bamboo floor, and a sample for him to touch.
Also samples of the Rastra foundation material and pictures of similar applications."

John & Cyndee M.
Bend, OR

Readers Say

"I was surprised how easy it was for me to get a contractors license for myself. It took $400 for the class and one day of time."

Joan L.
West Mountain, UT

Sources Say

"Lenders will probably require you to have cash equal to a down payment, but they probably won't require you to use it if you are successful in building equity as a general contractor."

From *Build Your Dream Home for Less*
(See page 259)

Shop for the Right Terms

With your proposal and presentation, you may find yourself uniquely well-received. My research with bankers tells me that you will be the most prepared owner-builder the lender has ever seen. This puts you in the driver's seat.

Your lender will want to make the loan, and so will other lenders in your area. Since you are no longer in a "hat in hand" position of subservience, you get to take your pick of the available lenders. It's no longer a case of "will they take me?" but of "who will I take?"

Consider the terms and conditions of the construction loans available before you choose. Lay out a spreadsheet of the loan differences discussed below and others you are concerned about. Before you see the lenders, call and ask their policy on the key terms. After you present your case to a lender, talk through their terms using your checklist. If you are considered a good candidate, the lender will negotiate any or all of the terms.

• Origination Fee

This fee can vary from zero percent of the loan amount to as much as three percent.

• Loan Rate

Readers Say

"I'm going through my credit union for the permanent financing, and a bank did my construction loan. My long term relationship with my financial institutions helped a lot."

Ivealia D.
Tulsa, OK

The interest rate could be fixed or adjustable, and pegged at some percentage over prime. Adjustable rates are less risky for the lender and more risky for you.

• Down Payment Required

Is the land you have secured enough of a down payment? Do you have to have the land fully paid for? Is additional cash required, and how much?

• All-in-one Loan

Some enlightened construction lenders are offering combination loans that you close on only once. When you finish construction, the long-term mortgage automatically kicks in and pays off the construction loan. These loans save on origination and some other fees.

• Interest Rate Locks

If you catch the market at a good time, interest rates may be temporarily low. Rate differences can mean thousands or tens of thousands of dollars on your interest costs on the long-term mortgage. You may be able to lock in a low future rate by paying a small fee. What rate can you get and what will it cost?

• Title Insurance and Other Fees

What will be the other charges on your closing statement? What will be the cost of title insurance (a big ticket item)? What other fees will you see?

• Draw Procedures

Construction lenders can make your life miserable with restrictive draw procedures. What does it take to get money to pay the bills? Does the lender require any home office or out of town approvals before disbursing funds? Are there completion percentage inspections required? How often can you get a draw? How much advance notice do they require? Is there a fee? Is the money paid directly to subs and suppliers, or to you? Who handles check writing and lien releases?

• Uninstalled Item Draws

Kitchen cabinets are often ordered weeks or months before installation, and a 50% deposit may be required. Can the bank deal with this, or will they be difficult with you about the fact that you make the deposit before the cabinets are installed? To get bargains on some other items such as ceramic tile, you may have to pay cash for supplies before they are installed.

• Cost for Inspections

Lenders want to have the project inspected periodically to see that the work they pay for has been done. Some lenders insist on an inspection before every draw, and make you pay for the inspections. Most lenders have a program of periodic inspections. Some lenders charge nothing for inspections; many, however, do.

• Title Update Fees

Some banks take a legal precaution of updating your title periodically. This limits the conditions under which subs and suppliers can file a lien and verifies that no creditor has any claim on your property. Do you pay for the procedure?

• Category Shifting

If you save money on one area of the project, for example excavating, can you apply the extra to another area, such as kitchen cabinets? How user-friendly is the procedure?

• Insurance Cost

The lenders have arrangements with various insurers that could save you money on course of construction insurance.

> **Readers Say**
>
> "I put my loan out on the Internet and asked lenders to bid on it. Construction to perm. The first company came back with $6,900 then one at $5,200, and then the third one at $800 plus interest during the term."
>
> Aaron & Daylene S.
> Heber City, UT

Sources Say

Your New House Lists eight questions to ask when getting a mortgage loan and four potential problems with mortgage loans.

(See page 260)

• Time Limit

With most construction loans, you get a loan on which you make no payments. A construction loan accrues interest as time goes by, and that interest is usually paid off by the long-term mortgage on completion. How much time will they give you before the loan is over and you must make interest payments? Six months is common, but very optimistic since the average owner-built house takes longer to build. Many banks give nine months on a custom home.

• Cost of Extension

If you go over, is there a fee for extra time before you have to make monthly payments? What will the interest rate be?

• Additional Amounts

If you need more money to finish your project than anticipated, and you qualify for it, can you get it? Do you have new origination or other fees to pay? Is there a change in interest rate?

• Disputes

What recourse do you have if there is a disagreement? Our loan was tied up for a month late in the project because the bank insisted that we had spent 92% of the funds but that the project was only 87% complete. We had subs that wouldn't do more work until paid, but the bank wouldn't advance a nickel. It turned out that their computer spreadsheet had a totaling error and they were off by six percent. We had no way of getting their attention in the meantime.

Review the items that concern you before you make a presentation to a candidate lender. Negotiate for the terms you want. With competitive information from other institutions, you have even more leverage. If you are not satisfied, reserve your final decision until later. See other candidate lenders, make your case and negotiate. Don't sign on the dotted line until you have found a package that suits you.

Chapter 12: Paperwork Before You Begin

Time line: One month before groundbreaking

Anatomy of a Lawsuit

We made the mistake of not having back-up plans for those budget categories where volunteers were to help on our project. One of the volunteers, someone to whom we had loaned money, never showed up to do the finish carpentry he promised. Since our project was already delayed, I moved hastily to find a replacement carpenter.

I hired someone I knew who was retired and seemed grateful for the work. He said he could finish the task with a helper in a week and a half. I agreed to pay him the hourly wage he asked for, with the proviso that payments would not exceed eight days for two men or 128 hours of work time. Since I knew the man slightly, I only made notes in my day book. We didn't sign anything. Then our nightmare began.

For one reason and another, the men kept telling me that it would take longer than expected to finish the work. At the same time they came to me every Friday and asked for advances on their pay, saying they would not be able to stay in their apartments or have transportation if they didn't have some money. The task dragged on,

Sources Say

"Don't count on getting anything you don't ask for in writing. Remember, 'Not written, not said.'"

From *The Complete Guide to Contracting Your Home*
(See page 260)

Sources Say

"If you allow contractors to insert an "or equal" clause in their bid, you are at their mercy."

From *Build Your Dream Home for Less*
(See page 259)

Sources Say

"Look for any situation that can void workmen's compensation coverage. For example, in some states, drywall subs experiencing accidents while using drywall stilts are not covered."

From *The Complete Guide to Contracting Your Home* (See page 260)

Sources Say

"Most states have special statutes that require builders, even when using subcontractors, to have worker's compensation insurance protection for anyone working on the building site. Since you are providing insurance to cover these workers on your site, make sure to deduct the amount of the insurance from the price paid to the subcontractor."

From *The Complete Guide to Contracting Your Home* (See page 260)

Sources Say

"Put payment amount and payment schedule in writing and have it signed by both parties."

From *The Complete Guide to Contracting Your Home* (See page 260)

and I eventually wrote out personal checks totaling 140% of the agreed amount, with only 65% of the work completed. Finally, on the advice of an independent inspector friend, I refused to pay any more. They left with curses and threatenings.

In a few weeks I got a notice that our place had been liened. We were almost finished with construction, so I called the mortgage lender and asked if this would affect anything. I was informed that an amount equal to two times the amount of the lien would be escrowed at the mortgage closing. We felt we owed the men nothing, but we would still have to escrow $5,000 at closing. I protested that under state law these men weren't qualified to file a lien as unlicensed contractors. I was told that it's a case where the owner is assumed to be "guilty until proven innocent."

Later we got registered letters from the carpenters' attorney stating that we were liable for Breach of Contract, Unjust Enrichment, Failure to pay a Mechanic's Lien, and violations of the State Bonding Statute. Much to our chagrin, the relative who had co-signed on our mortgage loan was named in the action. There was nothing to do but hire an attorney and respond to the motions that had been filed with the Court.

We were informed that these claims were standard in attempts by tradesmen (mechanics) to enforce a lien they file. We traded volleys with the other side, each time showing that the claims were groundless. But the other side wouldn't go away. They responded with a willingness to consider our "offer to settle".

During the months of this turmoil we felt unsafe in our own house. There was anxiety and insecurity prompted by unfamiliar and uncomfortable legal proceedings. The matter never came to trial. We eventually cleared the lien, but the damage was done; we suffered just because it was filed.

You, too, can have an unwanted experience with the courts. Fifteen percent of the owner-builders I interviewed stated that they had been liened at least once in the past. Their average estimate was that 20% of all owner-builders wind up getting liened.

What is a lien? It's a claim filed against your property for alleged nonpayment for materials or services. In our state a mechanic (tradesman) can file a Mechanic's Lien without paying a fee, or even showing identification. A second type of lien is a "Materialmen's Lien" which a supplier can file against your property, even if you are only late in paying his bill.

These liens have priority even against permanent financing, so the bank will ask you to pay the mechanic or materialman before you get your long-term mortgage. If you are unwilling to pay off the lien, you will be required to set aside money to pay for the lien later in the event you lose your case. The bank may escrow two or more times the amount of the lien, so that legal expenses are also covered.

You can be subject to a Materialmen's Lien if a tradesman procures material for your project from a supplier and fails to pay the bill subsequently. You are liable, and the supplier will lien you. This is one big argument in favor of your buying materials separate from labor when you build. In addition, even if you pay your mechanics and materialmen fully, you can still be liened. In our state, no proof of non-payment is required at the time of lien filing. It can be done to harass or intimidate you.

The magical key to preventing this misery is a "lien waiver". (See sample on next page.) Every time you make a payment to a supplier or a tradesmen, you can insist they sign a lien waiver which deprives them of any right to legally file a lien for non-payment. Many lenders incorporate the language of the lien waiver on the back of their checks. When a sub or supplier endorses a payment from that lender, they also relinquish any right to file a lien.

Get Good Protection

Most of the time nothing goes wrong, no one is injured, and you are not sued. But when you are sued, someone is injured, or you become the target of the unscrupulous, the loss can be very great. Although infrequent, these situations can be costly, and you can lose your house or your future income if you are unprotected.

You may not be aware of insurance requirements, and you may unwittingly hire an uninsured roofer, and he falls from the roof, and becomes permanently disabled, or worse. You have a builder's risk policy and you think you're covered. But it doesn't cover subcontractor personnel. A subcontractor is supposed to have a Workmen's Compensation policy for situations like that. Needless to say, if the sub doesn't have coverage, you become liable.

Before you engage subcontractors, you need to talk with your attorney, your lender, your insurance agent, and your state or province offices of lien recovery and Workmen's Compensation. Find out if any of the following requirements from around the U.S. apply to you:

Payment Protection

1. Lien Waiver Forms

Some states have a blanket lien waiver arrangement where once the necessary document is signed by all parties, the mechanics and materialmen can't lien you. In most states, you must get a lien waiver signed by the sub or supplier upon receipt of payment to be protected against liens. To be extra careful, you can have every employee of the subcontractor who works on your site sign a lien waiver before you make payment to the sub.

> **Sources Say**
>
> *Everything You Need To Know About Building the Custom Home*, written by an attorney, includes a sample contract with subs and a land purchase contract.
>
> (See page 259)

> **Readers Say**
>
> "I spent four hours negotiating a contract with a builder and he said afterward that it was the most thorough he had ever seen. Even though I'm an attorney, I used your book for that. The contract was put to the test right away when the fill dirt came out at $4,000 more than he estimated. He was obliged to absorb the overage."
>
> Mike V.
> Birmingham, AL

> The Lien waiver and the Contractor Agreement forms shown in this chapter are also available as a word processing document on our free Resource CD-ROM.
>
> (See page 270)

Lien Waiver

Customer Name: _____

Customer Address: _____

Customer City/State/Zip: _____

Customer Phone Number: ( ) _____ Fax: ( ) _____

Job Location: _____

Type of Work:_____

Contractor/Subcontractor/Materialman:_____

Contractor/Subcontractor/Materialman address:_____

Description of work completed to date:

_____

_____

_____

_____

_____

Total Payments received to date and/or Payment received on this date:

$_____

The contractor/subcontractor signing below acknowledges receipt of all payments stated above. These payments are in compliance with the written contact between the parties above. The contractor/subcontractor signing below hereby states payment for all work done to this date has been paid in full.

The contractor/subcontractor/materialman signing below releases and relinquishes any and all rights available to place a mechanic's or materialman's lien against the subject property for the above described work. All parties agree that all work performed to date have been paid for in full and in compliance with their written contract.

The undersigned contractor/subcontractor releases the general contractor/customer from any liability for non-payment of material or services extended through this date. The undersigned contractor/subcontractor has read this entire agreement and understands the agreement.

_____   _____
Contractor/Subcontractor Signature   Date

2. 1099 Filings

Currently in the U.S., if your subcontractors are not incorporated with a federal tax ID number, you must file a Form 1099 with the IRS for all payments you make to that subcontractor if he receives more than $600 for the work. You must provide the subcontractor with a copy of the 1099 form as well. If your construction lender is making the disbursements on your project, the lender must file the 1099 forms.

Insurance Protection

1. Builder's Risk Insurance

This coverage, also called "Course of Construction" insurance, is almost universally required by lenders. Be aware, however, that a policy might not cover everything. For example, one O-B told me that he filed a claim with his insurer over some stolen lumber, and discovered that unless the lumber was under lock and key, it was not covered if stolen.

2. Liability Insurance

You probably have some liability coverage under your current homeowner's or renter's policy. For a nominal sum you can increase the coverage to $1,000,000 or more for the duration of your project. Ask your agent.

3. Workmen's Compensation Policy

This coverage is issued by individual states or private insurers throughout the U.S. It provides for replacement income for a worker who becomes disabled due to injury. You need to verify that your subs have this coverage. You can ask for a certificate of insurance proving that they do. But even that sometimes backfires. One owner-builder became liable for a claim with a sub who had shown him the certificate. It was expired, and the O-B didn't look closely enough to notice.

4. Payment Bond

Your lender may require you to purchase a payment bond from your insurer that provides payment to suppliers in the event that your subcontractor should default or disappear during your project, leaving unpaid supplier bills. These bonds are expensive, and pretty rare for residential construction, but some lenders have told me that they require them.

5. Disability Insurance

If you become injured on your construction site and are forced to miss work, you can receive compensation through disability insurance. Many people have disability insurance as part of their employment benefits, but typically their coverage is for Long-Term Disability, not short-term. Check with your employer. You can purchase disability insurance from your insurance agent to replace your salary in the event of a disabling injury for a surprisingly small amount of money.

6. Term Life Policy

Some lenders want the additional protection, (it's not very expensive), of having a policy on your life and that of your spouse, with the bank as the beneficiary. Should you die during the course of construction, the bank would have to replace you with paid help to finish the project and recover their investment. At the same time you may want a private life insurance policy that would permit your survivors to complete the house, and possibly to own it free and clear.

Write Good Contracts

One very tough construction lender I met has made 75 construction loans to owner-builders over the years. They all had ten percent contingency reserves in their cost breakdowns. This lender made a bet with each of his borrowers that they would use the entire contingency before they finished. If not, he would buy them a steak dinner. He has only had to buy one steak dinner, and I interviewed the lucky winner, Mark Benson, a professional purchasing agent.

Mark Benson had a simple phrase that he wrote into each subcontractor agreement he signed. Here is his explanation:

"Get a signed contract on the dollar amount for labor, and for materials if you go that way. Have a clause: 'Will not exceed the quoted price'. I don't sign their proposal until I write it on there. We both initial and sign. I try to have the owner or principal of the subcontracting company sign it."

The second biggest regret (after insufficient planning) of O-B's I interviewed is that they didn't get more things in writing. Make sure that you have written agreements with your subs. These protect you against disasters, and they give you a very potent means of controlling the outcomes on your project.

There are some items that should be included in any construction contract to make project supervision easier. Examples are:

- Deadlines for completion – with possible penalties (liquidated damages) for delays.
- Start dates and possible reward for timely commencement.
- Detailed descriptions of tasks and level of performance expected.
- "Cost not to exceed $_____" with initials of both parties.
- Insurance the subcontractor must maintain.
- The subcontractor's license number.
- Responsibility for clean-up on the site.

The very useful book *Everything You Need to Know About Building the Custom Home*, coauthored by attorney John Folds, available on page 259 in the Resource Guide at the back of this book, explains six elements that are recommended for a good subcontractor agreement.

Owner-builder Jim Stark, who is a professional engineer and has built four times, stresses the value of describing performance in detail:

"Be clear about what you expect and hold them accountable for it. You are writing the check, you're in power. You can get rid of a tradesman after he starts. You have sequential payments in the agreement – performance, then payment. You can write him a check and he is done if you are not satisfied."

Most of the process of contracting with subcontractors revolves around fixed-price bidding. You can sometimes save money by paying your subs not by the bid, but by the hour, on a cost-plus or time and materials basis. Owner-builder Alex Acree, himself a commercial construction and maintenance supervisor, used this technique effectively:

"I had a painter who charged $10 an hour, and did the exterior of the house in a week. I had carpenters where the lead guy was very trustworthy. He had a super work ethic. I did some cost-plus contracting with him. I would monitor it on a daily basis, and if I thought it would take a lot more than he thought, I would limit it. Like crown molding. I let him do two rooms, and I saw it only took one day, so I said, 'do the whole house.' Keep scope in small manageable pieces when you do a cost-plus. He first quoted me $3,000. But I only let him do it in small chunks on an hourly basis, and it wound up being $1,500. He was unique, though. In areas where I have no experience, like plumbing, I always took a fixed-price bid."

In my own case, I naively accepted a time and materials arrangement with our plumber. I told him I was concerned about the bill getting too high, and he hooked me by looking concerned and saying to me with sincerity, "I'll just bill you for time and materials." He wound up charging me lots of money, and at least in one case reworking one of his own mistakes at my expense.

When you act as owner-builder, you are a "contractor", responsible for contracting with others to complete your project. Because of the liabilities and the need to control your project, this part of your work requires your serious attention.

City Permits

Provide enough time before your intended groundbreaking to procure all the necessary permits and authorizations from your city. I thought a week would be plenty, but it took about six weeks to get everything through the system in our case.

You will be paying thousands of dollars to meet all of the city's requirements. There are fees for connection to sewer, water, and power. There is a plan review fee in most jurisdictions, state or county fees, impact fees, and of course, the cost of a building permit. In our municipality there is a refundable deposit to pay for any sidewalk that you crack or break during construction. Our tab was nearly $5,000 for permits and fees. In some communities impact fees alone easily exceed $10,000.

If your construction plans include anything that requires a zoning variance from your city's Planning Commission, you may have to wait months to get on a meeting agenda, plead your case, and follow up before you can begin construction. Plan ahead, and maintain communication with the inspector who will be handling your project.

Contracting Agreement

_____, referred to as OWNER, and _____, referred to as CONTRACTOR, agree as follows:

CONTRACTOR shall perform the following services for OWNER: _____

_____

_____

Schedule Start Date: _____ Completion Date: _____

Not to exceed the following price: $_____. Owner Initials: _____ Contractor Initials: _____

Contractor shall be responsible for the following in addition to the workmanlike performance of the work stated above:

The materials and construction supplied by the CONTRACTOR shall meet the specifications as described on the approved blueprints and shall meet code.

The CONTRACTOR shall provide the following types of insurance matching or exceeding the amounts specified:

1. Worker's Compensation Insurance in the minimum amount of $_____.

2. General Liability Insurance in the minimum amount of $_____.

3. _____.

The stipulated contract price shall be paid as follows: _____

_____

The CONTRACTOR shall daily remove all trash and debris from the premises.

Any disputes arising out of or related to this agreement shall be arbitrated under the rules of the American Arbitration Association before a single arbiter.

This agreement may be terminated by OWNER upon substantial abandonment of the project, defines as at least _____ business days without substantial activity, except for delays caused by:

a. bona fine weather disturbances;
b. strikes;
c. shortages of material;
d. material delays not caused by the general contractor;
e. governmental delays except those caused by the fault of the contractor.
f. persistent failure of workmanship to meet high quality standards for which adequate assurance of correction is not provided.

In any disputes related to this agreement, the adjudication body may assess reasonable counsel fees to the prevailing party.

This is the entire agreement between the parties and this agreement may only be altered in writing.

Dated: _____

Owner: _____ Contractor: _____

Chapter 13: Six Months to Victory

Time line: Groundbreaking

"Integrate"

You remember the duties of a manager — POIMM — Plan, Organize, Integrate, Measure, and Motivate. You are two thirds through this book and you have only dealt with planning and organizing so far. This reflects reality, because a general manager should spend 65% – 75% of his or her time on the future. As the contractor for your home, you are about to get down to the present and handle your responsibility to integrate.

Integration is the coming together of the parts. It will be your job to get the people on your team to work together. You have selected people with a common work ethic and standard of construction quality. Nonetheless, there will need to be careful coordination to make your project run smoothly.

You will need to coordinate the trades by running the schedule smoothly and managing the site for efficiency. In many cases you will need to bring people and their required materials together in a timely manner. Take responsibility. If a portion of the work is not done in time to enable the work of somebody else who depends on it, you are responsible. If materials are not there in time for the next sub or the next step, you are the one responsible. You settle disputes and facilitate the work of others. Your function is to make things easier for everybody else on the team.

The average owner-builder I interviewed had a dozen different subcontractors to coordinate. It is possible to have up to 50 subs and up to 50 suppliers serving your project.

Step One

How do you begin?

After we had laid out all our plans for the project and came close to groundbreaking, I realized, believe it or not, that I had "nothing to wear". We headed for a thrift shop and bought a construction wardrobe for about $10. I found later that I fit right in.

In order for groundbreaking to occur, your lot needs to be staked and marked with the pattern of cuts that your excavator will dig. Staking lots is one of the few things that general contractors may actually do. My construction advisor supplied us the service, using an engineer's transit, a couple of long steel measuring tapes, metal stakes, string, a sledge hammer, and powdered lime to mark the surface.

A very good description of the task is found in *The Building Buddy* by John English. You can attempt to do it yourself with instructions, but I suggest having a surveyor perform the service. It is not a major task — less than half a day for a flat lot. Check prices by phone. If you are having an official survey of your lot performed, you can purchase the staking service as part of a package from a surveyor.

Once your staking is done, and there are no permit hold-ups with your project, you can break ground. When we got to this point, we held a groundbreaking ceremony of our own, took pictures, and watched while the excavator started. Within an hour, there were four inches of snow on the ground. Our intrepid excavator jumped down from the cab of his backhoe and dragged a booted foot on the ground in several places pulling the mud and lime into a smear that he could see. He finished the job perfectly even though the lines were covered with snow.

How to Get Subs to Show Up

The contract documents you have signed with your subcontractors provide you protection from unexpected loss, but they don't guarantee that you'll get what you want. As in any management situation or any human situation, results depend on reciprocity, relationships, and follow up. Owner-builder Gary Ziser explains:

"You run into the fact that things are often done in a kind of simple form. It's difficult to enforce a bid. You have to have a good relationship with contractors to have a meeting of the minds on things. Specifications on homes are not that detailed. That's why you need a meeting of the minds, and much is based on trust. This is one of the biggest problems faced by owner-builders because it is a one-time situation and expectations are not well-understood either way. I don't think you can cover it all on paper."

You will build trust and relationships with subs through a series of steps:

1. Through interviews, bidding, and checking references, choose trustworthy tradesmen.

2. Agree on contract terms including start and finish dates.

3. Send the subs a confirming letter indicating that you will do your part to make this a smooth project.

Indicate that you will keep the job clean, pay on time, and be on-site for fast answers and decisions. You will keep people out of each other's way as much as possible. You will have a phone on-site, and refreshments for workers. Remind the sub that 20% of the marketplace is owner-builders like yourself, and jobs like yours will help him build market share. If he fulfills his part of the bargain you will recommend him actively to others.

Under-promise and over-deliver on these items. This establishes reciprocity.

4. Call once a month before the target month, once a week until the target week, and two to three times until the target day. Call the night before the scheduled day.

5. If they miss an agreed time, call within hours. If they miss three promised show-up times, make arrangements to replace them with a back-up sub.

6. Don't pay until the work is done and inspected fully. Pay promptly.

Rules of Work

You know you have good subcontractors when:

△ They start on time.

△ They finish on time.

△ They do what they say they are going to do.

△ They have the right tools for the job.

Readers Say

"Our drywallers told us the place had to be clean when they started, or they would charge us for cleanup. We, in turn, warned our electrician. He left a mess, and the drywallers charged us $200, which we deducted from our payment to the electrician. He then charged the drywallers directly for each electrical outlet they had covered up, and he had to fix. He charged them about $200!"

Steve & Maria J.
Provo, UT

Sources Say

"It may take ten years to learn how to lay bricks properly, but only ten minutes to check the work for quality craftsmanship."

From *The Complete Guide to Contracting Your Home* (See page 260)

Readers Say

"The framer thought he was done, and I called for the clips and nails inspection. It wasn't done and it failed the reinspection. So I withheld his money until he got the page and a half of little items finished and passed. I had to stand my ground. I told him, 'this is my house, I want it right.' I have a business background, so I am used to standing my ground. Sometimes they tried to pull the wool over my eyes, and I would go to the car and call my site manager on the cell phone, and verify with him, then come back and say 'here is my decision.'"

Kathi D.
Tucson, AZ

Sources Say

"Make sure when paying cash for work that you keep documentation of the work done for the IRS. Write a check in the sub's name and have him cosign it. Then cash the check. This way you have an audit trail to prove that you paid the sub for the work done."

From *The Complete Guide to Contracting Your Home*
(See page 260)

△ The work is straight and sturdy.

△ There are no obvious flaws.

△ You could picture the work in a million dollar home.

△ You are satisfied.

Running the Job

One family from Tennessee (mentioned in Chapter 1) went on vacation while their house was in the framing stage. When they got back the roof was on, and they sat in the car for a moment admiring the structure. Husband and wife then felt a sudden sinking feeling as they realized that the framers had forgotten the second floor. Their two-story was a one-story.

Sometimes the input you make into the construction process is as simple as reminding the subs how many stories to build. If you are not a construction person, you may feel unqualified to run the job, but you're not unqualified. You have done detailed planning of budget, calendar, and specifications. These are the keys to a good project.

As the owner, you are really the most qualified to say if a thing is done right during construction. At the same time, you should avoid the temptation to be a know-it-all. By respecting the opinions of qualified subs you can learn much and get a better house. In management, there is a term for attempting to supervise the small details: "micromanagement". You will get better work out of subs if you don't micromanage their work.

Your job as contractor is to facilitate and coordinate the work of others. Make sure their materials are on hand and the preliminary steps to their task have been completed. The best way to do this is to be on-site. I found the work endlessly fascinating and stayed on-site full-time during our project. Most of the owner-builders I interviewed recommended half time, that is about four hours a day. Particularly the first and last work hours of the day. This schedule enables you to check on the work for the day in the morning and inspect it in the afternoon.

Subcontractors have often told me that it is important to have one person in charge of the project who can be decisive. If you are married, work out the decision-making roles of the spouses for the various phases of the project, and work within them. You will be called on to answer questions and explain plan details constantly. If you don't know the answer on something, you can talk it over together and network with people you trust in the evening. You can provide an answer the next day or very soon.

Part of your time on-site can be to inform affected trades of the upcoming schedule and arrange delivery of needed materials by phone. With current bargains available on wireless phones, you can easily carry one with you wherever you go. Take time to program in all the sub and supplier numbers you think you will need. Use the phone on-site to check prices on materials for which you haven't yet found a bargain price.

Check all deliveries that come to the site for completeness, quality, and pricing. Make sure the site is clean, and clear any obstructions out of the way of your subs. Should the work of subs not meet your standards its up to you to point out deficiencies and insist on remedies. Be prepared to let a sub go if it becomes necessary. It is your project.

Cost Accounting

The fourth function of managers, after Plan, Organize, and Integrate is "Measure". One of the key measures you will track on your project, the one that makes a difference to your wealth, is costs. You need to track every actual cost that goes into your house, and project expected costs.

Actual costs are the "as delivered" and "as performed" charges you pay for materials and labor on the project. Expected costs are the prices you will pay for items not yet delivered or performed. Together, the two costs give you an ever-changing total of the cost of your house.

You can use a computer to great advantage in measuring costs. Our computer spreadsheet reflected the total of all items by categories and showed the effect of any actual or projected change on the total construction budget. In some ways, the spreadsheet was cumbersome however, because of the sheer number of items we paid for. You can't really view all of your costs on one computer screen.

Perhaps a better system is the one we use to track our family finances. We have a financial management program called Quicken™ on which we enter every normal check, credit card, or cash expense, and categorize them. For instance, we might make a supermarket purchase and when entering the check into Quicken's register we specify that it falls under the "grocery" category. We can have Quicken™ report all grocery expenses for the past year with a simple command.

If you use a Quicken-type personal financial program to track construction costs you can create categories that make it easy to match up totals to your original budget. For example, you could have categories for "new house — electric", "new house — lumber", "new house — tools", and so forth. You can produce detailed reports by categories or time periods at any time.

It can be very valuable to track your expenses closely. You don't want to leave it to your lender, who produces periodic reports, for several reasons. First, the lender doesn't have knowledge of all costs on your project. By actual count, we purchased more than 500 items separately from our bank loan, even though the lender paid most of the big bills directly in our case. The separate purchases can make a big difference in your totals.

Sources Say

" . . . you've selected your subs. You're satisfied . . . that they are honest, trustworthy, and experts in their fields. Now let them work. Don't try to supervise every blow of a hammer, the placement of every stud. They know more about their trades than you do . . . they take pride in their work. Let them do it."

From *Be Your Own House Contractor* (See page 258)

Second, your tracking will provide you control and overall project savings. You may find mistakes in prices and quantities on some of your invoices, and usually not in your favor. You can change and adapt as individual costs go beyond their planned limit, in order to protect your overall total. When you find cost savings on some items, you can apply them immediately to reduce projected overruns in other areas, or spring for upgrades. None of your choices will be made in a financial vacuum.

Third, cost control brings you onto a par with professional builders. They have developed some sophistication in tracking costs for the purpose of protecting their profits. You, too, have profits (equity) to protect, and the effort you make tracking costs will likely exceed anything a general contractor can do on any one project.

Daily Record

Once your job begins, you will find it helpful to have a daily record of what happens on the job. Various tradesmen, salesmen, inspectors, and service representatives will visit the job site. Deliveries will occur. Promises, decisions, arrangements will be made. You may lose a phone number or forget an important fact. Remember that "a short pencil is better than a long memory."

Keep general time records of tradesman work. These proved useful to me in settling disputes. Keep specific time records of your own activity on the job.

Readers Say

"I use Microsoft Project but I don't like it. I use it for milestone scheduling. I now use Access and Excel. Project is the only one that has a scheduling feature. To make it non-intimidating to subs I make a bar chart sketch by week with tasks for the week written on the left and hang it on a stud on a nail and everybody pays attention to it. The subs get on each other about it. Like a 'gotcha' system."

Jim V.
Reno, NV

Time records help you track effort and redirect it. From a management point of view, they will tell you if you are really saving money. By knowing your time investment you can make your next iteration of a task, or process, or indeed, your next house more efficient. My time records tell me that I was on-site much more than I needed to be to do my job. The 800 hours we spent doing the electric work pointed up my painful lack of planning. I now figure that we could have done a month of planning on that task and saved nearly 500 hours overall. With that change, we could have done the electric work completely in 320 hours.

Owner-builders report over 1,000 hours of time spent on the job site and less than 300 hours of advance planning. This is backwards. I think with a thousand hours of planning, an O-B could spend perhaps 500 hours on-site and bring in a successful project. More money would be saved, and less effort expended.

James C. Maxwell said that, "To measure is to know." I would add to that "to know is to control". Your time records help teach you how to manage your efforts and accomplish more in much less time.

Your Video Camera and Other Unlikely Tools

What will be your most valuable tools in managing the construction of your house? For me, any project is an excuse to buy a tool, and building a house was a chance to buy more than a hundred tools. I started with new toolboxes and a tool belt, and enjoyed tremendously buying tools on sale and at contractor prices. In truth, however, traditional tools don't help you perform your role as general contractor for the project.

What I used the most was a broom. I bought a good "stand up" dustpan with a long handle that allows you to pick up without stooping. My five horsepower shop vac was also very useful for keeping the site clean.

I thought I would need a cellular phone, but budget constraints forced me to cancel that. With currently low wireless prices, though, you can put a cellular phone to good use. I thought I would need a pickup truck to haul things. That, too fell to budget constraints, and I never missed it. Most all of the suppliers provided delivery, and I accomplished a lot with the trunk of the family car. Once in a while I slipped down the highway with pipe or lumber traversing the passenger cabin and sticking out the front window, hoping not to get pulled over. The house got built without my owning a pickup truck.

The major management tools that you will depend on are your written budget and calendar, your plans and detailed descriptions. Your daily record will become a lifesaver as well. To this, I would add a long and a short carpenter's level and a long and a short measuring tape for checking the straightness and squareness of the work you inspect daily. A handy homemade tool is a corner of a four by eight-foot sheet of plywood. Cut it as a triangle with the two factory edges measuring about two feet. Cut a hand hole in the middle of the triangle and shove it into corners as a shorthand way of determining straightness and squareness.

A computer can be a very powerful tool for managing your project. You can shop, plan, estimate, track and communicate with the aid of a computer. A video camera is another electronic friend to an owner-builder. Use it to document work and to record what is inside the walls of the house and underground. Narrate your pictures with explanations of the decisions you made when building.

The video camera came in very handy for us. During construction we placed a conduit pipe inside the wall of the laundry room to receive wires for the eventual electronic lawn sprinkler controller that would go in that room. After the house was sheetrocked we couldn't locate the pipe until we reviewed the construction video. By using the known thickness of wall studs as a scale of measure we figured the location of the top of the pipe within one inch. We have also used the video for locating underground pipe when making changes to the sprinkler system. We didn't own a video camera — we borrowed one. But we did own a computer.

Emotional Roller Coaster

When we built our house we were surprised at the intensity of feeling the project brought to us as first-time owner-builders. There was real anxiety and disappointment. When my schedule was blown away by a boundary dispute with the neighbor I was tremendously disappointed and angry. For the first time I can remember, I cried myself to sleep that night.

Readers Say

"I use Microsoft Project. My wife and I did quite a bit of prep work. She moved to our land in the mountains to be on-site supervisor, and handled the finances. She did the phoning, and gofer jobs for the builders. We had a cabin on-site there, and didn't need a portapotty. We built a 4,000 s.f. house. With 2,200 s.f. finished for $190,000."

J.M. & Nancy B. Kirkland, WA

Sources Say

"Have materials delivered early so they can be exchanged or corrected before they are needed..."

From *The Complete Guide To Contracting Your Home* (See page 260)

Sources Say

The Complete Guide To Contracting Your Home gives list of things to have at job site, like first aid kit, extension cords, hose, trash can.

(See page 260)

Readers Say

"60 years ago a house cost 75% materials and 25% labor. Today a house is just the opposite: 75% labor and 25% materials. With the new use of skill saws, portable drills, staple guns using compressed air, paint sprayers, the dumbest SOB can be taught to be an expert rock hanger, linoleum layer, etc. A thinking person who watches it done once can do it himself. He not only avoids 50% of the cost of the home, but he avoids the interest he would have to pay to borrow the money."

Bill R.
Moses Lake, WA

There were real fears about performing adequately and building a respectable house. Many times I veered into areas of uncertainty where I experienced an unaccustomed lack of control and felt lost and inadequate. I felt alone and lonely many times and wished for support from anywhere. Very little was forthcoming.

When the house was built, Elaine and I both felt tremendous pride and satisfaction over the accomplishment. It was a kind of glow that stays with us continuously. I could say that the project, however frustrating and painful, yielded the most enduring satisfaction I have ever known.

All of this became reason to write this book. We wanted to help others to steer around the pain and loneliness that we felt with so little guidance planning and building our house. As we met and talked with numerous others who shared the experience we learned that we were not alone in any of these emotions.

Owner-builder Debbie Crosby stated her feelings articulately:

"This was our first owner-built house. It was scary to sign paperwork to owe this much money. I was sick to my stomach. There is a fear to be able to build what you have in your mind. It's exciting to see your dream materialize. You anguish over almost everything, that you made a wrong choice. I redid my window in the kitchen three times. It wasn't coming out like I wanted. I tried using two windows, and stared at the gap between them. I tried a garden window — not right. Then I just got a big picture window. I had to eat the cost of one of them. I really stressed over that window."

Other common owner-builder emotions:

- Worry over staying on budget, running out of money

- Fear of not meeting the deadline

- Friction between spouses

- Self-doubt

- Aggravation

- Miss the family because of so much time away

- Disappointment over those who intend to help but don't

- Uneasiness over decisions made without adequate information

- Discomfort over many incomplete tasks and nothing finished

Although good preparation makes every bit of this easier, you will still feel a surprising intensity of emotion when you build for the first time. You are not alone.

Chapter 14: Smooth Execution Saves Money and Improves Quality

Time line: Three to five months out

Other Daily Duties

With you as the contractor, there are a surprising number of things nobody will take care of but you. You oversee the details that, taken together, make a clearly successful project. There is a saying that "God is in the details." Every day you should:

1. See that people are showing up.

Make phone calls to subs who are about to begin the night before they are to show up. Call subs who will be coming soon in the evenings or in the early morning before work. When you get to the site, if people are missing, call right away from the site. Your records should include cellular phone numbers for each of your team.

Sources Say

"The first steps, such as digging the foundation and pouring footings, will have more impact if done improperly than if a door is hung to swing in the wrong direction. Hence, your utmost care should be taken at the beginning of the project when every step is critical – particularly through the framing stage."

From *The Complete Guide to Contracting Your Home* (See page 260)

2. Check the work.

One owner-builder who is a physician from Atlanta paid a premium of $10,000 to upgrade his cabinetry from Georgia pine to solid cherry wood. He left the office to check on the installers in the middle of installation day. He discovered that they were installing particle board with a cherry veneer. They claimed he was getting what he had ordered. He had it in writing, and stayed on the vendor with calls and visits until the solid cherry was furnished a few days later.

Check the work on your job daily and in detail. See that:

a) It is straight, square and sturdy.

Carry a tape measure to verify dimensions. Measure the square dimensions of the house by running a tape measure diagonally from corner to corner. The opposing measurements should be identical if the work is square. You can check doorways, walls, window openings, and the outline of the house itself this way. Use a corner of a sheet of plywood to check the squareness of small corners like doorways and windows. Shove the factory edges of the plywood into a corner and observe if the edges are all flush. Use a four to six-foot level to check the plumb of all doorways.

b) Proper materials are used.

One owner-builder found the electrician installing aluminum wire, when he was paying for copper. Several others found that carpenters tried to install basic moldings instead of the more elaborate upgrades they thought they had ordered. There are many variations in quality in each building component from windows to shingles. Check constantly.

c) Proper designs and approaches are used.

Never trust your subs completely. Always question their motives when they make choices about the work. For example, they may say, "This is what you need", when it is a material or an approach that is simply cheaper and less work for them.

d) The quality of the work is as expected.

3. Give clear directions.

Be available to answer questions and provide direction. If you are not on-site all the time, spend a block of time in the beginning and end of each day to provide direction. At the end of the working day, review with the subs on-site what has been done to determine if it is what you expect. If there are questions you cannot answer, take them home and call your trusted advisors or your inspector for input. If possible, bring back clear direction the next morning for that sub.

4. Anticipate needs.

Anticipate needs for tomorrow, for a week out and for a month out. Make sure the materials needed tomorrow will be delivered on time, and that the needed subs will be there. Look ahead to subs and materials needed in the next week, and touch base with the necessary parties. Look ahead to completion dates and goals for the next month and anticipate them. Inspections may be difficult to schedule and require lead time. Once you have a date set for the next inspection, keep everyone informed of it and on schedule.

Have a "Plan A" and a "Plan B". Alex Acree, an owner-builder from South Carolina, observed his framing carpenters floundering and somewhat at a loss to handle the work after a few days. He provided them clear direction, but anticipated their possible failure on the job. He paid them only for work completed and made calls to line up possible back-ups. The framers walked off the job, but the back-up framer was on the site promptly.

5. Keep the site clean.

A clean site is safer and more productive for everyone. Dispose of packing and scrap materials. Lay down scrap wood or crushed packing boxes for footpaths in and out of the site. Sweep or vacuum dirt and sawdust regularly from the structure. Keep it free of water, snow or ice.

6. Meet inspectors on-site.

Be on-site to meet your inspector for scheduled inspections. Many times the inspector will waive a problem item after a suitable explanation by the owner. Flagged items are easier to resolve if you have the chance to query the inspector about them on the spot.

7. Receive deliveries.

Make sure the deliveries are complete and accurate. Check that you are being charged accurate prices for each line item. If you were shopping for a pair of pants, you would be very concerned if the price came out to be $300 instead of $29.95. But delivery invoices can be off by hundreds of dollars and often go unchecked. Also check materials for quality. Reject what you don't like such as crooked lumber or chipped cabinets.

8. Pay bills on the spot.

You can pay subcontractor bills on the spot if you have been inspecting work daily, if it meets your expectations fully, and there are no questions about its suitability for follow-on work. However, you should withhold a portion of the fee. Many builders hold back ten percent as a precaution until after the house is finished and a Certificate of Occupancy is issued. If it needs to be inspected by the city or tested by follow-on subs (as a sheetrocker needs to verify a framer's work, for example) you can make a partial payment pending inspection if you are satisfied.

9. Observe the work.

Generally, people work more carefully and meticulously if they are observed and appreciated. Every aspect of the work seems to go better if you are close at hand.

Why You Need to Be On-Site

The on-site tasks of an owner-builder are what management types would call "non-trivial". The owner-builders I interviewed spent an average of 1,068 hours on-site — far more than they anticipated. You need to plan to be able to handle the commitment. If you have planned fully, you may be able to get satisfaction from a 500-hour effort. This means four hours per working day, during working time, for a six month period.

The 500 hours I recommend do not include any trade work whatsoever. You must add to your 500 hours the time it will take you to do the trade work, and that too is non-trivial. For example, electric work took us 800 hours. For many O-B's site time is a way of making up for failure to plan. It can run to much more than 500 hours if you haven't settled everything you possibly can in advance, before you break ground.

The first reason you need to spend so much time on-site is to prevent disaster. An amazing number of things can go wrong, and will. The lack of communication is a common problem on a construction site. You must explain, explain, and explain. One couple in Florida took a vacation during construction and patiently told the framing crew before they left that they wanted the family room to be six feet longer than the plans specified. When they returned they found the family room had been built six feet shorter than the plans specified.

Some trades will not show up consistently or when promised. You have to keep after them to get the work done. In some cases you will have to hunt them down to get them to show up. You learn that even a written contract guarantees nothing. Conscientious supervision gives much more assurance. You need to keep after the subs, remove barriers, settle conflicts and prevent disasters through your supervision.

The second reason to spend time on-site is to get a better house. Several O-B's told me the more time they spent, the better they did. Like planning time, the more time you spend, the more money you save, the better the quality, and the more features you get.

You save money because of opportunities that come to your attention while on-site. As an eager O-B I always offered to help the subs and to help the vendors with deliveries. The concrete sub took me up on my offer, and allowed me to tie reinforcing steel before the footings were poured. I benefitted in several ways from the experience — I made sure the steel was tied more than code required, I reduced my footings bill by $300 in exchange for my efforts, and I kept track of delivered concrete. When the amount of concrete for footings and foundations turned out to be much less than originally thought, the sub agreed to further reduce my invoice by $350.

Quality improves in many ways because of your supervision. You make certain that implementation of the house corresponds to its use. For example, since you know how each room will be accessed you can ensure that light switches are placed on the correct side of doorways, and not blocked by open doors. You see that electrical outlets and phone jacks are placed where they will be convenient to your use. You catch doorways that may interfere with planned stairs or windows that would interfere with future walls.

In spite of your efforts at planning, your perspective on-site is better than the abstract visualizing you did during the planning stage. We caught a planned window at an early stage and had it moved to a different wall to capture a beautiful mountain view — rather than a view into the neighbor's upstairs bedroom.

You will get more extras, greater quality, and improved comfort out of your house by your thoughtful time spent on-site. Many opportunities present themselves to add extras, conveniences and improvements, sometimes at no cost, if you are on-site to seize them. You need to participate in the process while it is happening to make a variety of small changes. Some of the opportunities we grabbed were:

- Stuffing insulation behind shower units and between rooms
- Placing water lines under footings, rather than through walls
- Installing nailing blocks inside walls where needed
- Putting sleeves under walks and drives for future sprinkler pipes
- Doubling sheetrock in rooms where quiet is important
- Moving access to crawl space to free up a pantry space
- Installing electric outlets in floors where furniture would be placed away from walls
- Using balusters instead of half-wall on bridge over family room to improve view
- Placing heating vent under tub and shower
- Moving rocks from around property to foundation cavity to improve drainage and facilitate landscaping
- Stuffing insulation into outside framing corners before covered over
- Putting pesticide granules on sill plate behind walls
- Pouring drives and walks early to keep mud out of structure
- Sheetrocking portion of garage early to allow doors to be installed and house to be secured
- Widening halls where door frames didn't accommodate molding
- Creating a camping equipment shelf instead of a high uninterrupted wall in garage
- Turning garage with high ceiling into sports court
- Creating electrical path from crawl space to attic for future wiring
- Adding heating and cooling vents in garage and crawl space

Readers Say

"I found it to be very tiring. Many times subs are there at 5:00 a.m., and go to 2:30 p.m. I have trained myself to get up early. By being there I've been able to catch a lot of things. But I would do it again, and pull your book out and go from cover to cover again and again."

Kathi D.
Tucson, AZ

Sources Say

"If you cut down trees yourself: Cut them four feet from the ground. The bulldozer needs a good piece of the tree to pull the roots out of the soil."

"Trees to be saved should be marked with red tape or ribbon. Also, remind your excavator to be careful about knocking the bark off of trees to be saved. This could kill the tree or invite wood-hungry pests."

From *The Complete Guide to Contracting Your Home* (See page 260)

Consensus Breeds Creativity

How will you manage your subs?

For some, particularly those O-B's with a construction background, the temptation is to tell them what to do. Some general contractors are this way. They "micromanage" people, telling them what to do in detail and the way to do it. For others, it seems safest to go with whatever the sub wants and does — a "laissez-faire" attitude.

Remember your responsibilities as manager: Plan, Organize, Integrate, Measure, and Motivate. The "integrate" is the coordinating of all the members of the team, with their disparate needs and wants. Left to their own devices, the subs you hire may get into each other's way, damage each other's work, and become hostile and alienated.

Owner-builder Debbie Crosby describes a situation that arose on her project:

"The plumber did not work well with others, and if something was in his way he would saw right through it. We might have seen these things if we visited the site at midday. He sawed through some of the framing and a gas line also. I told him the master tub was not level, and he busted a big hole in the drywall to level the tub, and I said he would be responsible for repairing it, and he refused. I figured he made the hole, he should fix it — just one of the things you learn in kindergarten. I said I would retain part of his fee, he threatened a lawsuit, and I said, "see you in court." He came back, apologized, and fixed the hole."

The best way to manage subs is to show them you respect their abilities and need their contribution. Some take responsibility well and can be given a lot of freedom. Some need close attention. Where possible I apply consultative and consensus styles of management.

A consultative decision-making process is one in which the members of the team have been asked to provide their information and suggestions, but one member — you — reserves the right to make the final decision. A consensus decision-making process is one in which the resolution is achieved only when all members of the team agree that it is the best possible decision given the available information. Every member has the authority to veto the decision until, in fact, each member has found it possible to agree on a solution.

After a 15 year career as a management consultant and ten as a manager, I believe you get the best cooperation from a team by a consensus approach where everyone, including yourself, has an equal say, and decisions are unanimous. I named my company after the concept. However, in a construction situation, the members of the team change rapidly, and you are the only common denominator over the course of the project, which suggests that you should reserve the right to decide.

One day I stood in the dirt in front of our partially finished structure and joined in a debate between my concrete man, who is a respected general contractor, my construction advisor, also a general, and the area's largest interior door supplier. I had to make a decision about hollow-core or solid-core doors for the house. All three of them told me they had hollow-core doors in their houses. I wanted solid-core, but it would cost $2,000 more. I relented and accepted the hollow-core doors, out of respect for the three men. It turned out to be a poor decision, because my house is an open design, and much more sound travels inside than in their houses.

Better to have used a consultative approach, thank them for their ideas and say that I would get back to the vendor with a decision. The doors didn't pan out perfectly, but each of my helpers got the message that I respected their ideas, and many more ideas came from them after that day.

Many of the writers who have tackled the subject of owner-building in the past have minimized the need to be on-site. Most of these are contractor-authors who have a natural resistance to being overseen. Most people want unlimited freedom in their behavior. You want a smooth project, a quality home, and the greatest possible savings. These things don't happen on their own. You need to manage your subs consultatively to provide a good working environment wherein you will achieve all of your goals.

Clean Job Saves Five Percent

One of the unglamorous but valuable functions you can perform is to ensure a clean and organized job site. General contractor Matthew Rittmanic, an unusually perceptive builder I interviewed provides his reasoning for the claim that a clean job saves five percent of the cost of construction:

> "When it's clean, the sub has a better feel for the job, and gets in and out faster. It raises his standard of meticulousness, elevates the spirits of the team, fosters an atmosphere of cooperation and reduces rework. Missing supplies that might cause delays in upcoming work are more readily apparent. The inspector likes it better and is more helpful. It streamlines the final bidding process for bids that get finalized during the course of the project like insulation, drywall, cabinets, floor coverings, finish carpentry, and painting. There is a reduction of waste. Parts that arrive early and are needed later like finish covers of all types and door and cabinet hardware are protected. Ultimately useful remnant specimens of shingles, tile, carpet, hardwood, balusters, paints, and wallpaper are not damaged or lost."

Construction experts say that 70% of the dust that will ever get into your house is there when construction is finished. You can do a lot to keep that dust to a minimum.

We used scrap material and broken down packing boxes laid down as walking paths to keep mud from being tracked into the structure at early stages. I placed fresh bales of straw as steps into the house which helped brush work boots clean. At an early point we had our sidewalks and drives poured, and kept them swept. We used a shop vac to clean up sawdust and plaster dust. Before we painted and before the carpet was laid we even wet-mopped the floors. The result was a pleasant work environment and the peace of mind that our house was deep cleaned before occupancy, not to mention the savings.

The Inspector Is Your Friend

My advice is not to fight with your building inspector. Consider him a member of your team and check with him far in advance of the need. The building inspector's job has historically been to protect future owners from unwise, unsafe building practices. You are the future owner, hence the inspector should be on your side. Likewise, you are on the inspector's side because you want your house to be of the highest quality.

Nevertheless, conflicts can and do arise. O-B Jay Sevison described one situation he had with his inspector:

> "He failed a wall on a nailing inspection three times. He failed it because you are supposed to have screws *and* nails and there were only screws in the sheetrock. I said screws were better, but he didn't let it pass, even though I was the owner and contractor. His supervisor said it was a question of shear strength when I called him. I replied you don't need it on this inside wall. Persistence paid off for me — the policy was changed, and I wound up with a different inspector."

I have heard inspectors denigrated many times by contractors and occasionally by owner-builders. As in any trade there are better and worse practitioners. And there may be personality conflicts. The inspector can help you and can make observations and suggestions you will get from no one else. It pays to cultivate the inspector even before the start of your project. Make it a point to be present whenever he performs an inspection.

When you meet with the inspector before groundbreaking, ask what he will be looking for, what inspections your city or county requires, and how to schedule them. We had inspections of:

1. Temporary electric
2. Footings
3. Underground plumbing
4. Shear walls
5. Framing and electrical, plumbing, HVAC rough-ins ("four-way" inspection)
6. Insulation
7. Final electrical, plumbing, HVAC

One municipality described in Jim Hasenau's book, *Build Your Own Home: A Guide for Subcontracting The Easy Way*, required more than 30 inspections. When you meet with your inspector, check off the inspections from the "master list" on page 208 that you will be required to undergo.

You Can Get Independent Inspections

There is a class of inspectors known as independent construction inspectors who can be of great help to you. These are paid professionals who represent your interests in inspecting a house during the course of construction. Unlike city inspectors, these specialists can be sued — they are liable for their opinions.

For many owner-builders, the independent inspector may be the key to a successful owner-built home. Consider using one if you are not knowledgeable about all phases of construction. Their advice may be the key to admitting you to the fraternity of construction privilege and greatly increased net worth.

The independent inspectors I interviewed say they come out to inspect a house under construction an average of ten times for an overall average fee of under $1,000. Some come out as many as 20 times on a typical custom home. Most of them are former or retired contractors with a lifetime of experience in construction. They know the business, they know the habits and culture of the industry, and they inspect not for city code, but for quality in construction techniques and material.

One independent inspector I interviewed, Beryl Ford, from Tulsa, Oklahoma, showed the tremendous detail that can be studied in an independent inspection. Ford is a "forensic inspector" who is often hired by insurance companies to investigate the causes and origins of structural failure in houses. He describes his approach to evaluating a composition shingle roof:

> "You have to nail it right, nails in the right place, the right fasteners, in the right pattern and quantity, or the warranty won't be valid. Right pressure on nail gun, right angle and depth. Below the seal strip. If you have a material that deteriorates, they will not honor that warranty unless you meet the standards. If you don't have the right deck to receive the shingles, if it's not nailed properly, it will hump up. Proper ventilation in attic space. One and a half inches of ventilation space for every 100 square feet of space in the attic. Moisture migrates from the living space via ducting over jacuzzi's, over cooking area, over laundry areas; it migrates to the attic, and if doesn't discharge right it will condense and collect on the back sides of the shingles. On a hot day the moisture is drawn through the shingles and deteriorates the belting. In the winter the moisture on the back will freeze and expand and destroy belting fibers. Environmental creep will eventually destroy it prematurely. You want 20 years of useful life on a 20 year warranty. Valleys should have a liner: roll roofing with composition shingles, or metal with cedar shakes, clay tile, and masonry types. If you use metal with composition shingles, due to differences in the coefficient of expansion, it will slide. You'll see wrinkles, humps, and hollows."

The independent inspector can be a key to evaluating the performance of your subs and verifying that you have received what you are paying for. There are so many potential pitfalls in construction quality and technology, that I find the assis-

Sources Say

"The best inspectors are retired contractors or licensed engineers with residential construction experience. Such individuals would be most likely to spot problems with new construction. Many home inspectors specialize in evaluating older or re-sale homes; their cursory, "cosmetic" inspections would not be appropriate for a new home construction project."

From *Your New House*
(See page 260)

Sources Say

Your New House lists key inspection points, six sources for finding an independent inspectors, and questions to ask independent inspectors.

(See page 260)

The inspections checklist shown on the next page is also available on a spreadsheet on our free Resource CD-ROM.

(See page 270)

Inspections Checklist

Inspection	Required ?	Date	Notes
Building			
☐ Footing open			
☐ Rods in footing			
☐ Grade			
☐ Ready for backfill			
☐ Floor joist			
☐ Before sub flooring is applied			
☐ Truss on ground			
☐ Rough framing			
☐ Sheathing			
☐ Lath			
☐ Final grade			
☐ Final			
Electrical			
☐ Rough			
☐ Finish			
Heating			
☐ Rough heat			
☐ Insulation			
☐ Final			
☐ Plumbing			
☐ Septic tank & field			
☐ Sewer			
☐ Underground plumbing			
☐ Inside drain			
☐ Shower pan			
☐ Rough plumbing			
☐ Water test			
☐ Well water test (in case of well)			
☐ Final			
Concrete			
☐ Forms			
☐ Compaction			
☐ Rods or wire			
☐ Basement floor			
☐ Back fill			
☐ Forms outside (walks and drive)			
☐ Final			
☐ Other			
☐ Other			

Notes

tance of an independent inspector a relief and a bargain. They can answer your questions, make suggestions, even point out construction savings you have overlooked. Their fee pays for itself quickly in promoting a smooth project, ensuring quality, and in reduced replacement and operating costs.

Staying on Schedule

> **Sources Say**
>
> "Don't try to do too much of the actual physical work yourself. Your time and skills are often better used managing the job."
>
> From *The Complete Guide to Contracting Your Home* (See page 260)

It's actually possible to build a house in one day. It has been done by Home Builders Associations several times as a public relations event. They pour the concrete the week before and blitz the project on a Saturday with dozens of craftsmen. Some general contractors routinely finish projects in under four months. But you might not believe that when you are in the middle of your project. Schedule overruns are common for generals and for O-B's. Occasionally a house project goes two years or more, despite the best intentions of the owner-builder.

If you have done detailed planning as suggested, you will not be far off, but you may need a little encouragement during the construction phase. You should know your schedule by heart and what's coming up. Know what week of the schedule you are on by number. ("This is week seven. Where are the roofers?") It's not too complicated. If you are building in six months, you are dealing with 26 weeks.

We adopted a tradition when we built our house of wearing different ball caps every month of the schedule. We put on fresh ball caps on the first day of every month and discarded them ceremoniously on the last day of the month. The next day we started with new caps. The ball caps were easy to get because most construction materials vendors have logo caps they will give to their customers.

> **Sources Say**
>
> "Your choices are many. You can hire out everything, or do everything. Usually the middle ranges make the most sense, so you end up doing some aspects of the project – maybe the design and carpentry – and "subbing out" (subcontracting) the rest."
>
> From *Independent Builder* (See page 259)

This is a good time to review the procedure for keeping the subs on schedule. Call the subs once a month to remind them of your schedule until the month before they are due. In the last month, call them once a week to report progress and verify that they are still on schedule to show up as planned. In the week before their start time, call three nights before to verify that they will be there. If they can't do it, scramble to line up a replacement that night. The night before they are to start, call and confirm that they will be there in the morning. If they don't show within three days of the agreed time, for whatever reason, replace them immediately.

Staying on schedule is one of those things that takes your active management. "It's easy if you work it hard, but it's hard if you work it easy."

If You Do Self-Work — Control It

Benefits and Trade-Offs

> **Readers Say**
>
> "When you start to do labor, everything else stops."
>
> Lucy & Ivan B. Provo, UT

Occasionally I see a whimsical sign on the wall in a print shop or service provider's office reading:

"Do you want it good, fast, or cheap? Choose two."

You want your house "good", and as an owner-builder you likely are motivated by saving money ("cheap"). To get it built "fast" usually costs more. This is the problem with self-work on your house. For most of us who are inexperienced at the trades and are juggling a house project with full-time employment, extensive self-work is prohibitive.

The average owner-builder I interviewed did three to four of the trades (3.7) on his or her own project. The savings were very impressive, an average of 62% off the quoted price for each trade. The O-B's estimated 534 hours spent on 3.7 trades, which equals 144 hours per trade performed.

Elaine and I didn't work nearly that fast. We are fairly dedicated at measuring work hours, and we find that people often underestimate time spent. Our fastest trade was ceramic tile work, which we accomplished in about 100 hours. This includes taking a class (twice), reading a couple of guides to tiling, shopping for tools and materials, doing the work, and clean-up. Our slowest trade was electric, which took us 800 hours of work.

Painting is an often underestimated trade which took us 650 hours of work, the bulk of which was spent after we occupied the house. Painting is almost all prep work, and we sanded and patched and caulked until our fingertips literally bled. The woodwork in a custom colonial house is very extensive, and the gorgeous high gloss trim paints available today show off even tiny flaws.

Our fourth trade was landscaping, a 350 hour effort, performed after we occupied the house. The most popular self-worked trades by O-B's we interviewed were:

1. Finish carpentry
2. Electrical
3. Painting
4. Ceramic tile
5. Pre-wire (alarm, telephone, cable or satellite TV, network cabling, home theater, house audio).

For us, the trade work was a matter of economic necessity. We couldn't fit the budget under the borrowing limit the bank imposed on us, and we had to cut back. In the relaxed environment before groundbreaking, self-work seemed like a nice way to save money. It did extend the time of our house completion, by perhaps two frustrating and anxious months. But it cannot be said that construction interest ate up our savings because we saved about $5,000 average on each trade we did and spent only $2,000 of interest on the two months of delays.

In business, a decision like the one to do self-work is called a "make or buy" decision. A manufacturer can sometimes do better by allowing outside suppliers to provide some components rather than make them in-house. Factors like cost and capacity have to be weighed. Look at savings versus interest costs when you decide, and be realistic about the time it takes. I would urge you in any case to strive for project completion in six months.

Readers Say

"We hired a site manager. $1,200 to $8,000 was bid by various guys. One of the candidates tried to sell me on a $17,000 fee, and presented me with a list of "contractors that I use all the time". I knew this was a good old boy thing, so I eliminated him. The guy I got was $1,400 and I was able to call and ask about scuppers, for example. I was able to ask for any information I wanted. He comes out for inspections, and any information I want to ask on the phone. He doesn't seem to mind giving me lots of info, sometimes taking 45 minutes with me on the phone. He helped with some technical things on the plans. Things that people were resisting doing, but they are in the plans. He does 7-8 inspections."

Kathi D.
Tucson, AZ

Rather than let self-work gobble up the calendar, make your self-work highly efficient. Recognize that it will take you from two to ten times as long as an active tradesman to do any trade. Utilize the Greenewalt Principle which states that "one month spent in planning will save from three to four in execution". Plan your work thoroughly and manage your performance closely.

Risks, Dangers and Difficulties

In our city last year, an owner-builder died tragically while working alone late at night at the construction site. This man had kissed his wife good night and returned to his site at a late hour to put in a few more hours of work. On-site were typical stacks of sheetrock leaned against walls where they would be hung in a few days. The man was doing some work on hands and knees when a stack of sheetrock fell over on him, crushing him under its tremendous weight. His wife had gone to sleep at home, and didn't notice his prolonged absence until dawn. His body was discovered in the early morning.

It saddens me very much that a courageous owner-builder would die trying to build his house. It is a lonely occupation, and sometimes working alone is very risky. Fatigue can be a big factor, along with inexperience and the improper use of tools. Many injuries and sometimes fatalities result.

We were surprised at our limitations when we began to do self-work. I began to set junction boxes for electrical outlets about one month into the project. I went on hands and knees and used a hammer to pound in the boxes after sighting their heights with a "story stick". As I nailed in the first box my knee began to ache with throbbing pain. I had had knee surgery three months before and had thought I was fine. I hurried out to buy knee pads, but continued to experience pain with each kneeling task.

Doing electrical work also involved climbing a tall scaffold to make connections in vaulted ceilings over 20 feet from the floor. It was painful to climb the scaffold. When I got up the first time, I discovered I had an almost paralyzing fear of the height.

We all have some limitations in doing physical work, be it inexperience or inefficiency. Allow for your limitations and for the unexpected, like bad weather, illness, or injury when making your plans. You may find the work surprisingly complex. Most household tasks involve a very few steps to completion. Construction tasks can involve dozens of steps, posing a challenge to even the brightest among us.

The world's greatest chess players are able to envision as many as 30 moves ahead of the present move. Most normal people have trouble seeing beyond six or seven steps ahead. The result is frustration for a first-timer. I counted 30 steps to complete a minor electrical task, installing a single duplex electrical outlet in the roof soffit over the deck:

Get tool belt, find an unused duplex outlet and cover, get ladder, look for safety glasses, clean safety glasses, get boom box, plug into next outlet, flip possible breakers until music stops on radio, mount ladder, test if power's on, strip sheath of Romex, strip ends of black and white wires, loop ends to fit around screws, place black wire under bronze screw and tighten, place white wire under silver screw and tighten, place bare copper wire under green screw and tighten, push back into box, secure outlet with mounting screws, replace and attempt to screw in face plate, climb down, search for longer plate screws, remount ladder, screw in face plate, dismount ladder, reactivate power, mount ladder with boom box, plug in to see if music plays, put away boom box, tools, and ladder.

This task took me about an hour. It can be unsatisfying and frustrating to deal with the cumbersome steps in a complex task for members of our "instant gratification" generation. You must learn to be satisfied with a single step as an achievement instead of an outcome as an achievement.

Another phenomenon that surprised me in doing unfamiliar self-work is called "the learning curve". Initial attempts at tasks invariably took much longer than subsequent repetitions. For instance, installing the first recessed can light in the family room ceiling took me two hours. The second took one hour, the third one-half hour, the fourth took 17 minutes. All the rest took less than 15 minutes each. When I taped over the first window unit before spray painting, it took two hours, the second, 45 minutes, and eventually less than five minutes each. When sanding walls with a pole sander, the first wall took 30 minutes, then 20, and on down. Each repetition was better than the last.

Consider the learning curve when planning your work or if you get discouraged. Your work will improve in quality and speed as you persist.

Rules of Self-Work

At first, unfamiliar work is a novelty, then it's boring, and then, if you stay with it, it becomes like a drug. You wonder how you can live without it. To paraphrase Karl Marx, "Self-work is the opiate of the owner-builder".

1. Be a good learner. Gather materials and organize your study of the task. Pay an expert for advice if appropriate.

2. Plan the task in detail before you start.

3. Allow enough time overall. If you don't have enough time, let someone else do it.

4. Don't worry how long each step takes.

5. Redo something if you're not satisfied.

6. Do one thing at a time.

7. Use good materials.

Sources Say

"Resist the temptation, even on a big lot, to bury the stumps off in a corner somewhere. This extends the scarring on the landscape and usually makes later work both necessary and difficult. Trucking stumps away is preferable."

From *The Well-Built House* (See page 260)

Sources Say

"I think there are two, maybe three keys to success in taking on construction tasks yourself. One read up, do your homework. There are good books on everything. Two, don't take on too much. Three, get the backup or support you need."

From *Independent Builder* (See page 259)

8. Assemble all needed materials first.

9. Use good tools.

10. Assemble all needed tools first.

11. Keep all tools in good condition, sharp, oiled, and operating well to promote quality and safety.

12. Do the important thing, the hard thing; don't just stay busy.

13. Start early.

14. Keep at it until you're done.

15. Pause to rethink your approach.

16. Keep the area clean.

17. Work a full day and don't leave your task.

Accomplishments and Satisfactions

One of the satisfactions of doing self-work is that you constantly invent things when you build. I devised little paper circles I cut to trace a hole for a can light above the front porch. I used a strap tie to hold up a heavy fluorescent can while I secured it on a high ceiling. I put a screw in the framing and hung my drill by a strap while my hands were busy with other tools working on a high ladder. A friend and I struggled to make a stubborn electrical supply cable reach to the wall panel. We finally turned the rear panel mechanism upside down, and it reached. You get meaning from solving constant problems and from constant striving.

You have to laugh at yourself and marvel that you ever finished any of the projects. Our electrical consultant checked our work after we finished wiring the master bath. He studied the wiring quietly for some moments and said, "I was looking at this wiring, Mrs. Smith, and what you've got here is that two of these vanity lights will be on at all times regardless of the switch. And the fan light in the johnny room will only operate when the switch is thrown for the vanity lights in the main bathroom."

When I tour people through our house I enjoy pointing at the ceiling fan high above the family room and saying that Elaine installed that fan. We had a tall scaffold set up in the room and we both climbed up to put the fan in place. I stood up to screw in the mounting bracket and my knees began to shake from fear of heights. Elaine volunteered to take over, but at the very peak of the ceiling height, she too got unsteady. So I sat down and hugged her legs and she worked with one hand while firmly gripping my hair with the other. From such things are lasting satisfactions made.

Sub Recognition

The last of your P.O.I.M.M. responsibilities as a manager is to "Motivate". You motivate your team from the very earliest point by respecting their opinions in interviews and in the bidding process. Throughout the job it is your responsibility to provide a work environment that motivates the team.

Studies consistently show that respect and job challenge rank over wages as motivators. You show respect for the subs by seeking their opinions and giving them the deserved freedom to operate. Respect their needs for an orderly schedule and clean work environment. Run a job where the subs can get in and out quickly. Little things like helping to unload material will facilitate this.

Inspect early and pay fast, which is a great sign of respect. If you ask them to do extras, be free with additional payment. Many things that you will want done are not clear on the plans or in bids. Pay for these promptly. One O-B who saved nearly 40% on his project kept a $1,000 – $2,000 fund available in 50 and 100 dollar bills. When the schedule slipped, he asked subsequent subs to put in extra hours or weekends and offered them cash for the extra effort. He got amazing productivity.

Your subs may want to erect their signs at your site or use you as a referral to get future business. Go to extra lengths to facilitate this for responsible subs. I provided a word processed letter of recommendation on my letterhead to several without being asked.

Some O-B's buy lunch once a week, or have daily refreshments on-site for the subs. Think of what you appreciate in a working environment and do likewise for your team. Two cautions: 1) Don't allow alcoholic beverages on your site. Alcohol and construction don't mix. 2) Don't get too "chummy" with the subs. Maintain an appropriate relationship of mutual respect.

Readers Say

"I rented a Bobcat to do some of my own dirt work. It was on the incline which slopes toward the lake behind our place. I got off, and it started to 'click' and move. I jumped in to set the brake, but had not familiarized myself with the brake. I fumbled with it as it picked up speed. I decided in a panic to start the thing and put it in reverse, but forgot that the seat belt had to be engaged for the starter to work. It rolled smoothly into the lake. The lake bottom dropped off steeply, and it rolled 30 feet into the lake, covering the top of the cab by five feet. I swam to shore. Linda came around the house and looked at me soaking in my clothes and said, 'Where is the Bobcat?'"

Gary & Linda Z.
Stansbury Park, UT

http://www.OwnerBuilderBook.com

Some messages from Owner-Builder Connections:

SUBJECT: New in NJ

Hi, We are in the final stages of closing on our land. I would like some information specific to NJ area. Can you help us? I am looking for reliable subs etc. Please reply if you have some time to share information. Thanks in advance. Sri

SUBJECT: Closing in NJ

Hi...What area are you located in? Michel

SUBJECT: O-B from NJ

Hi, Thank you for replying. We are buying the land in Lawrenceville. It is the next town to Princeton. My e-mail address is ... When did you start/complete your O-B home? I need some info specific to NJ. Can you share your experiences? Thanks in advance. Sri

SUBJECT: RE:O-B from NJ

Hi Sri,

I am from the Woodbury area of South Jersey so my contractor connections won't be helpful. I found some great subcontractors through a general contractor who is retired. I obtained three bids that included the ones he suggested and 7 out of 9 won out with their bids. It was more their recommendations that got them the bids and their prices were 25 to 50% lower than the ones with so-so recommendations.

This is my retirement home and the three bids I got from builders were all really high. So I took the leap and went ahead being my own general. I had no previous experience but good organizational skills. That has paid off. I keep notes on everything and do "Things to get done" lists everyday and try to complete each list entirely...or else things would have piled up on me very quickly.

I started two and a half months ago and break ground next month. I anticipate building my 1,700 sq. ft. Cape Cod with a full poured concrete basement in 3-4 months. I had researched my wish list for almost 9 months before going to builders, so I knew what I wanted. In the last two months I've spent 40 hours a week on the paperwork and research. I research everything on-line about each trade before I picked my subcontractors. The cost of the concrete work was the biggest surprise. The Owner-Builder budget was actually closer to the %'s than I thought it would be on a lot of the line items. Go ahead and order the CD-ROM if you don't already have it.

Suggestions: Go to job sites of new homes that match your standards and ask who's doing the work. Then find them and ask them if they're interested in bidding on your job. The idea is that they will do the work for you for the same price as that builder without the builder adding on his additional overhead. Order extra sets of prints so the process goes faster. In the long run it's money worth spending. I negotiated prices for materials and saved money almost every time. Bids can also be negotiated. And if you find a contractor that will agree to walk you through the process as a consultant...it would be worth paying for. My consultant has been invaluable since otherwise I would have had trouble knowing which step to take next.

I have taken on quite a task but am proud of myself for going at it with 100% commitment to building a home that will be my dream home. If there are any questions I can answer I will try to get back with you as soon as I can. Michel

SUBJECT: Owner-Builders

Hello, We are in Valencia and about to begin our search for a lot. How has things been for you in this area as owner builders?

SUBJECT: Land Prices

Hello.... we live in Saugus, but have been looking all over SC Valley.... so far, it just looks very pricey. :(We are not actually intending to Owner-build for several years (too many young children in our household right now), but we wanted to shop for land early -- hoping to have something by the end of next year. So far, we are not seeing anything that is a good price, let alone a bargain. That is, unless you want to move way out to Green Valley, and even those lots are small. How is your search? We were thinking about checking some land auctions around the beginning of next year, and getting in touch with the assessors office.... have you tried that yet? Keep in touch... would love to hear how your Owner-building experience goes.

SUBJECT: Phoenix

I'm beginning to get bids for my new house in Phoenix. I was wondering if you had any comments and/or could recommend any subs. Thanks, Tom

SUBJECT: RE: Phoenix

Hi Tom,

If you have time to grab a cup of coffee or something, I would like to talk to you about your planning process and how you handled the loan situation. We're putting our plan together right now and any information sharing I could do at this stage would be wonderful.

Best Regards, Matt

Chapter 15: Mistakes You Can Avoid and Successes You Can Achieve

Time line: Six months out

Mistakes

During the course of our construction, I kept a notebook of mistakes we made. Some of them were items that came out okay, but not as I'd hoped. For instance, the stairs in the garage step down straight out of the mudroom. This was as originally planned, but it cuts a foot or two out of the basketball playing surface in the garage. I wasn't thinking too clearly the day they poured those, or I would have had them form a landing and turn to parallel the garage wall. After being in the house we see that the smoke alarms go off occasionally from excess kitchen smoke. Next time I would put a 200 cubic foot per minute fan in the wall or ceiling to supplement the downdraft range.

Most of the mistakes were items that didn't go smoothly — where the process could be improved next time. My biggest were:

Readers Say

"It's a good idea to mark on the floor with spray paint where every outlet is located so the drywallers can pinpoint them."

Steve & Maria J.
Provo, UT

-relying on donated labor or the return of favors from volunteer helpers;
-waiting too long for subs who didn't show;
-not hiring an electrical consultant soon enough;
-allowing the consultant to do some actual work;
-paying some subs on a time and material basis without an advance estimate;
-allowing the plumber to supply some materials which were marked up heavily;
-hiring some "no-goods" as subs because I got in a hurry when the first choice didn't show;
-not having a written agreement to protect me from the no-goods;
-giving some subs too much payment before they were finished.

The owner-builders I interviewed cited five principal mistakes repeatedly:

1. Self-work problems.
2. Insufficient planning.
3. Using friends or hiring someone as a favor to someone else.
4. Not picking subs carefully.
5. Not putting more things in writing.

Disasters

Sometimes the mistakes lead to disasters. In my case, the mistake of hiring dishonest carpenters led to a small disaster. I compounded the mistake by making progress payments instead of one payment at completion. I then compounded that mistake by not having them sign a release of lien for the payments. The result was a lien on the house and a lawsuit — considerable aggravation.

One owner-builder I interviewed made the same mistake of paying his framers weekly. He compounded the mistake by paying fully, not partially, on work done. After receiving two payments the framer didn't show up for two weeks. When the O-B hunted him down the framer said "Go ahead and fire me". He had nothing to lose.

Another O-B made progress payments to his bricklayer. The bricklayer then failed to show up for four weeks, or stopped in to do a little bit of work and left. When challenged he asked for a payment three times as large, which the owner refused to pay. It turned out the bricklayers went out and spent the money each time getting drunk. The owner fired them but had no back-up plan, and it was very difficult to find a new bricklayer.

One O-B remembered to schedule all his inspections except the insulation inspection all municipalities make just before sheetrock goes on the walls. The inspector put him through the unwanted experience of tearing out sheetrock in several locations around the house to expose the insulation for inspection.

Sometimes the disasters are big ones. One O-B, who was in the Bobcat™ equipment business, bought land in Florida that had been a dump and was very settled. He used his equipment to level the land himself, and never got a survey to see if it was sitting at the right elevation. It was four feet below road level. Subsequent rain filled the lot up and went into the house. After experimenting with retaining walls they gave up and tore the place down.

Several lenders told me about projects that got started and dragged on for years. One lender told me about two O-B houses he knew of that took over ten years to complete. Lenders also tell stories about people who start the house planning to save money by self-work, and get injured on the job. One of these got a hernia, one broke his back. The houses wound up costing much more than planned.

In the "top this" category is a story from California about a couple that also failed to get a survey before breaking ground. They got the entire house finished before they discovered it was on the wrong lot. I think that would ruin your whole day.

Successes

Remember Vince Miner, the college tennis coach mentioned in Chapter 1 who saved 52% on his construction costs?

Vince Miner built a custom house some years ago for $87,500 that had eight bedrooms and four baths, amounting to 4,000 square feet. ($22/foot) He framed it as a helper, helped pour all the flatwork, insulated it, and made sure everything was ready for each sub as they came along. The house appraised at $225,000 immediately, or about $56/foot when finished. (Allowing for land, a 52% savings.) He did the things he wanted — wide hallways and stairways, high ceilings, and lots of extra insulation. He has two feet of blown-in insulation over the ceiling. He didn't bother to install air conditioning; in that house, ceiling fans are adequate. His heating bills are negligible.

He was required by the neighborhood CC&R committee ("Covenants, Conditions, and Restrictions") to put cedar shake shingles on the house, and he called around and found a supplier in Montana who trucked down a load of "short" shakes at a discount that were more than adequate. These saved him $1,000. Many people were out of work at the time, and he got deals on subs. The roofer was in between jobs and put the roof on for $25 a square. The tile sub was a student from the college where Vince taught. Vince never had anybody show up late on the schedule. The result was that he built the house in four months. One luxury was a professional estimator from a lumberyard who did his budgeting and scheduling, and found him some deals, for a $3,000 fee. I have toured Miner's house and was very impressed with the workmanship. His savings are off the charts for a civilian owner-builder.

Another house with even greater savings that I toured was that of a tradesman, a sheetrocker who owner-built a high-end custom house. His house is valued in the $100 per finished foot range, but he built it for $60 a foot. He traded for all the services he could and further reduced the out of pocket cost to $30 a foot. It took some time to fulfill all the trades, but he occupied his home at a 70% cash savings.

Another tradesman I know built a 3,800 square foot custom home for $88,000 in construction costs ($23 a foot). He traded extensively to achieve this. I have toured the two year-old home of owner-builder Jay Sevison, the software manager mentioned earlier. It is an absolutely posh custom home built on an amazing $38 per square foot budget.

I asked one naysaying lender who refuses to do owner-builder loans how his past O-B loans came out. He said they typically went over budget but admitted their projects were done at a savings. I asked him to describe a successful project and he described a woman owner-builder who came in right on her $180,000 construction budget, ran a smooth project, and finished in eight months. Her secret to success? She had three written bids for each trade when she applied for the construction loan. She didn't work and ran the job full-time.

One lender told me about a couple where the husband was an engineer and the wife ran the job full-time. It went so smoothly they did another, and earned handsome profits. The woman got a license as a general contractor and now builds for a living.

Several lenders described to me projects that saved 35% off estimated costs. One lender in Alaska told me of a couple who saved 50%. A lender in Florida told me that every owner-builder he has financed has moved in with a minimum of 20% equity.

Success in residential construction is to come in on budget, on schedule and on specifications. For owner-builders, I would add: at a savings. The owner-builders I interviewed saved an average of 35% off the estimated costs of construction or appraised value. To me this dispels the myth that owner-builders can't save money over using a general contractor.

We did some things right on our house that we consider successes. One was the use of a spreadsheet budget. We got a lot of mileage out of the computer and fax capabilities that saved us money. We had a very clean job site and beautiful finished product. We found some stellar subs and used very good material. We were able to upgrade many of the components to the very best available. We ran over our budget but got a satisfyingly overbuilt house. We saved 44% over estimated cost, and because we managed to pay for the land in advance have an overall equity of nearly 60% in the property.

How to Score Yourself

Budget

The most important measure of your success as an owner-builder is how much money you saved building your house according to specifications. You can score yourself if you know what your construction costs are estimated to be by general contractors in advance. Or you can take the appraised value of the house (minus land) immediately after you complete construction to compare it. Use the college system, and give yourself a letter grade: "D" if you beat the estimate by ten percent (a 1.0 grade point average), "C" if you beat the estimate by 20%, "B" if by 30%, and you get a 4.0 average, an "A", if you beat the estimate by 40%.

In my case, the house was estimated at $85 a finished foot, which we calculate at $90 to reflect landscaping, construction interest, window coverings, and other items which the builder did not include. We built the house for about $50 a finished square foot, a savings of $40.

Estimate: $90/ft.

As-built: $50/ft

Savings: $40/ft

Percent: 44%

Grade: "A"

Schedule

In order to compare apples to apples, let's look at what it takes to build the average American single-family home. The average home in 2001 came in at 2,324 finished square feet, according to the U.S. Census Bureau. The average time to complete for general contractor projects was 6 months for the same year, according to the National Association of Home Builders.

Let's combine those two statistics and make one of our own. 2,324 square feet divided by 6 months to build equals 387 square feet per month. ("F.P.M.") This is the rate of production of the average general contractor. This is a fairly poky pace of building. Some builders in the NAHB study came out building homes at 878 feet per month by my calculation. But let's use averages to score owner-builders.

The average contractor-built home came in at 387 feet per month of building. To score myself, I calculate that my 3,500 finished square feet were built in eight months for a production of 438 feet per month:

Finished square feet: 3,500 square feet

Months to complete: 8 months

"Feet per month":   438 f.p.m.

National builder average: 387 f.p.m.

Percent over average: 13%

Grade ("1.0")   "D"

The "Ten Commandments" shown on the next page have been expanded into a series of DVD's.

(See page 264)

My own score was an "A" for budget, and a "D" for schedule. Score yourself when your project is over. Let us know how you did. Visit us on the Web at www.OwnerBuilderBook.com and tell us of your success.

If You are Married

No report card tells the whole story of success. How your project affected your personal life is not measured by grades on schedule and budget. There are many stories about marriages and families suffering during home building projects. A common saying is: "A marriage that survives building a house will survive anything." One architect told me he contracts separately with both husband and wife in case they divorce.

Owner-builders I interviewed acknowledged the stress, but often said that the project was ultimately a bonding experience. Some mentioned added closeness with children who were involved in various ways in the undertaking. Elaine says that our project brought us closer together and was very enjoyable. I think she has a short memory, but I am grateful for her attitude.

One O-B told me that he got so upset at his wife when they were hashing out details that he left the car and walked all the way home from the job site (three miles) on several occasions. I have heard similar stories from others who have built homes, with or without a contractor.

I remember yelling about something one day on the job site, and when the dust settled looking around red-faced to notice that we were in the middle of a busy neighborhood in a house without doors or windows.

The antidote to serious marital friction in building a house is planning. As experienced owner-builder Jim Stark of Nebraska City, Nebraska (mentioned in Chapter 5) says: "Building a house will stress any marital relationship. Making choices is a strain. We put together a notebook of what it will look like before we even start. We get most of the arguing out of the way. We take pictures as we plan and turn it into an album. We use the album to develop specs."

Georgia Architect Robert Byington adds: "If the marriage is not stable, don't start. If you can decide on a plan, and become almost concrete with that plan, you will succeed. Pre-planning is paramount. The average person does not understand the effect of moving a wall three feet. Planning lessens the number and complexity of the problems."

The Ten Commandments of Owner-Builders

1. 1,000 hours of planning

2. Written list of features

3. Spreadsheet budget and expense tracking

4. Written schedule

5. Three bids on all sub and supplier items

6. Signed agreements and lien releases

7. Buy materials directly

8. Constant communication with subs

9. Be on-site

10. Run a clean, organized job

Project Notes

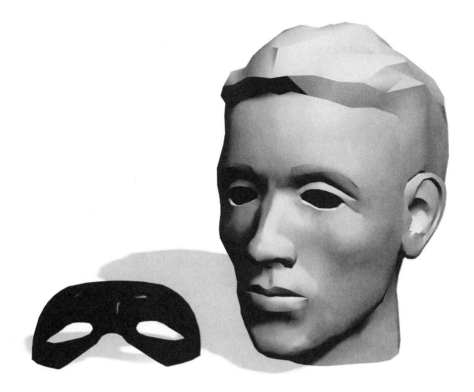

Chapter 16: If You Decide to Use a Contractor

There Are a Lot of Reasons to Use a General

An experienced construction lender whom I admire puts his loan applicants through hoops to make sure they are prepared to begin building. He insists on thorough preparation and a commitment to the time gobbling process of on-site supervision. If the candidate can't make the commitment, he steers them to the use of a general contractor. 65% of his candidates wind up going with a general.

Perhaps you are in the category of the 65% who intend to owner-build but acknowledge that they can't make the commitment to succeed. It involves too much time or disruption. You may be under a tax or land contract deadline that impels you to move more quickly than you can prepare properly.

It helps to be honest with yourself. You know the facts. You can save a great deal of money, but only if you conscientiously take the steps needed to effect the savings. You know the time commitment involved. You know the tasks involved and can make an informed and mature choice.

Readers Say

"I'm doing an owner-builder with a site manager - project manager. He's a full contractor. He gets 10% on everything bid through him at the end of the day, and he does the foundation."

Jay B.
Pacific Palisades, CA

Sources Say

Your New House gives13 questions to ask a general contractor before using him.

(See page 260)

You may want to go through a contractor-built process before attempting to solo. Like me, you don't want to do something half-way. Life is long — there are many chances to implement your growing knowledge.

For many people personal time is scarce, and realistically, there is a good-sized part of the public for whom money is more abundant than time. You may be in the happy circumstance of being able to afford all the house you want to build, general contractor notwithstanding.

How to Hire a General

You may choose to dedicate the limited time you have to do a thorough job of hiring a general contractor. You have a good deal of knowledge of the "system" from reading this book, and you won't go into this process naively. Like the steps in the owner-builder process, you need to be organized and tenacious to get what you want.

Start by interviewing possible general contractors. Don't invite them to give you a sales pitch yet, just interview them as "background" before deciding what to do. Use the subcontractor interview form on page 89 as a guide and add other concerns you have to the interview. Be professional about this — much is at stake. Follow the suggestions in Chapter 7 for a well-documented interview. If you go to the trouble of interviewing many generals, say six to ten, with the same form, a picture will emerge of their differences and your preferences.

Select the generals from whom you will solicit bids. Follow the guidelines in Chapter 3 for a detailed bid from a general. You will supply written descriptions and specifications along with your plans to elicit a detailed bid. The generals will supply line item pricing and a written schedule.

You don't want any of the many contractual disasters that owners have endured with their generals. Thus you will ask for the keys to a thorough evaluation of your builder from a financial and legal standpoint:

- Evidence of workmen's compensation insurance.
- Evidence of liability and builder's risk insurance.
- Evidence of performance and completion bondability.
- Identities of the likely subcontractors.
- References of three most recent customers.
- Recent credit report.
- Three trade references.
- Bank reference.
- Copy of state contractor's license.
- Terms of House Warranty.

Experienced California construction lender Jan McClary explains:

> "Hire an experienced contractor. Check their license. Do they have workmen's compensation and liability insurance? He's responsible to make sure that every sub has the insurance, and that the policies name the owner as additionally insured. Two years down the line, the neighbor comes over and says, 'your contractor did this to my property, and it will cost $10,000 to fix'. If the owner has the certificate of insurance naming the owner as additionally insured, (and the bank, too) then, even if the contractor is out of business, it will be covered. He has to make sure that every sub has the worker's compensation and general liability insurance naming the owner and certificate holder as additionally insured. Require a performance and completion bond. Check out him and his documentation. Credit report, three references, two trades, bank and license boards. Have a consultant do a cost breakdown review, and the general contract, and check out the insurance."

Take the time to check the references you get and to record your findings. Ask past customers of the general: Did you have problems? Did he service problems promptly even after you occupied? How long have you been in, and what kind of problems have you had? What was it estimated for, and what did you wind up paying for it? How were relations during the project? Was your move-in date met?

If the references have been in their homes for a long time, the contractor didn't give you the three most recent like you asked. He may have given you an aunt or a cousin. Pass over that contractor, or get fresh references from him and try again.

Who's Got the Risk?

There are several contractual arrangements under which homes can be built by general contractors. The first and most well-known is the contract bid. 90% of all residential construction is contracted this way. The general tells you the price and signs a contract saying he won't go over it. Theoretically there is a risk for the builder that it will cost him more than what he has agreed and he will lose money.

But what is the reality of the situation? Here's a multiple choice question:

If the budget starts to go over, the builder is likely to:

a. Shop for bargains.
b. Cut corners.
c. Hit you with change orders.
d. Take a loss.

(Answer: He will resist a and d. If you resist c, he will go to b, whether you know it or not.)

Generally the risk returns to you in any of the major contract formats, but there are differences:

You decide what you want for yourself. You are under no obligation to accept a contract bid arrangement from a general. You are in the driver's seat and you call the shots, even if it takes passing over several builders until you find the one you can work with.

Major Construction Contract Types

	Owner-Builder	Fixed Fee	Cost-Plus	Contract Bid
Description:	No contractor	You hire and buy. You pay a fee to contractor.	He hires and buys. You pay a percent of costs as fee to contractor.	He just charges you the agreed amount.
Risk:	Yours	Mostly yours, reduced technical.	Mostly yours	His
Quality of House:	High	High	High	Low
Savings:	High	High	Medium	Low
Control:	High	Medium	Medium	Low

In any case it is good to permit the builders to estimate your project in the normal way, where they estimate the costs in a contract bid. With cost estimates in hand you can reflect on the best way to proceed.

You could turn to a cost-plus arrangement where you pay the costs directly for the subs and materials used. If the costs come out to $200,000 and you have agreed to a ten percent fee, you pay $20,000 to the contractor at the end. Review the discussion on cost-plus in Chapter 3 to understand why this is not a high savings approach.

Fixed fee, however, is a winner if you handle it right. Without specifying fixed fee you can entertain the bids of several good generals. You can then negotiate with your preferred general. With his estimated costs in hand you can ask how much profit he will make on the job. The answer will come back as 10%, 15%, or some number that is certainly negotiable. Ask, "Then to build this house with a ten percent fee, you would expect to earn $20,000? If so, would you be willing to accept that as a fixed fee and let us pay the subs and suppliers directly?"

Under this arrangement you would receive and pay the invoices for subs and suppliers directly without any mark-up or profit to the general. You are free to substitute your own subs or suppliers in any category and to negotiate with the general's usual subs. You can do any self-work you wish. Since your general is not getting mark-ups on subs and materials, he may ask for more than customary profit — something to cover overhead. If he doesn't — don't offer it. If he does, it is now a negotiable number, which is an advantage to you. If you have several contractors vying for the work you have leverage in setting this fee.

Any agreements like the above need to be settled with your contractor in advance of construction, while he is in the position of vying for the work. Let the contractor know that you intend to have a well-defined relationship in the beginning, and get protections that are very solid. You will be in a very rare and enviable position among residential construction buyers.

It does pay to shop and negotiate, even if you think you have a very good deal before you. When I was restoring my house in Ohio in 1983 after a house fire, I got a bid from the insurance company who said flatly: "This is what we will pay to restore your house." I decided to get a second bid, from a restoration contractor. He found several additional items that he suggested be included in the restoration.

I called the insurance company one morning from work and described five or six items to them that they hadn't considered. The conversation took about 15 minutes and resulted in the insurance company paying $7,500 more than they had planned. This resulted in an improved payout of $500 for each minute of the phone call. In DSDE dollars, I would have had to earn $75,000 to add that much to my net worth. That would have taken me a year and ten months at my then salary of $42,000.

Prior to finalizing your contractor choice, before you sign the agreement, take time to do some telephone shopping to check with other generals on your acceptable list to see how close they would come to the terms you can get from your first choice.

Bide your time. Based on normal market fluctuations, experts tell me that your bid for the same work could be 15% higher or lower. It may pay to be patient, or to be ready to move if the numbers are right. Your preparation will help you to recognize a bargain.

You Know What You Are Getting Into

Having read this book, you know all about the planning steps involved in a thorough custom home project. The planning work is like shooting foul shots at the end of a basketball game when you are behind. You can score without taking time off the clock. You can reduce your costs substantially before a shovel of dirt is turned, and before the interest clock starts ticking. Even if you hire a contractor.

You can decide after you do all the prep or at any point along the way if you want to go the contractor route. Keep your options open at first. Everything you do and all you learn will help you at points along the way, and give you a better finished product and more equity.

A recent story in the newspapers in Phoenix, Arizona was about a homeowner in the historical district. The owner there got a licensed remodeling contractor and gave him $55,000 to remodel the home and never saw him again. Don't be casual about a decision to use a general contractor, thinking that you can place yourself in his hands and relax. You must be vigilant to use the legal safeguards of contracting described in Chapter 12, including the rule of not paying before work is done.

Review "Contractor Games" in Chapter 3. Be savvy in looking out for your own protection.

Readers Say

"Many of the builders have their own architects. If you enter into the agreement properly, you can cut out the architect, and then have greater control over the materials used. You can set it up to make progress payments subject to satisfactory completion of each stage. Architects would charge professional fees for monitoring all that, and it could cost from $50,000 to $100,000 on a high-end home. You could take care of that yourself and save that money."

Jim & Diane B.
Telford, PA

Sources Say

Independent Builder has a chapter on contract types.

(See page 259)

Readers Say

"Some of the other books out there wind up telling you to go see a contractor after you've got your plans. That's ironic, because using an architect or a contractor are the two biggest things that add to your cost."

Ron D.
Cortland, NY

Project Notes

Afterword: Once You're In...

Minimize Punch List

As a quality control on the house, make sure that items aren't hanging over after you occupy. They can become enormous. I had six pages of punch list (unfinished or incorrect items needing fixes before the contractor can "punch out") after my house restoration in Ohio, and refused to make my last payment until it was completed. The contractor didn't want to take care of the little things so he decided not to pursue collection of the last several thousand dollars. I took care of the items at a big savings.

You don't have that advantage as an owner-builder. You will be stuck with whatever is not right when all your subs have gone home and you have paid them. The little items can linger for a long time. My list on the Riverbottoms home was over 100 items, most relating to my imperfections as a painter.

If you have a list, manage it. Use the worksheet on page 232, or put the items on a spreadsheet with a column to tally an unfinished item count. Track your progress to completion.

The punch list checklist shown on the next page is also available on a spreadsheet on our free Resource CD-ROM.

(See page 270)

Punch List

Task	Notes
25% 50% 75% 100%	
25% 50% 75% 100%	
25% 50% 75% 100%	
25% 50% 75% 100%	
25% 50% 75% 100%	
25% 50% 75% 100%	
25% 50% 75% 100%	
25% 50% 75% 100%	
25% 50% 75% 100%	
25% 50% 75% 100%	
25% 50% 75% 100%	
25% 50% 75% 100%	
25% 50% 75% 100%	

Punch List

Task	Notes
25% 50% 75% 100%	
25% 50% 75% 100%	
25% 50% 75% 100%	
25% 50% 75% 100%	
25% 50% 75% 100%	
25% 50% 75% 100%	
25% 50% 75% 100%	
25% 50% 75% 100%	
25% 50% 75% 100%	
25% 50% 75% 100%	
25% 50% 75% 100%	
25% 50% 75% 100%	
25% 50% 75% 100%	
25% 50% 75% 100%	

Punch List

Task	Notes
25% 50% 75% 100%	
25% 50% 75% 100%	
25% 50% 75% 100%	
25% 50% 75% 100%	
25% 50% 75% 100%	
25% 50% 75% 100%	
25% 50% 75% 100%	
25% 50% 75% 100%	
25% 50% 75% 100%	
25% 50% 75% 100%	
25% 50% 75% 100%	
25% 50% 75% 100%	
25% 50% 75% 100%	

Punch List

Task	Notes
25% 50% 75% 100%	
25% 50% 75% 100%	
25% 50% 75% 100%	
25% 50% 75% 100%	
25% 50% 75% 100%	
25% 50% 75% 100%	
25% 50% 75% 100%	
25% 50% 75% 100%	
25% 50% 75% 100%	
25% 50% 75% 100%	
25% 50% 75% 100%	
25% 50% 75% 100%	
25% 50% 75% 100%	

Lower Your Property Taxes

Many owner-builders find themselves in the position that I did on moving into their new homes. The new house is assessed much higher for property taxes than their former residence. My new assessment resulted in much higher property taxes than I anticipated. I went down and appealed my assessment before the Board of Equalization for my municipality and got a generous adjustment.

You are in a uniquely opportune position to get an adjustment as an owner-builder, and it can be a big savings. My evidence before the Board was that my home cost less to build than they assessed it for. They accepted that argument along with my statement about costs. I interviewed assessors in several locations around the United States and they all acknowledged that receipts for construction costs would be considered good evidence for adjustment.

The value of your adjustment can be substantial because reassessment does not occur for as many as ten years in some localities, according to Peter Sepp at the National Taxpayers Union. If you save $400 a year, your savings may mount up to as much as $4,000. Mr. Sepp told me he is constantly amazed at the citizens who will not make the effort to prepare and present a case for adjustment, no more than a half-days' work. Four hours expended for $4,000 saved is $1,000 saved per hour.

Better than Wall Street

Some homeowners are surprised to learn that mortgage interest usually exceeds the cost of the house itself over a 30 year period. With interest, your home can cost you three times its original price over the life of the mortgage. (At an interest rate of 9.5%) For instance, principal and interest payments on a $250,000 loan at 9.5% interest would amount to about $750,000 over 30 years. At six percent interest the payments would equal $541,000 over 30 years.

There is a loan amortization calculator available on our web site.

By planning carefully, you can turn this phenomenon to your advantage. One way to make a quick reduction in overall interest is by setting up your mortgage over a 15 rather than a 30 year period. Principal and interest on a $250,000 loan at six percent for 15 years are $380,000. Another approach is to make balance reduction payments periodically in addition to your regular mortgage payments. By making one extra mortgage payment per year, you can pay off a 30 year loan in 22 1/2 years.

On a $150,000 loan at 9% for 30 years, principal and interest payments are $1,189 per month. If you made an extra payment of $100 per month, you would spend $27,000 to reduce the mortgage by 7 1/2 years. You would save $86,729 in interest over 7 1/2 years thereafter. The return on your $27,000 is $86,729, and unlike stock market returns, it's guaranteed!

Help Someone Else

By following the steps in this book, you, the courageous owner-builder, will accomplish one of the most substantial achievements available in our society. You will gain all the advantages and status of owning a well-designed and meticulously constructed home. Your personal wealth will jump substantially. Share your good fortune. Put your knowledge to work on behalf of someone else.

Coach another owner-builder. Show up to offer on-site support and assistance. Help build a Habitat for Humanity or Christmas in April house or similar charitable construction project. Join a church or civic group in repairing the home of an elderly or disadvantaged person.

Be sure to thank, in writing, the subs and suppliers who made you a success. Share their names and business cards with others. Promote their success as they did yours.

Join us on our web site at www.OwnerBuilderBook.com. Contribute your ideas to our Forums. Add to your knowledge and help others to "beat the system". Allow us to help you with further materials or answers to your questions. Call us toll-free at 1-888-333-BUILD.

Now go build.

"Whatever you can do, or dream you can, begin it. Boldness has genius, power and magic in it."

Goethe

Slashdot
www.slashdot.org

Following a review of *The Owner-Builder Book* on www.slashdot.org, a website with more than 50 million page views a month, 200 pages of comments were generated. Here are a few excerpts.

Re:DIY
by sbaker on Wednesday June 19, @03:50PM

We built our house in Texas where all but about two of the people who actually did the work didn't speak a word of English. My wife took Spanish classes just so she could talk to the workers. Beer, soft drinks, Big Mac's and Pizza were all provided - most on a daily basis. It's DEFINITELY worth doing that. We asked the contractor if we could have a fancy herringbone pattern worked into the brickwork under the windows - and he wanted to charge us an extra $1K for doing it...well, about $10 spent at McDonalds got us it 'for free'.

We'd also visit the site at least daily - often to find the bricklayers sitting around because they'd run out of sand or something...it was our mobile phone that got things moving again by getting the damned contractor to get off his duff and get some delivered. Getting friendly with those guys was well worth it.

Re:Contractors...
by libre lover on Wednesday June 19, @02:09PM

Even a nerd is smart enough to build equity.

And when I moved into my starter home (town house, actually) I was fully on the DIY kick. I pulled down wallpaper, put up drywall, changed and added light fixtures, and painted, good lord how I painted!

Now we're planning on adding a deck in the backyard and we spoke to different contractors. After getting the used-car-salesman "what can I do to make you sign the contract today?", the run-around, the week-to-week price change, and the shady "we'll drive around in my truck and I'll point out the one's I've done, you don't NEED references!" - I've decided to build it myself.

For a savings of $1,500-3,000 USD (depending upon whose estimate you believe).

So this book is right up my alley!

Re:Living through it right now
by jdevons on Wednesday June 19, @01:40PM

I actually got better prices than all of my subs could get. There wasn't a one that could beat me... And I even told the suppliers that I was an owner-builder.

Re:I suppose....
by Avwar on Wednesday June 19, @12:02PM

I built my own house, spent a lot of time instead of money; and haven't spent a lot of time bellyaching about a contractor ever since.

Very simple
by Black Aardvark House on Wednesday June 19, @11:12AM

You're doing the work the contractor does. Not everyone will have the patience to run through all the steps in the book. Therefore, people hire contractors to do all this for them.

This book will appeal to a rather limited audience who has the time and energy to do all this themselves. Despite the savings, most people would rather "take the easy way out".

Special Report #1

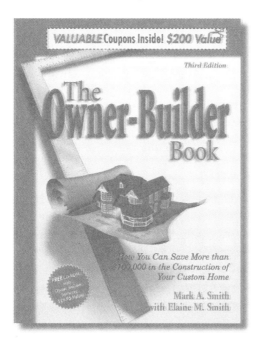

The Owner-Builder Book

Mark A. & Elaine M. Smith

House features that netted us $140,000

The right features rank with budget and calendar as your core tools in making money on your home. The four ways of increasing your wealth through your home rank as:

1. Reduce cost of construction
2. Improve resale with right features
3. Appreciation
4. Pay down mortgage

Traditionally your house adds to your wealth in only two ways. The most important way is through appreciation, which has averaged 5.5% per year in the U.S. for the past twenty years. This is a valuable source of gain, much better than a savings account. If you have a $200,000 house, and made a typical down payment of $20,000 to buy it, your 5.5% gain is measured against your $20,000 down payment. That returns $11,000 per year on $20,000 or 55%. Your savings account pays 5% or less on average.

The second way your home adds to your wealth is through retiring your mortgage. For most of us this is a small but steady gain. You hold a $200,000 mortgage, you make $2,000 payments, and you reduce the mortgage by a thousand or two per year in the early years.

On my last house I got $67,000 of appreciation in twelve years, or $6,000 a year. I had paid down my mortgage by more than $10,000 or $1,000 a year during the period. Compared to savings this was a superior gain for us, but small compared to the gain afforded by owner-building.

"We have an A-B-C list of what features we want. 'Must have', 'like to have', and 'if we can afford'..."
Ernie C.
Hill AFB, UT

"Other features of our house include: hurricane roof truss hangers, Simpson Strong ties affixing the main floor to the foundation, all concrete is mixed with fiber mesh to reduce cracking, four foot stairwell with lighting at treads, heat recovery ventilator, hot water heat in all bathrooms, whirlpool tubs, concrete tornado shelter, natural daylighting via Sun Tubes, 12-gauge wiring, whole-house vacuum , whole-house stereo, video, intercom, computer and telephone, 14 different heating zones, security system."
Dave & Sheila A.
Boone, IA"

As a remodeling contractor, I try to talk people out unusual ideas for their houses because they will probably resell within seven years. I would emphasize more the idea that you're building your house for resale. Really spend a lot of time trying to visualize what it's going to be like."
Bill R,
Redmond, OR

Owner-building opens up two additional areas of gain. The first is keeping the costs down, and the second is pushing the value up. The latter is done by building a house with market appeal, one which sells better and for more money. This is where selected, researched features come in.

On our custom home, we added $140,000 to our net worth in the eight months it took to build it. And the special features we managed to incorporate will enhance the price at sale. We built the house which was estimated at $90 a foot for $50 a foot using the techniques described in this book. But because of the strategic features we incorporated we were told that the house is currently worth $150 a foot in some markets. One architect told me that the right design and features will add 15% to the value of a house.

We selected the features for our custom home by a process of successive approximation over several months. We began by listing the features we had recorded in our dream home notebook. We then studied Parade of Homes houses in our area, taking pictures and making notes. We then compared the features to those listed in the Multiple Listing Service® for houses in our intended price range. We then called ten realtors and asked them to rank the features we had preselected for desirability and marketability.

To this process we added the consideration of which features were available at a bargain price. If our selected feature was overly costly to buy and install, we downgraded our plan. If a superior feature was available at the planned cost, or less, we upgraded our plan. As owner-builders we were free to make last minute additions and upgrades, and to include items that take a little extra time or effort to implement.

The following features found their way into the house we built for $50 per finished square foot in 1996:

Riverbottoms House

Summary of Features:

- 3,500 square foot two-story on .29 acres in the Riverbottoms
- Fully finished 780 sq. ft. garage
- 4 bedrooms
- Four baths: two full, one three quarter, one half
- 250 amp electrical service with upstairs and downstairs service panels
- 55 separate circuits for load balancing and convenience
- 12 gauge wiring and 20 amp circuits reduce resistance and fire risk
- Sports court in garage with metal halide lighting

- "Camping shelf" for item storage in garage
- Formal dining room/office
- Paneled breakfast nook
- Laundry room
- Mud room
- Walk-in pantry plus cabinet pantry
- Main floor master
- Walk-in master closet with hexagonal outside window
- Individual reading lights with bedside controls in master and guest suite
- Quoizel vanity lights in all baths
- Operable windows in master bath and guest bath
- Wolverine Monterrey IV Restoration Line
- .044 vinyl siding exterior
- Three piece vinyl corner posts
- Smooth finish vinyl
- Restoration beaded soffit entry
- Exterior architectural millwork
- Exterior recessed soffit downlighting
- Optional future exterior porch lighting stubbed in
- 25 year architectural asphalt shingles
- Aluminum roof drip edge
- 30 pound asphalt roofing paper over entire roof deck
- Heavy-gauge aluminum gutters and downspouts
- Formal entry with recessed lighting and hardwood flooring
- TJI "Silent Floor" joists
- Wiring and bracing for optional future entry chandelier up to 200 lbs.
- Recessed lighting throughout house
- Prewarmed Lasco Luxury Line jetted tub with 1 1/2 HP pump motor
- Silent cast-iron plumbing down pipes
- Moen Monticello plumbing fixtures
- Rain Bird lawn sprinkler system with programmable electronic timer
- Sprinklers installed with line drains and flexible head risers
- No-scald pressure balancing plumbing valves in all baths
- Two-sided gas fireplace with thermostat controls and variable blower fan
- Fireplace rated 48,000 BTU's and direct-vented to exterior
- Two quarried marble fireplace surrounds
- Solid maple mantel in family room
- Solid maple stair newels, rosettes and hand rail
- Seismic straps and extensive footing pads for earthquake resistance
- Extra wide footing piers and rebar in excess of building code
- Ten inch facia on exterior, with ribbed aluminum facia cap
- Bullnosed drywall corners
- 5/8" Type X fire retardant drywall throughout garage
- Alarm system with two motion detectors
- Two 90 Plus gas furnaces
- Two 12 Seer Day & Nite A/C units 2 1/2 ton up, 1 1/2 ton down
- Two programmable Honeywell electronic thermostats
- Insulated heating and air conditioning ductwork
- Two 40 gallon gas water heaters with seismic straps

"When we talk to builders and others in the business, they give us the same modest earnings description you mention in the book, but I can see how we can save much more. We are very enthused about this. What stands out to me is the helpful lists that professionals recommend for quality features. I had not even considered something like dual furnaces. Great for energy conservation. We are going to step up with this next house. 2,400 feet, but we want to fill it with quality features. People are tending to build big houses here, but it's all paint grade woodwork, hollow core doors and the like."
Lyn & Phil S.
Kansas City, MO

"Built our house and we're in it. It went great, very few problems. People tell you can't do it, but you really can. You run into a lot of obstacles, but if you are prepared for it, it goes well. He had a flexible job, and I was home with the children. I got involved a lot, and with the small kids, I couldn't be there a lot, but I could do a lot of errands during the day, but I could check up on things, and make calls. Picked up a lot of supplies, researching carpet buys, etc. It wasn't supposed to be our dream home, but it turned out so well we could really stay here for a long time. We would do the generalling next time, but subcontract out more of it. Started June 5, and occupied Nov. 14th. We did it for $111,000 and it appraises for $180,000 Equity is around $40,000, because we owned the lot. Did many upgrades, so is not a true starter home. 1,530 s.f. on upper, and now almost finished with basement. We will soon start on landscaping. Some of the custom features are upgrade carpet, tile work, laminate flooring, no vinyl, Marble bath counter tops, cultured marble Some of the custom features are upgrade carpet, tile work, laminate flooring, no vinyl, Marble bath counter tops, cultured marble tub surround, and windowsills, built in island stools, Trex deck, walk out basement, fabulous carpet. Upgrade lighting, track lighting, wall sconces, extremely nice front door, Thermatru, Insulated garage, we didn't cut

- Two story family room with East window wall
- Vaulted ceilings upstairs and in family room
- Cable TV to each room
- 24 gauge steel two inch thick Raynor
- Decade Showcase garage doors with 9.17 R-Value and lifetime panel warranty
- Insulated glass panels in garage doors
- Two Moore-O-Matic chain drive garage door openers with independent light controls and keyless entry pad
- Two 2 button garage door remotes
- 17 telephone jack locations
- Two active phone lines to each telephone jack expandable to four
- GE super quiet Profile dishwasher
- ISE Badger 5 1/2 HP garbage disposal
- Dramatic views of Provo Peak, Timpanogos and Squaw Peak
- Jenn-Air countertop downdraft gas range
- Gas range hookup convertible to electric
- Electric clothes dryer convertible to gas
- Stub-in for natural gas grille on deck
- Modular melamine and wire rack closet systems in all closets
- Master closet design includes drawers and wire laundry baskets
- Food bar seating at kitchen island
- Maple kitchen desk and pantry unit
- Stacked GE Profile microwave and convection wall ovens
- Solid granite kitchen countertop and island
- Two built-in maple cutting boards
- Solid granite bathroom counters and maple vanities
- Solid maple entertainment center with surround sound home theater
- Walk-in "nook" storage in two upstairs bedrooms
- Custom cabinets with solid maple frames
- Cabinets have crown moldings, fluted columns, rosettes and plinths
- Dramatic custom wood accent color contrasts in cabinetry
- Rabbeted wood cabinet joinery
- Self-closing cabinet drawers with 3/4 inch wood shelving
- Cabinets fully lined with fused melamine
- Abundant cabinets in kitchen island
- Solid maple furniture grade toe kicks
- Bake center with appliance garage and handicap accessible work seating
- Bake center wired for optional task lighting
- Switchable under-cabinet halogen lighting at kitchen range
- Marble candy-making counter surface at bake center
- Undermount Francke stainless steel sink in kitchen   *3 sink system*
- Pull-out Moen kitchen faucet with spray handle
- "Repair Kit" includes replacement tiles, shingles, balusters, carpet remnants, touchup paint, hardwood flooring, and wallpaper pieces
- Construction video depicting stages of construction and landscaping
- Owner's file with all appliance and product manuals
- Slide-out garbage can in cabinets
- Fully landscaped with more than six inches of rock-free topsoil
- Extra wide sidewalk and all flatwork poured with six-bag concrete mix

start here

Appendix I

- Chain-link fence with vinyl privacy inserts on two sides of property
- Wall to wall carpet with premium pad
- Dal-Tile Lithos Verde ceramic tile floor
- Ceramic tile floor in garage entry/mudroom/laundry/powder room
- All tile over cementitious underlayment
- Pedestal sink in powder room
- Two inch wood and metal privacy blinds
- Six-bag concrete patio
- Solid vinyl Brock Dock deck
- Library shelves in the family room
- Wenco thermal vinyl windows with 7/8" spacers and low-E protection
- Windows provide almost double the R-factor of other thermal windows
- Christmas light outlets on exterior front with single inside switch
- Roof heat tape outlets on exterior rear with single inside switch
- Hunter ceiling fans in bedrooms, family room, and kitchen nook
- Master and guest suite ceiling fans with dual bedside controls
- Guest suite with private bath
- Two-tone paint interior
- Nine foot ceilings upstairs
- Home theater speaker cavities prewired
- House stereo system prewired to master and guest suites
- Weatherproof back yard outside speaker connections prewired
- "Future proof" house wiring with accessible path from foundation to attic
- Hub and spoke pattern for cable, electrical, security, stereo, phone wiring
- House "overwired" with extra outlets, alternating circuits in rooms
- Tiled seat in shower
- High capacity fill at master tub
- Two exterior garage man doors
- Hard-wired smoke detectors in each bedroom and hall
- Hard-wired carbon monoxide detector
- 3M furnace-mounted air cleaner
- House wrapped in Typar to prevent air and dust infiltration
- Shaklee Bestwater two stage whole house water filtration system
- Whole house vacuum
- Chair and crown molding in formal dining and living room
- Beaded board wainscoting in dining room and kitchen nook
- Crown molding in master bedroom
- Fluted door casings with rosettes and plinth blocks
- Triple hinged interior doors
- Oversized colonial base moldings
- Extra depth and two story ceiling in garage
- Decorative wallpapering
- Open house design with oversized windows for light look
- Two sets of french doors to deck off family room facilitate entertaining
- Lights in all closets, with wall switches
- Eyeball lights over south wall of family room, and kitchen island
- Maple cabinets in laundry room
- Laundry room wall prefitted and prewired for pull-down ironing board
- Fluorescent lights in laundry and sewing room

anywhere. 3,100 finished s.f."
Chuck & Laura L.
Providence, UT

"The half million dollar homes here are no better than the $150,000 houses, only bigger. They have laminate countertops, standard appliances, and no upgrades on the cabinets or anything. My dad built his own home, did a lot of the work himself. A $275,000 house, and he didn't spend half. My neighbor Laura saved 20% owner-building a half million dollar house."
Kathryn & James H.
Kansas City, MO

"We were advised that with blown in cellulose insulation, and with gluing the sheathing to each exterior stud, we would not need housewrap for our house. In fact, they said it might cause problems preventing the out-migration of moisture from the house, which can make the insulation rot or mildew."
John & Jessica N.
Lehi, UT

Some of the items I found for my owner-built house: Pre-Stressed Concrete Foundation: look under superiorwalls.com. Pre-insulated to R-5 and comes with a 15-year warranty. TJI Silent Floor Trusses: 3/4" in multi-ply plywood. Screwed and glued. Enercept Structural Insulated Panels www.enercept.com. Super energy efficient and EASY to erect. Ten of my friends erected the house walls last Saturday. We erected the garage in four hours the next day. Hot Water Heat: look under wirsbo.com. Energy-efficient and super comfortable. Four of us installed the basement circuit in one day and saved $3,800. It's done right too. The gentlemen who sold it to us engineered the system and helped us install it. Fiberglass Framed Windows: Look under accurate-dorwin.com. Triple-Paned, 2 low-e coatings and 2 argon gas cavities. Super energy-efficient and the price is very competitive with quality window manufacturers. We did a lot of research here and believe we have made the right decision. Icyenine Foam in attic and rim-joist: Look under prairiefoam.com. Will seal the home from potential air leaks, which will add big time to the comfort and efficiency. Aquapex Plumbing: Look under aquapex.com. Too many advantages to list, but the best part is that I can run the feed lines myself! Heat Recovery Ventilators: look under thermal associates.com. Recovers energy and cleanses the air. Other features include: hurricane roof truss hangers, Simpson Strong ties affixing the main floor to the foundation, all concrete is mixed with fiber mesh to reduce cracking, four-foot stairwell with lighting at treads, heat recovery ventilator, hot water heat in all bathrooms, whirlpool tubs, concrete tornado shelter, natural day lighting via sun tubes, 12-gauge wiring, whole house vacuum, whole house stereo, video, intercom, computer and telephone, 14 different heating zones, and security system. A few items of Interest: "Builder's Guide, Cold Climate, 1997" eeba.org, published by the Energy Efficient Building Association (EEBA). Visit the EEBA web site to order your copy. Ask EEBA about membership. EEBA has annual meetings that provide an opportunity to upgrade building and HVAC skills, something of interest to me. Straw bale is the way I wanted to build, but I couldn't convince my better half. See www.mcgill.ca/mchg/straw/index.html."

Dave & Sheila A.
Boone, IA

- Bullnosed drywall
- Freezer hookup in garage
- Wide door to master suite
- Therma-Tru security entry door with full length side lites
- Schlage colonial entry lockset with deadbolt
- Decora rocker switches on all lights
- Lighted toggle switch for crawl space lights
- Custom six-bag concrete walks and drive
- 2X6 exterior framing, R-19 insulated walls, R-38 ceiling
- Extra countertop outlets in all baths
- Oversized flushmount plate glass mirrors in master and kids' bath
- Neo angle showers in guest and master baths
- Custom tiled showers and tub enclosures throughout
- Two Kohler sinks in master bath
- Built-in benches in master closet and mudroom
- Door knob stops
- In-wall blocking for hand rails, towel bars, bedroom shelves and draperies
- Brass hooks in master bath and closet
- Convenience hooks in mudroom, pantry, hall closet and garage
- Sealed acrylic burnished brass Schlage door hardware
- Waterproof light fixture in master shower
- Enameled cast-iron tub in upstairs bath
- Linen closet in upstairs hall
- Linen cabinet in guest bath
- Mop and broom storage in pantry and garage closet
- Vacuum cleaner hose and parts rack in utility closet
- Double joisting under master tub
- Reading lights over both tubs
- Heat lamp/fan in master bath
- Quiet-flush 1.6 gallon toilets
- Sound insulation in bathroom walls and around toilet drain plumbing
- Insulated switches and outlet boxes on exterior walls
- Hot and cold water tap for car washing in garage

Index

Symbols

12-gauge, 81, 254, 258

A

A/C, 44, 75, 81, 240
Absorption, 81
Accomplish, 210
   Accomplishment, 212
Accounting, 209
Accurate, 85
   Bidding, 102
   Deliveries, 215
   Estimates, 113
Acoustics, 76
Acres, 102, 137, 240
Addition, 44, 100, 119
Adjustable loan rates, 194
Administration, 135
Advance
   Notice, 195
   Planning, 210
   Specifications, 86
Advantage of Planning, 85
Advisor
   Construction, 38, 184,
      191, 206, 219
   General Contractor, 20,
      120
Advocate, 17, 134
Aesthetics, 93, 97
Agencies, 72
Agenda, 203
Aggravation, 212, 232, 268
Aggregate, 87
Agreement(s), 26, 232, 280
   Change Order, 83
   Construction, 191
   Contracting, 204

Lien Waiver, 200
   Non-Disclosure, 20
AIA, 92
Air-to-Air Heat Exchanger,
   76
Air Tight, 80
Alarm System, 76, 115, 126,
   225
Albums, Project, 286
Alternate, 104, 120, 184
Alternative Building Materi-
   als, 270
Aluminum, 80, 96, 214,
   255
Amps, 88, 254
Analysis, 28, 275
Angle(s), 90, 221
Angry, 211
Anguish, 212, 267
Animals, Subs like, 99
Annual, 27, 30
Anti-depressants, 205
Antidote, 236
Anxiety, 48, 198, 211
AppleWorks™, 112
Appliance, 75, 117, 130, 135,
   170, 178
Appraisal, 201
Appraise(r), 19, 100, 112
Apprentice, 162
Approvals, 195
Aptitude, 25
Aquapex.com, 258
Arches, 33
Architect, 43, 54, 67, 88,
   100, 163
   Interviews, 268
   vs. Designer, 91
Architectural, 19, 91, 255
Argon, 258
Argument, 198, 250
Art, 175
Arthritis, 75
Article, 94
Artificial, 77

Artistic, 93
As-Built, 118, 235
Asking, 88, 109, 201
Aslett, Don, 76, 273
Aspect, 86, 174, 216
Asphalt, 100, 255
Assembling, 99
Assess (ment/ors), 175, 186,
   250
Association, 22, 72, 101,
   174, 235
Assumptions, 28
Attic, 107, 117, 130
Attitudes, 19, 20
Attorney, 100, 193, 198
Auctions
   Construction, 155
   On-line, 155
Audio, 76, 138, 225
Audiotape, 284
Author, 21, 29, 81, 272
Authority, 218
AutoCAD, 166
Automobile, 16

B

Back-up Plans, 184
Backfill, 114, 122
Backhoe, 206
Backsplashes, Tile, 70
Balance, 28, 74, 92, 149,
   153, 250
   Loan, 149
Bale, 258
Balusters, 135, 169, 217
Banisters, 75
Bank, 32, 86, 118, 188, 202,
   225
Bargain(s), 18, 32, 43, 102,
   109, 134, 135, 154, 172,
   224, 243
Barter Club, 146
Basement, 68, 89, 118, 155,
   178

Basketball, 231, 243
Bathroom, 58, 80, 88, 108, 137, 154, 228
Baths, 54, 70, 71, 77
Battery, 76, 150
Beam, 38, 77
Bedroom, 26, 39, 69, 73, 79, 90, 97, 108, 166, 217
Beneficiary, 202
Benefits, 18, 27, 99, 154, 189, 201
Bid(s), 35, 91, 109, 113, 144, 279
  Comparing, 283
  Contract, 242
  Fixed, 21
Bills, 215
Blinds, 76, 147, 257
Blocking, 80, 89, 156
Blown-in Insulation, 233
Blueprint(s), 68, 92
Bond, Payment, 201
Boneyard, 135
Bonus, 73, 76, 186
Borrow(ing), 26, 153, 189
Brass, 90, 258
Breakdown, Cost, 190
Brick, 23, 75, 96, 113, 125, 146
Budget, 20, 109, 113–122, 151, 192, 234, 267, 283, 286
  Amount, 119
  Spreadsheet, 141, 279
  Worksheet, 119
  Written, 143
Buildability, 91, 93
Building
  Codes, 270
  Green, 270
Built-in, 130, 163
Buy
  Direct, 147
  Land, 269
  Materials, 280

Buying Group, 163

C

"Cold Sweat" Equity, 17
Cabinet, 136, 163
Cable, 56, 77, 113, 138, 157, 225
  Network, 225
Cafeteria-Style, 161
Calendar, 60, 110, 173, 208, 226
Camera, 211
  Video, 210
Canada, 118, 141, 169
Cantilevering, 95
Can Lights, 164
Card, Frequent Flyer, 168
Carpenter, 100, 139, 169, 197
Carpentry, 16, 116, 126, 197, 219
Carpet, 18, 58, 95, 147, 156, 209
Casualty, 34
Catalogue, 158
Caulk, 86, 166
CD-ROM, 284
Cedar, 71, 148
Ceiling, Ceiling Fans, 19, 33, 70, 107, 157, 231
Cellular, 40, 211, 213
Cellular Phone, 40, 211, 213
Cement, 20, 37, 87, 119, 157, 216
Ceramic Tile, 75, 89, 111, 116, 129, 225
Certificate, 201, 241
Certificate of Occupancy, 215
Chandelier, 157, 255
Changes, 83, 84, 86, 138, 157
Charges, 22, 37, 122, 144,

195
Charitable, 156, 251
Cheating, 20, 21
Checklist, 49, 70, 194, 221, 222, 245, 284
Checks, 17, 198, 199
Choose subs, 283
Churchill, Winston, 25, 76
Circuit, 76, 258
Circulars, 152
Claim, 42, 195, 198, 201
Classifieds, 169
Clause, 197, 202
Clean-up, 114, 157, 178, 220
Clearing, 62, 122
Climate, 106
Closet, 20, 69, 73, 96
Closings, Store, 152
Club, Barter, 146
Co-sign, 198
Codes, Building, 20, 91, 155, 167, 217, 270
Commission, 203
Communication, 25, 175, 185, 203, 216
Communities, 169, 203
Compact Fluorescent Lighting, 81, 96, 164
Comparing Bids, 283
Compensate, 26, 154
Competition, 143, 147, 169
Competitive, 37, 84, 120, 163, 188
Compliance, 200
Computer, 85
  Schedule, 142, 175
  Spreadsheet, 39, 119, 176, 209
Concentrator, 98
Concrete, 20, 75, 84, 100, 146
Conduit, 76, 157, 211
Congress, 17
Coniferous, 81

Consensus, 218
Conservation, 78, 96, 255
Considerations, Quality, 78
Construction
 Advisor, 191
 Auctions, 155
 Contract, 242
 Loan, 148
 Work Schedule, 178
Construction Bargain Strategies, 128-158, 269
Consultant, 36, 50, 136, 228, 241
Consumer, 36, 154, 160
Contingency, 84, 113, 117, 118
Contract
 Bid, 242
Contract, Construction, 242
Contracting, 274
Contracting Agreement, 204
Contractor, 272
Contractor, General, 269
Contractor, House, 272
Contractors, Drywall, 267
Contractors, Foundation, 267
Contractors, General, 109
Contractors, HVAC, 267
Contractors, Insulation, 267
Contractors, Siding, 267
Contractor Discount, 150
Contractor Returns, 164
Contractor Show, 147
Contracts, 202, 284
Control, Cost, 188
Control, Job, 188
Cooperation, 218, 219
Coordinate, 23, 46, 103, 205
Copper, 136, 214, 227
Corian™, 18, 75

Cornice, 178, 182
Cost
 Control, 188
 Tools, 153
Cost-Effective, 95, 165
Cost-Engineering, 145
Cost-Plus, 37, 203, 242
Costs
 Breakdown, 190
 Insurance, 195
 Life-Cycle, 96
 of Extension, 196
 Operating, 96
Counselors, 110
Countertop, 146, 155, 178
County
 Fees, 203
 Inspector, 220
Coupon, 151, 152
Coverings, Floor, 166
Credit, 189, 240
Creditor, 195
Cultured Marble, 138
Cupboards, 136
Curb Appeal, 75, 146
Customer, 19, 36, 84, 134, 154, 200

D

D.S.D.E., 32
Dangers, 226
Deadline, 110, 173, 212, 239
Deciduous, 81, 96
Decision-Making, 208, 218
Deck, 72, 125, 256
Design(er), 78, 88, 91–92, 163, 190
 Home, 270
 Interviews, 268
 Teacher, 166
Developer, 21, 50
Directories, 142
Disability Insurance, 201

Disasters, 232
Disbursements, 201
Discount, 135, 147, 150, 151
 Contractor, 150
Discount Tools
 Tools, 153
Disputes, 196
Do-It-Yourself, 56, 142, 158
Door, 178
Downlighting, 255
Downspout, 100
Downturn, 161
Down Payment, 194
Draws, 195
Dream Home, 273
Dream Home Notebook, 67, 140
Driveway, 125
Drywall, 116, 126
Drywall Contractors, 267
Duties, 45, 48, 205, 213
DVD, 278–283

E

Earthquake, 255
Economic, 34, 41
 thinking, 33
Economy, 161
Elevation, 92
E-mail, 142, 155
Employment, 25, 33, 166, 201
Energy, 75, 96, 164
 Saving, 80, 164
Energy Smart, 164
Engineer, 190
 Structural, 100
EPA Exam, 167
Equalization,
 Board of, 250
Equity, 43, 111, 148, 161, 188
 Sweat, 17. *See also "Cold Sweat" Equity*

Escrow, 198
Estimate, 28, 54, 242
Estimator, 275
Exam, EPA, 167
Excel™, 112
Expenditures, 122, 141
Extension, Cost of, 196

F

Facia, 129
Factory, 147
Fasteners, 138
Fax, 141, 161, 185
Features, 54, 69, 253
   House, 269, 283
   List of, 278
Features,
   Multiple Listing, 70
Features, House
   House, 284
Fees, 195
   Impact, 168
   Origination, 194
   Title Update, 195
Fencing, 130, 138
Fiberglass, 107
Filings, 201
Finance, 31
   Financial, 26, 28, 32
   Financing, 122
Firing, 174
Fixed-Bid, 21, 37, 203
Fixed Fee, 242
Flatwork, 125, 178
Floor Coverings, 166
Flyer, Frequent, 168
Footings, 87
Forms
   Interview, 284
   Lien Release, 190
   Lien Waiver, 199
Forums, 286
Foundation, 122

Foundation Contractors,
   267
Framers, 267
Framing, 178
Free Stuff, 156
Frequent Flyer Card, 168
Furniture, 269
Future-Proof, 74

G

General Contractor(s), 109,
   159, 186, 187, 200, 218,
   224, 239, 241, 269
Goethe, 251
Green Building, 270
Gutters, 138

H

Heating, 138
Henry David Thoreau, 113
Hire, 162
Home Center Stores, 150
Home Design, 270
Home Show, 147
House Features, 269, 283,
   284
How-To, 278–284
HVAC, 96, 100
HVAC Contractors, 267

I

"Illegals", 162
Impact Fees, 168
Independent Inspections,
   221
Inspection(s), 155, 195, 221,
   222
Inspector(s), 100, 215, 220
Inspectors(s), 268
Insulation Contractors, 267
Insurance, 21, 39, 92, 100,

   195
   Disability, 201
Insurance Cost
   Cost, 195
Insurance Protection
   Protection, 201
Integrate, 205
Interest Rate, 194
Interior Decorator, 101
Internet, 142
Interview(s), 54, 140, 268,
   283, 284, 286
Invoice, 39
Itemize, 106

J

Job Control, 188

L

Labor, 17, 37, 95
Labor, Student, 165
Land, 160, 166, 269
Landscaping, 266
Lawsuit, 197
Legal Precautions, 283
Lender(s), 187, 191, 268
Liability, 201, 240
Liens, 140
Lien Waiver(s), 190, 199,
   200, 280, 284
Life-Cycle Costs, 96
Liquidated Damages, 186,
   202
List of Features, 278
Loan(s), 22, 23
   Construction, 148
   Negotiate, 149
   One-Close, 149
   Presentation, 193
   Proposal, 189
   Rate, 194
Low-E, 80

Lumberyard, 38, 150

M

Mail Order, 158
Manufacturers, 142, 147, 169
Margin, 41, 85, 176
Mark-Up, 43, 145, 242
Market, 68
Market-Driven, 68
Masonry, 122
Material(s), 54
 Alternative Building, 270
 Buy, 280
 Recycled, 156
 Salvage, 155
 Separate from Labor, 145
Measure, 45, 205, 209
Mechanical Trades, 22, 139
Medicine Chests, 117, 130
Micromanagement, 208
Microsoft® Project, 210, 211
Middleman, 159
Mill-direct, 147
Misconceptions, 23
Mistakes, 231
Money, bank, 188
Money Saving Strategy, 159
Moonlighters, 162
Mortgage, 18, 28, 253
MP3, 284, 287
Multiple Listing Features, 70

N

Negotiate, 149, 243
Network, 153, 208
Network Cabling, 225
Newsletters, 286
Notebook, Dream Home, 140

O

Off-season, 161
On-line Auctions, 155
On-Site, 145, 168, 191, 207, 216, 281
One-Close Loan. *See* Loan(s)
Operating Costs, 96
Organized, 145, 268, 281
Origination Fee, 31, 194
Osmond, Donny, 18
Overruns, 20, 210, 224
Owner, Sell By, 269
Owner-Builder, 21, 23, 25, 30

P

P.O.I.M.M., 46, 205, 229
Package Plan, 160
Paint, 269
Parade of Homes, 69
Pawn Shops, 153
Payment, Down, 194
Payment Bond, 201
Payroll Deductions, 30, 32
Permits, 62, 203
Piggyback, 154
Plan, Package, 160
Plan-Ahead, 157
Planning, 278, 284
Planning, Advance, 210
Planning Advantage, 85
Planning Steps, 268
Plans, 156
Plumbers, 266
Policy, Term Life, 202
Porches, 115, 125
Pre-wire, 74, 126, 225, 269
Precautions, Legal, 283
Preparation, 187, 212, 239
Presentation, Loan, 193
Prices, 20, 39
Price Matching, 151
Pricing, 140, 142
Procedures, Draws, 195

Project Albums, 286
Property Taxes, 250, 267
Proposal, Loan, 189
Protection, 199
Protection, Insurance, 201
Punch List, 245, 246–249, 284

Q

Qualifications, 25, 188, 191
Quality, 188, 268
Quality Considerations, 78
Quattro Pro™, 112
Quicken™, 209
QuickTime®, 284
Quit-Claim, 193

R

Radiant Heat, 81, 146, 147
Rate, Interest, 194
Rate, Loan, 194
Realtor, 73, 100
Recommendations, 49, 54, 93
Recycled Materials, 156
Recycling Center, 73
References, 93, 105
Refund(s), 140
Releases, Lien. *See Lien(s)*
Remodel, 155, 270
Renovation, Home, 272
Resale, 67, 74
Research, 134, 143
Résumé, 191
Returns, Contractor, 164
Rights, 193, 200
Risk(s), 188, 226, 241
Roofing, 129, 178

S

Salvage Material, 155
Savings, 96
Savings Account, 34, 253
Savings Suggestions, 268
Scaffolding, 154
Schedule, 142, 144, 173, 176, 185, 191, 224, 235, 267
Schedule, Creating a, 283
Schedule, Work, 178
Schedule, Written, 185, 191, 279
Schedule Worksheet, 180
Seed, 130
Self-Work, 48, 142, 158, 192, 224, 227
Sell by Owner, 269
Sewer, 203
Shade Trees, 164
Sheathing, 19, 223
Shop, 194
Shops, Pawn, 153
Show, Contractor, 147
Show, Home, 147
Shower, 129, 223
Siding Contractors, 267
Single-Family, 65, 235
Sketch, 94
Slab, 88
Soffit, 116
Software, 138
Solar Home, 165
Solid-Surface, 73
Special Reports, 266, 287
Specifications, Advance, 86
Specs, 190
Spreadsheet(s), 141, 143, 279, 283, 284
   AppleWorks™, 112
   Excel™, 112
   Quattro Pro™, 112
Sprinklers, 80
Steps, Planning, 268
Store-wide Sales, 151

Stores, Thrift, 156
Store Closings, 152
Strategies, Construction Bargain, 128-158, 269
Strategy, 28, 29
Structural Engineer, 100, 190
Stucco, 71, 100
Student Labor, 165
Subcontractors, 140, 190, 206, 229, 280, 283
Successes, 233
Superintendent, 191
Suppliers, 74, 137, 138
Surplus, 148, 155
Surveyor, 100
Sweat Equity, 17

T

Tax, 16, 29
Taxes, Property, 250, 267
Teacher, Design, 166
Technical, 242
Telephone, 141, 225
Template, 284
Terms, Right, 194
Term Life Policy, 202
Theater, Home, 225
Thoreau, Henry David, 113
Thrift Stores, 156
Tile Backsplashes, 70
Title Insurance, 138, 149, 195
Title Update Fees, 195
Tools, 138, 153, 155
Tools, Cost of, 153
Tools, Discount, 153
Trees, Shade, 164
Trusses, 19, 95, 138, 144
Tub/Shower, 117, 129

U

Underestimate, 23, 120
Upgrade, 157
Utilities, Temporary, 178

V

Valuation, 28
Vanity, 76, 117, 156, 228, 255
Variance, 62
Vendors, 85, 142, 147
Vent, 130, 217
Video Camera, 210
Vinyl Flooring, 116

W

Wainscoting, 70, 257
Waiver, Lien. *See Lien Waiver*
Wallpaper, 116, 129
Warranty Deed, 190
Waterproofing, 87, 100, 114
Wholesale, 50, 148
Work-at-Home, 98
Workman's Compensation, 104, 199, 201
Workmanship, 95, 186
Worksheet, Budget, 119, 124
Worksheet, Planning Steps, 50
Worksheet, Schedule, 180
Workshop, 282
Work Schedule, 178
Wrecking Yard, 137
Written Budget, 119, 143, 190, 211
Written Schedule, 185, 279
www.OwnerBuilderBook.com, 142, 235, 251

Z

Zones, 71, 254, 258
Zoning, 62, 167, 203

DVD's

III. How to Create Your Spreadsheet Budget

List Price: $24.95   Your Price: $19.95

The biggest bugaboo of owner-builders can be really easy and satisfying –

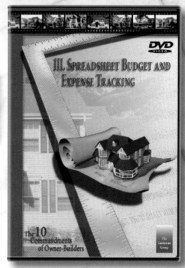

building a spreadsheet budget to control your project. Here we show you how to do your spreadsheet in detail. Starting with the Owner-Builder Resource CD-ROM, you will gain confidence using a spreadsheet to plan and control your project. Your cost to build doesn't have to be a mystery! Meet a couple who got good at it and who used creative bartering to save a ton on their home. Release date: May, 2003

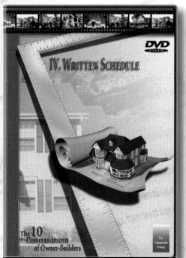

IV. How to Create Your Written Schedule

List Price: $24.95   Your Price: $19.95

After written features and budget, the third principal task of an owner-builder is a written schedule. Meet a couple of owner-builders who broke the code and built faster than the average general contractor. How to use our Resource CD-ROM to build a computer schedule. How successful owner-builders get cooperation from subs and vendors to make the schedule come true. Practical and money saving ideas from a 25 year old owner-builder and a tour of the amazing custom home that brought him a quarter million dollars in equity. Release date: June, 2003

V. How to Get Three Bids from Subs and Suppliers

List Price: $24.95   Your Price: **$19.95**

Visit a seven-time owner-builder couple from Tennessee who made $100,000 on their last house. Learn their system to make it enjoyable and profitable every time. How to get and negotiate good bids from both subs and vendors. How to find qualified bidders. How to get enough bids even in a busy market. How to handle the paperwork of bidding in a timely way. Also meet first-time owner-builders who managed to build an outstanding starter home for less than $30 a square foot. Release date: July, 2003

Resource Guide

DVD's

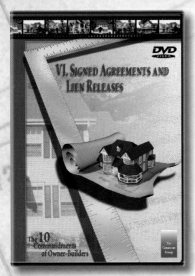

VI. How to Make Good Contracts and Lien Releases

List Price: $24.95   Your Price: $19.95

When you sign on your chosen subs, what written agreements and forms do you need to protect yourself and facilitate a smooth process? How do successful O-B's go about it? Meet one from Arizona who has owner-built several times and is approaching the "legal limit" of a half million dollars of tax-free gain in a single project. You've gotta see this house. How to manage the paper and the money and get what you expect.

Release date: August, 2003

VII. How to Buy Materials Directly

List Price: $24.95   Your Price: $19.95

Here's where we meet a vendor turned owner-builder from Idaho who knows a lot about procuring the products and services you'll need to build at a big savings. Husband and wife have a flair for self-work too, and demonstrate for us their tile and electrical work. How to buy materials direct and arrange the labor-only services that make for smooth construction and a quality home. Visit another family who saved money building a custom home with Structural Insulated Panels.

Release date: September, 2003

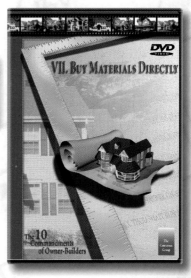

VIII. How to Communicate with Subcontractors

List Price: $24.95   Your Price: $19.95

John and Jessica Norton, owner-builders who kept a job diary with photos on our web site, show us their completed home and describe their ingenious strategies for getting the right subs and keeping them on task. Communication via e-mail, fax, telephone and internet brought them very good job control for first-time owner-builders. How they settled a potential subcontractor disaster. How to set up a program to keep the subs happy and get you a better house for less.

Release date: October, 2003

Resource Guide

DVD's

IX. Why You Need to Be On-Site

List Price: $24.95   Your Price: $19.95

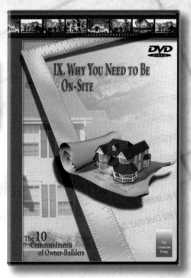

Elaine and Mark Smith tell the story and show footage from the building of the Riverbottoms house. How to get involved in construction to build it right. Opportunities for savings that you miss as an absentee manager. How to keep your job and still build your house on schedule and on budget. How to enhance your house "behind the walls" for added function and value at little cost. Also tour a log home under construction and learn from a hands-on woman owner-builder.

Release date: November, 2003

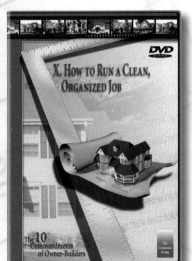

X. How to Run a Clean, Organized Job

List Price: $24.95   Your Price: $19.95

Gary and Linda Ziser tell how they built their lake front home in under four months with impeccable quality and serious savings. How veteran owner-builders do it smoothly and sanely. Your daily duties as general contractor. How to keep costs in check. How to check each aspect of the work for quality. How to keep the subs showing up on time. Special Bonus: How to sell by owner for huge gains, even in a down market.

Release date: December, 2003

Resource Guide

6 DVD's!

Planning/Workshop DVD Combination: The first three DVD's of the "Ten Commandments of Owner-Builders How-To" Series and "The Owner-Builder Workshop Videos" on DVD (6 DVD Set!)

Cover Price: $149.70   Your Price: $74.95

Six DVD combination comprises the three "Planning" DVD's ("1,000 Hours of Planning") and the three DVD's of our "Workshop Videos". For a starter set, this gives you the essence of planning and an overview of the construction process at a good price. The DVD technology makes this a super training combination and very entertaining as well. Includes many $1,000 Ideas and our embarrassing outtakes.

Workshop Videos on DVD

Digitally remastered

The Owner-Builder Workshop Videos on DVD (3 DVD Set!)

Cover Price: $74.85   **Your Price: $38.95**

Three DVD set is loaded with entertaining instruction. Mark and Elaine instruct a lively class of 81 owner-builders, half of whom had previously owner-built. The DVD technology makes this a valuable learning tool that is fun to use. The workshop teaches how to do a budget, how to develop a schedule and how to make it all work.

Viewer Comments:

"This is home building for dummies. (Just what I needed.)"

Derek White

"It really lets you know what you are in for as an owner-builder."

Elaine J. Smith

"Very valuable information for the novice up to the veteran homeowner."

Craig Martindale

"I can't wait to build. Thanks for making it sound attainable and fun!"

Lisa Dombrosky

"Both the book and workshop take all aspects of owner-building and tie them into a nice package. The end result - our own home with more in equity!!"

Dr. Lon Miller

"This book and workshop makes my dream house become a realistic possibility."

Liz Maxfield

"This has helped me take disorganization and put it into an organized path to follow. Thank you!"

Joel Taylor

"The Owner-Builder Workshop got me excited to get started on my own home. I feel like I can do a better job than anyone else as a contractor."

Anna Turley

"Having researched for over 1 1/2 years before beginning our home, we found The Owner-Builder Book to be the BEST source of information and guide to the whole process. Mark and Elaine's workshop really gives a great, detailed guideline for owner-builders at all levels. Even contractors can benefit from their insight."

Kathy Morita

Resource Guide

Workshop Videos on DVD

What you will learn:

- ✔ Creating a schedule
- ✔ Building a budget
- ✔ Comparing bids
- ✔ How to use a spreadsheet
- ✔ How to find subs in a tight market
- ✔ How to interview subs and vendors
- ✔ Sub and vendor presentations
- ✔ How big a house can you afford
- ✔ Legal Precautions
- ✔ Your contracting duties
- ✔ How to select house features
- ✔ How to choose subs
- ✔ Emotional Resilience
- ✔ Savings after you build

Super DVD Combination: Complete 12 DVD "Ten Commandments of Owner-Builders How-To" Series and "The Owner-Builder Workshop Videos" on DVD (15 DVD Set!)

Cover Price: $374.25   Your Price: $169.95

We don't think you'll get bored watching all of these DVD's. Each one brings you to new owner-builders who have been where you're going and have much to teach the rest of us. Each one contains original ideas that will bring you greater equity and project success. No program like this is available elsewhere. A great way to learn and gain confidence.

Resource Guide

Free Resource CD-ROM

Another Freebie

For years we offered a Resource Diskette for $19.95 plus shipping and handling that includes the spreadsheet templates used in this book to plan and manage your home construction project. Now we are providing this software plus much, much more to our readers free of charge on a CD-ROM for your home computer.

You may order the Owner-Builder Resource CD-ROM (a $19.95 value) at no charge other than our flat shipping and handling fee of $3.

The CD-ROM allows us to provide you with many resources that are difficult to offer even on our web site. We provide spreadsheet templates to manage your project on your own computer. There are tools and examples for specifying features, developing a schedule and creating a budget for your new house, remodel, or addition. We include highlights from The Owner-Builder Workshop DVD's and trailers from our other DVD titles.

The Resource CD-ROM is designed to work on either Windows® or Macintosh®.

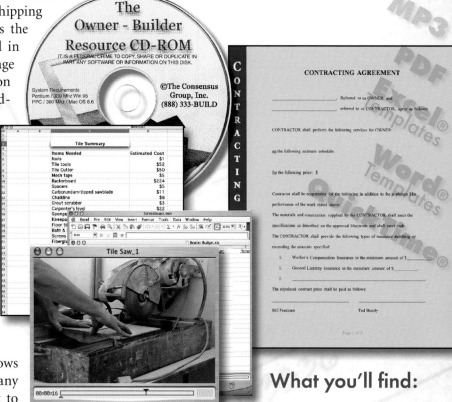

What you'll find:

- Entire classic first edition in digital sound
- DVD trailers
- Web site preview
- Spreadsheet templates for budget and schedule
- Checklists, contracts, lien waivers
- Interview forms
- Workshop highlights
- House features sample
- Punch list
- Planning spreadsheet template
- Job diary template

2nd Edition CD-ROM Release date: December, 2003

Free E-mail Newsletter

Address: @| Register at www.OwnerBuilderBook.com › go

OwnerBuilderBook.COM 1-888-333-BUILD (2845)
N E W S L E T T E R

Mark. A Smith Editor   Spring 2003, Volume 19, Number 2

NEW IN THIS ISSUE

* CD-ROM now available
* Recent Forum Posts
* Win a free trip
* New on our website
* Construction Bargain Strategies

BOOKSTORE SPECIALS

* Owner-Builder Book
* Building our Home
* Complete Guide to Building Log Homes
* How to lower your Property Taxes

Talking Points
You Get What You Pay For?
by Mark A. Smith

I've grown to despise the expression "You get what you pay for." It's a favorite of general contractors who condemn owner-building. It's spoken with some gravity as if it were a higher truth known to the wise.

But it just isn't true. We see people saving 35% by owner-building every day of the week. They have the same house, the same kitchen sink, the same garage door, the same sliding window as the person who used a contractor and spent 35% more.

What is it about that kitchen sink that makes it better when you've spent $338 instead of $220 like Elaine and I did? Or heaven forbid, if you paid $450 or $600, the listed "retail price"? When a contractor is running the job, you have an excellent chance of paying retail for house components, although they are widely available at deep discounts.

Yes, you pay more for a general contractor and what does it get you? A better design? No, that should be the province of the designer working closely with you. Better quality? Not if you are checking the work that goes into the job each day. The average custom contractor provides on-site supervision only a couple of hours a week when you're building. Expertise? You can hire an independent inspector for that who will provide objective input. Peace of mind? Yes, if you are clueless about the process.

But you won't be clueless. A successful owner-builder plans thoroughly before breaking ground. You wind up knowing your house and what's in it better than any third party can. Along the way you resolve design issues to your satisfaction and see better ways and better components to meet your needs.

The reward for this is not well understood. You pay less, but you get the same equity as a contractor-built house. On an average home, you would save more than $50,000. Mind you, this is pure equity, it is tax-free wealth. Did you get what you paid for? You paid less, but got much more. I prefer the saying, "The best things in life are free."

SPECIAL ANNOUNCEMENT

CD-ROM now available.

The Owner-Builder Resource CD-ROM, ISBN: 0966142861 is now available free through our Bookstore. You pay only our flat shipping charge of $3 (for any size purchase.) This multimedia disk includes resources priced separately at $120 and two ten-minute videos not previously available.

The Owner-Builder Resource CD-ROM

* Software templates for budget, schedule, features for your project
* The entire Owner-Builder Book on Tape in crisp digital sound
* Video Tour of The Riverbottoms house
* Highlights from the Owner-Builder Workshop Videos
* Previous editions of The Owner-Builder Book in electronic form (not printable)
* And much, much more.

The Resource CD-ROM is protected by copyright. Copying or duplication of contents is prohibited except for personal use. This free offer is limited to one per household. Note: The CD-ROM will automatically be included free with any first time bookstore purchase or can be ordered by itself. Click here to order.

Resource Guide

www.OwnerBuilderBook.com

www.OwnerBuilderBook.com

We put together a web site because owner-builders need a place to share enthusiasm and blow off steam. Come to our site to find the ideas of many other O-B's. Let us know where you find bargains, how you solve problems, and what you'd never do the same way again.

The web site gives you the opportunity to comment and add to every section of this book, and to our Special Reports and future books. You'll find blow by blow accounts of other projects, pictures and first person stories. We have some freebies for you, and you can order any resource we offer for sale in our on-line bookstore.

Free Newsletter

Use our web site to register for our electronic newsletter. The newsletter will be sent to you via e-mail. (See page 271)

Some Web Site Features

• Tour of Riverbottoms house
• Photos and budgets of reader projects
• Reader forums of owner-builder topics.

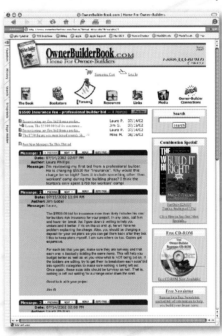

• E-mail notification if a response is made to a question or comment you post
• Database of past newsletters
• Newspaper columns on owner-building
• Database of owner-builder interviews
• On-line Bookstore where you can post your own reviews of books
• Project albums with owner-builder comments and photos
• Finished house tour

www.OwnerBuilderBook.com

• Interviews with owner-builders
• Take your own interview
• On-line bookstore books, software and DVD's, Special Reports, book combinations and specials
• Progressive sales specials
• Search command

Sample search:

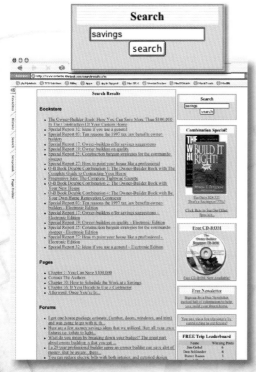

• Links to hundreds of resources updated by us.
• Find O-B's anywhere via Owner-Builder Connections

• Database of reader comments
• Feedback to the authors
• Book reviews
• Slashdot database
• Ask the expert
• Cover essays
• Database of Construction Bargain Strategies
• Downloadable MP3's
• Video clips of Owner-Builder interviews

• Free DVD's for Forum Tip of the Week
• Free trip for annual Forum winner

Resource Guide

Paperless Coupons

Do Not Tear Out • Just Enter the Coupon Code on our Web Site or Call in by Phone

FREE!

The Owner-Builder Book Electronic Download (Adobe® PDF file)

Cover Price: $19.95
Special Offer: FREE
You Save: $19.95
Coupon Code: 032072

FREE!

Electronic Download of a Special Report (Adobe® PDF file). Limit One.

Cover Price: $5
Special Offer: FREE
You Save: $5
Coupon Code: 092273

$15 off

Any DVD. Limit One.

Cover Price: $24.95
Special Offer: $9.95
You Save: $15
Coupon Code: 111896

Look for more coupon specials in our free e-mail newsletter

$45 off

The Owner-Builder Workshop Videos on DVD

Cover Price: $74.85
Special Offer: $29.85
You Save: $45
Coupon Code: 041598

$5 off

Any Book in our Bookstore. Limit One.

Cover Price: various
Special Offer: $5 off
You Save: $5
Coupon Code: 091076

$85 off

Super Reader's Library

Cover Price: $212.83
Special Offer: $127.95
You Save: $85
Coupon Code: 080643

Call Toll-Free: 1-888-333-BUILD

The Owner-Builder Book

Resource Guide